Author-ity and Textuality

LOCUST HILL LITERARY STUDIES
NO. 14

Locust Hill Literary Studies

Author-ity and Textuality

Current Views of Collaborative Writing

Edited by

James S. Leonard
The Citadel

Christine E. Wharton
The Citadel

Robert Murray Davis
University of Oklahoma

Jeanette Harris
University of Southern Mississippi

LOCUST HILL PRESS
West Cornwall, CT
1994

Library of Congress Cataloging-in-Publication Data

Author-ity and textuality : current views of collaborative writing /
  edited by James S. Leonard ... [et al.].
    p.   cm. -- (Locust Hill literary studies ; no. 14)
    Includes bibliographical references and index.
    ISBN 0-933951-57-4 : $30.00
      1. Authorship--Collaboration.   I. Leonard, J. S. (James S.)
  II. Title: Authority and textuality.   III. Series.
  PN145.A97 1994
  808'.02--dc20   94-15111
                                                             CIP

Printed on acid-free, 250-year-life paper
Manufactured in the United States of America

Contents

Acknowledgments

The editors gratefully acknowledge the assistance of the Citadel Development Foundation, which provided funding for research and manuscript preparation for this volume. We are especially grateful to Citadel Vice-President George F. Meenaghan for his aid and encouragement. Thanks also to student assistants Mark Little and Michael Socha for their excellent work on the manuscript.

Laura Brady's "Collaboration as Conversation: Literary Cases" is reprinted here with permission of *Essays in Literature*, where it appeared in Volume 19 (1992). Jewel Spears Brooker's "Common Ground and Collaboration in T.S. Eliot" is reprinted with permission of *The Centennial Review*, where it was published in Volume 25 (Summer 1981). Tom Inge's "The Art of Collaboration" appears here with permission of Bowling Green State University Popular Press, publisher of *Eye on the Future*, edited by Marilyn F. Motz, John G. Nachbar, Michael T. Marsden, and Ronald J. Ambrosetti (1994), in which the essay first appeared.

Contributors

Laura A. Brady—Assistant Professor of English, West Virginia University; coauthor of articles on collaboration and composition; dissertation (U of Minnesota, 1988): "Collaborative Literary Writing: Issues of Authorship and Authority."

Jewel Spears Brooker—Professor of English, Eckerd College; author of *Mastery and Escape: T.S. Eliot and the Dialectic of Modernism* (U of Massachusetts P, 1994); coauthor of *Reading "The Waste Land": Modernism and the Limits of Interpretation* (U of Massachusetts P, 1990); editor of *Approaches to Teaching T.S. Eliot's Poetry and Plays* (MLA, 1988), *The Placing of T.S. Eliot* (Columbia: U of Missouri P: 1991), and *T.S. Eliot,* American Critical Archives (Cambridge UP, forthcoming).

Robert Murray Davis—Professor of English, University of Oklahoma; author or editor of fourteen books on twentieth-century fiction, most recently *Playing Cowboys: Low Culture and High Art in the Western* (Norman: U of Oklahoma P, 1992), *Brideshead Revisited: The Past Redeemed* (Twayne, 1990), and *Evelyn Waugh and the Forms of His Time* (Catholic UP, 1989); editor of two special issues of *Genre* (Dec. 1972 and Summer 1985); author of a volume of poems and of *Mid-Lands: A Family Album* (U of Georgia P, 1992).

Jeanette Harris—Professor of English and Director of Composition, University of Southern Mississippi; author of *Expressive Discourse* (Southern Methodist UP, 1990); coauthor of *The Simon & Schuster Guide to Writing* (Prentice Hall, 1994), *Contexts: Writing and Reading* (Houghton Mifflin, 1985, 1988, 1993), *Interactions* (Houghton Mifflin, 1991, 1994), and *A Writer's Introduction to Word*

Processing (Wadsworth, 1987); coeditor of *Writing Centers in Context* (NCTE, 1993).

Linda K. Hughes—Professor of English, Texas Christian University; author of *The Manyfacèd Glass: Tennyson's Dramatic Monologues* (Ohio UP, 1987); coauthor of *The Victorian Serial* (U of Virginia P, 1991).

M. Thomas Inge—Blackwell Professor of the Humanities, Randolph-Macon College; author or editor of numerous books on American literature, humor, and popular culture, including *Huck Finn Among the Critics* (University Publications, 1985), *Comics as Culture* (UP of Mississippi, 1989), *Faulkner, Sut, and Other Southerners: Essays in Literary History* (Locust Hill, 1992), and *Perspectives on American Culture: Essays on Humor, Literature, and the Popular Arts* (Locust Hill, 1994).

Fred Kemp—Assistant Professor of English/Director of Composition, Texas Tech University; Director of Texas Tech's Computer-Based Writing Research Program; formerly Director of the Computer Research Lab at the University of Texas, Austin (1985–88); member of CCCC Committee on Computers and Writing; recipient of Educom/NCRIPTAL award for best writing software ("Daedalus Instructional System") for 1990.

Ellen Andrews Knodt—Associate Professor of English, Pennsylvania State University, Ogontz; author of *Writing: Process and Purpose* (Macmillan, 1986), *Making Progress: From Paragraphs to Essays* (HarperCollins, 1991), and articles on teaching writing in *Teaching English in the Two-Year College* and other NCTE publications.

James S. Leonard—Professor of English, The Citadel. Coauthor of *The Fluent Mundo: Wallace Stevens and the Structure of Reality* (U of Georgia P, 1988); coeditor of *Satire or Evasion?: Black Perspectives on Huckleberry Finn* (Duke UP, 1992); editor of the quarterly *Mark Twain Circular* (since 1987).

Michael Lund—Professor of English, Longwood College; author of *Reading Thackery* (Wayne State UP, 1988) and *America's Continu-*

ing Story: An Introduction to Serial Fiction, 1850–1900 (Wayne State UP, 1993); coauthor of *The Victorian Serial* (U of Virginia P, 1991).

Shirley K Rose—Associate Professor of Rhetoric and Writing Studies, San Diego State University; author of articles on literacy and stylistics.

Michael Schrage—Nationally syndicated columnist for the *Los Angeles Times*; formerly of *The Washington Post*. Has been a contributor to the *Harvard Business Weekly*, *The Wall Street Journal*, *Fortune* magazine, *Institutional Investor*, and *International Economy*. Author of *Shared Minds: The New Technologies of Collaboration* (Random House, 1990).

Robert P. Steed—Professor and Chair, Political Science, The Citadel. Coeditor of nine books on politics in the South, most recently *The Disappearing South?: Studies in Regional Change and Continuity* (U of Alabama P, 1989), *Political Parties in the Southern States* (Praeger, 1990), and *The 1992 Presidential Election in the South: Current Patterns of Southern Party and Electoral Politics* (Praeger, 1994).

Christine E. Wharton—Lecturer in Philosophy, The Citadel; coauthor of *The Fluent Mundo: Wallace Stevens and the Structure of Reality* (U of Georgia P, 1988) and articles on the relationship of literature and philosophy.

INTRODUCTION:

Let us not to the marriage of true minds / Admit impediments

James S. Leonard

What is collaboration? Does it work? If so, how? Does collaborative activity have broad social and/or philosophical implications? This book brings a variety of perspectives to bear on such questions. Its broad-spectrum approach to the subject—including essays by rhetoric and composition specialists, a business and technical writing specialist, a journalist, literary critics, and a political science researcher—looks at problems and benefits that may accrue from collaboration and considers specific applications in scholarly writing, literary writing, business writing/decision-making, and student writing.

Collaborative writing is today far from the norm either in actual writing practice or in theoretical constructions of the writing process. Yet the past decade has seen a considerable growth in interest in the practicability of collaborative endeavor as an alternative writing strategy. The greatest interest has occurred within the realm of composition pedagogy; in fact, the topic of collaboration is enjoying a certain vogue in rhetoric and composition circles, as demonstrated by the number of sections and papers on the subject at recent writing conferences and by the publication of such in-depth studies as Lisa Ede and Andrea Lunsford's jointly authored *Single Texts/Plural Authors: Perspectives on Collaborative Writing* (Southern Illinois UP, 1990), Anne Dyson Haas's edited collection *Collaboration Through Writing and Reading* (NCTE, 1989), and Karen Burke LeFevre's *Invention as a Social Act* (Southern Illinois UP,

1987). Moving beyond the academy, Michael Schrage's *Shared Minds: The New Technologies of Collaboration* (Random House, 1990), focusing on a growing interest in collaborative methodologies for business and management, examines collaborative production of text as a reasonable response to both the demands and the opportunities of contemporary existence. And though literary and scholarly writers (outside the sciences) have shown and continue to show a reluctance to recognize the legitimacy and workability of collaborative writing, that reluctance is itself becoming a topic of some interest—as evidenced by such works as Jack Stillinger's *Multiple Authorship and the Myth of Solitary Genius* (Oxford UP, 1991), which reveals the hidden or partly hidden collaborations that lie behind many putatively single-authored texts of the past two centuries. The present volume is intended to distill these various initiatives into a hard look at collaboration as such, whether the arena be the literary world, the academy, or even that most formidable of playing fields: the "real world."

Section I introduces the topic by asking, "Who Collaborates?" In "The Art of Collaboration," M. Thomas Inge recasts the question with respect to literary productions, redefining the *ars poetica* tradition in terms of an often-unacknowledged substratum of collaborative textual production. Inge examines a variety of literary and quasi-literary forms—from film to comic strips, to animated cartoons, to modernist poetry, to impressionist painting, to the nineteenth- and twentieth-century novel. He finds in each a fabric of group effort, textual compromise, and editorial reworking that constitute a collabortive reality at odds with the popular notion of heroically individual authorship of text.

Michael Schrage's "Writing to Collaborate: Collaborating to Write" approaches the question of collaboration in terms of "shared space"—by which he indicates an environment within which individuals can jointly create text. Schrage looks at the modes of collaboration and attitudes toward collaboration that have generated successful, if in some cases not fully acknowledged, collaborative products in the past and proposes new perspectives on "collaboration-friendly" technology that establishes new possibilities for writing together. He finds that collaboration is itself a "medium" and that its intersections with technological possibilities on one hand and the writers' needs on the other open onto avenues that lead to a reevaluation of the writing process.

Section II, "What Does It Mean to Collaborate?," takes a look at philosophical aspects of collaborative versus individual authorship, asking whether the choice to write either separately or in combination has any significance beyond the practical. Does our continuing devotion to the ideal of individual authorship rest on hidden assumptions that need to be examined, or does it simply reflect our experience that separate authorship is the most effective approach to writing?

The first essay in this section, "Breaking the Silence: Collaboration and the Isolationist Paradigm" (James S. Leonard and Christine E. Wharton), considers in its broadest terms the paradigm of the writer as lonely genius, tracing the path by which that model has been carried forward from nineteenth-century Romanticism to New Criticism and into much of the current thinking on textuality and the writing process. The essay discusses collaborative writing as a critique of the Romantic model by virtue of its substitution of a transactional model for the more traditional writer-as-isolationist and considers philosophical implications of the isolationist/collaborationist dichotomy in relation to the legacies of Nietzsche and Heidegger and the more recent contributions of Barthes, Foucault, and Derrida.

"Union and Reunion: Collaborative Authorship," by Linda K. Hughes and Michael Lund, examines the problem of authorial attribution, considering the "author" as both more and less than any text. The essay includes an extensive discussion of Hughes and Lund's experience in their coauthorship of *The Victorian Serial*, including their gradually diminishing sense of the distinctness of individual contributions. On the basis of that and other experiences, Hughes and Lund weigh the degree to which explicitly collaborative writing constitutes an undermining of authorial authority.

The final essay in the section, "Common Ground and Collaboration in T.S. Eliot," by Jewel Spears Brooker, finds in the poetic practice and critical theories of T.S. Eliot a ground for evaluating the significance of collaborative activity. Brooker, centering on Eliot's view of art as essentially collaborative, discusses his assumption that the writer, though writing alone, collaborates in three ways: (1) with auditors or readers, (2) with philosophers, theologians, and others who develop major worldviews, and (3) with other artists. Her analysis details the network of ideas, tech-

niques, and shared understandings within which Eliot sees the
artist working. Eliot praises Dante as a "borrower" and, on the
other hand, criticizes Blake as a mere "fabricator" who is unwilling
or unable to collaborate. He particularly emphasizes the importance of attending to collaborative effort in periods (like Eliot's
own) when the "common ground" of shared beliefs and assumptions seems to have dissolved.

Section III, "How Does Collaboration Work?," realigns the focus from collaborative writing's significance to its workings. This
includes examination of the effectiveness of collaborative endeavor, description of how collaborative decision-making and collaborative production of text can be accomplished most efficiently,
and consideration of the ethical questions and practical consequences involved in sharing a writing task or relying on collaborative pedagogical techniques.

Jeanette Harris, in "Toward a Working Definition of Collaborative Writing," first considers the sense in which all writing can be
seen as collaborative, then narrows the scope to collaboration in
the actual construction of text. Distinguishing the stages of collaborative text construction—interior text (pre-writing), generative text
(writing-in-progress), and completed text (revision)—she looks at
the practical implications of collaborative activity at each stage.
Harris further discusses the effects of current trends, such as the
increasing use of computers in writing and teaching, with respect
to encouraging or discouraging collaborative work. Perceiving a
growing acceptance of collaboration for pragmatic but not for aesthetic writing, she calls for a more thorough "legitimizing" of collaborative undertakings.

Shirley K Rose, in "A Model for Collaborative Writing," argues
for the need of collaborators to adequately and accurately describe
their individual roles in the joint production of text. In response to
this perceived exigency, she uses several collaborative writing scenarios to delineate a spectrum of possible types of collaborative
procedure. Using participants, propositions, and decisions as her
fundamental terms and categorizing the types of writing decision
(the ultimate step in collaboration) as proposing, reviewing, responding, canceling, and asserting, Rose designs a general model
to define and assess individual responsibility for the joint product.
She discusses how the model would work specifically for coauthorship, ghost writing, cooperative writing, and peer-response

groups—categories corresponding to the situations of her initial scenarios.

The third essay in the section, "The Ethics of Computerized Collaboration in the Classroom," by Fred Kemp, discusses problems involved in pedagogical methods which promote student responses to the writing of other students—including questions of privacy, ownership of text, and evaluation of the final product. Kemp considers rights of the student with respect to her/his own text and the degree to which exposure of that text to the scrutiny of others is an unwarranted intrusion into the writer's private domain. The essay also focuses at length on the question of "exploitation" of student writing: to what degree and under what circumstances can a writing teacher-researcher feel justified in quoting, citing, or otherwise appropriating text produced in a collaborative learning situation?

In "What Do You Think?: Collaborative Learning and Critical Thinking in the Business Writing Class," Ellen Andrews Knodt turns to the question of effectuality of collaborative effort. Knodt first reviews current literature on the pedagogical value of collaborative writing assignments for students, then presents her own method for student collaboration in business writing. With respect to the theoretical aspect of such methods, she discusses the value of the "public" nature of collaborative writing as an aid to critical thinking. In pursuit of adequate practical applications, she describes actual assignments and results, showing more thorough and generally better performance by collaborators and suggesting that the value of collaborative work on one project may carry over into subsequent projects.

Section IV, "What Makes a Collaboration Successful?," presents a number of examples of literary and scholarly collaborations, both successful and unsuccessful. Following the clue of these examples, the authors in this section seek to determine the conditions under which collaborative effort thrives and those in which it fails. On this basis, they ask to what extent collaboration is worthwhile and what its documented successes and failures teach about not only collaborative possibilities but the nature of the writing process in general.

Robert Murray Davis, in "Kicking Dr. Johnson's Rock: An Inductive View of Collaboration," proposes the practical explanation that a writer collaborates out of necessity—to achieve greater efficiency or to make up for her/his shortcomings. To describe how these pragmatic gains are achieved, he discusses the various types of collaborations, which he identifies as the assembly-line model (individuals producing different portions of the text), as-told-to (division of labor between style and content), and senior partner-junior partner (one writer assisting another). To consider how these function, he divides the collaborative process into three stages (which are the same as those for any writing)—preparing, producing, polishing—and analyzes the problems resident in each. On the basis of specific examples of literary collaborations, such as Joseph Conrad-Ford Madox Ford and William Butler Yeats-George Moore, he analyzes the effect of collaboration on future works of collaborators, including future individual works. And finally, he asks how the lessons of collaboration can be profitably applied to the teaching of writing.

"Collaboration in Political Science: The Research-Writing Nexus," by Robert P. Steed, moves us away from the literary and into the realm of the social sciences. Steed, a political scientist who has participated in a number of projects involving both collaborative data-gathering and collaborative production of text, discusses joint effort as fundamental to scholarship in political science, but notes that collaboration in actually producing final text has become common (or commonly acknowledged) only during the past half-century. He sees the importance of collaboration in social-sciences research as a function of the size of the tasks involved, geographical obstacles to data-gathering, need for a range of specialized knowledge, and need for funding from multiple sources—all of which make data-sharing and cooperative production of text the most (perhaps the only) practicable route. Steed discusses his specific experience in collaborative research and writing (for studies of delegate attitudes at political conventions), touching on problems and their possible solutions in collaborative data-collection, writing, and editing.

Laura Brady's "Collaboration as Conversation: Literary Cases" analyzes collaborative fiction-writing in terms of authority, agreement, dialogue, and negotiation. Brady examines three coauthored novels as examples of the monologic (only one voice heard at a time), dialogic (alternating dominance of authors working cooperatively but writing separately), and conversational (discussion and consensus throughout). She finds that the monologic (*The Whole*

Family, Henry James et al.) fails due to competitive attitudes and a lack of common goals and purposes. The dialogic (*The Gilded Age*, Mark Twain and Charles Dudley Warner) achieves a much greater compatibility of separately authored parts but still fails to achieve sufficient continuity and consistency. The conversational (*Love Medicine*, Louise Erdrich and Michael Dorris), which emerges as Brady's model for collaboration, succeeds, through total integration of text production, in creating a consistent and seemingly single-voiced text. Thus the three types of collaboration establish a kind of hierarchy of efficacy directly proportional to the degree of integration of effort between coauthors.

The concluding essay, M. Thomas Inge's "Mark Twain and Dan Beard's Collaborative *Connecticut Yankee*," extends the interrogation of textuality by examining the nature and impact of Beard's work as illustrator of Twain's *A Connecticut Yankee in King Arthur's Court*. Inge's analysis of this celebrated case of author-illustrator collaboration categorizes Beard's illustrations as (1) purely illustrative, (2) extensions of the text, or (3) departures from the text. He assesses the degree to which they often yield meanings different from those of the written text itself. Inge speculates that Beard often captured elements of Twain's intention that Twain was not willing to express himself but was glad to have included with/in the novel. He shows how this dual-medium collaboration raises questions about authorial intention, non-linguistic meaning, and ownership of texts.

"Collaborative Writing: A Browser's Bibliography" brings together entries from rhetoric and composition theory, literary biography, literary criticism, and a smattering of other topics deemed relevant to a broad consideration of collaborative writing. The result is a rather odd assemblage, but one which we hope will be useful to readers interested in exploring the diverse aspects of collaborative endeavor identified and discussed in the essays that comprise this volume. The entries are, with a few exceptions, annotated.

This book itself is, obviously, multiply collaborative, having more than the usual accumulation of editors, a collaboratively compiled bibliography, and two (explicitly) jointly authored essays. Like other collections of essays by different authors, it offers an example of multiple viewpoints turning a subject many ways and finding in each a perspective worth considering. However, unlike most collections the present one, by self-consciously scrutinizing collaboration's unity-from-multiplicity, directly faces the textual/authorial questions involved in such an enterprise. This volume both practices and espouses the doctrine that collaboration works, that it may be invaluable, that its riches have in the past been unjustly ignored or denied by major players in the textual production game—as enforced by institutions which we (all of us who play or aspire to play that game) both are and are dominated by. We suggest that the rules of the game are, for the sake of both collaborative possibilities and collaborative necessities, beginning to change in ways which will alter our relation to writing and to ourselves.

Section I

Who Collaborates?

The Art of Collaboration

M. Thomas Inge

Individualism has often been noted by cultural historians as one of the salient features of the American character. From before Frederick Jackson Turner's celebration of individualism as a product of the frontier experience in his influential address of 1893 down to the lone figures of the film screen such as John Wayne, Dirty Harry, and the Batman of 1992, Americans have praised the solitary individuals willing to strike out on their own, take the law into their own hands, rise above the common crowd, and chart a unique path for themselves. True creativity and innovation are the products of those gifted individuals who break the pattern of tradition and the commonplace to lead us into new directions of enlightenment and achievement—or so goes this line of thought. Thus collaboration, group creation, or mass production are likely to result in the ordinary, unexceptional, and unimaginative. Who wants an assembly-line product when you can have a hand-made one? Why settle for Taster's Choice when you can grind your own coffee beans at home?

In the areas of art and literature, these ideas have connected with the concept of the creator as prophet and conduit of divine inspiration and led to the veneration of the alienated and misunderstood artist who refuses to barter his talent for the vulgar taste of the ordinary populace and the demeaning demands of the capitalistic marketplace.

Herman Melville has often been cited as a case in point. The traditional view of Melville has been to see him as a writer "damned by dollars" and the economic necessity of earning a living, who because of his individual genius and talent was unable to adapt to the prevailing patterns of popular fiction in his day, and who was rejected by his readers because he refused in *Moby-Dick*, *Pierre*, and other works to compromise by writing down to his mass audience. He has been the darling of the high-brow literary establishment because he demonstrates the fate of the artist unwilling to sacrifice his integrity for popularity. I should note, however, that this view may soon change in the light of forthcoming research that demonstrates Melville was actually drawing directly on existing popular narrative forms in these works, intended to address himself to a wide readership, and was himself very much a part of mainstream antebellum popular culture. Melville collaborated with his cultural and economic world, in other words, out of intention as well as necessity.

The truth is that most of the culture of this century, probably of the nineteenth century, and possibly since the Industrial Revolution has largely been the product of the art of collaboration rather than the art of the individual. From the time movable type was developed, another individual has stood between the writer and the reader—the printer. As soon as the type-setter began to regularize the fonts and impose systematic grammar and spelling on the contents of manuscripts for the sake of expediency and readability, the books produced were collaborations.

It is the lack of recognition of this simple fact that has often led scholars in wrong directions in the newly emerging study of popular culture. With no history of scholarship or methodology to follow in the beginning, they often relied on those approaches already established in the separate disciplines. Thus popular fiction was read by historians for its reflections of social change and historic events as one would read primary documents, or by literary critics for variations in character, plot, style, and theme as one would read established classics. Whatever was current in historiography or literary theory was brought to bear, more often than not with a sense of disappointment. It was quickly evident that works like *Uncle Tom's Cabin* offered neither sound history about the South and slavery nor an artistic match for such novels about the same topic as William Styron's *Confessions of Nat Turner*. Like its later sister novel *Gone with the Wind*, the importance of *Uncle Tom's Cabin* resides outside history and literature.

The very first film courses I remember being offered in universities where I taught were called "Fiction into Film" or some variation thereof. A selection of novels and films based on those novels were taught, usually by a professor of English, and both were explicated in the new critical style for plot, structure, theme, and characterization as one would literary texts. Needless to say, the works of fiction by individual authors inevitably proved superior to the films produced by the collective labors of Hollywood. The students came away convinced that reading books was superior to viewing films and that all efforts to film classic works were doomed to failure. I even heard such statements offered to curriculum committees as justification for teaching such courses in English departments—they would work to benefit literature by turning students away from movies and back to books (we now know they were never even in competition with each other). Such attitudes contributed little to a proper appreciation of the artistic qualities of film.

A film, of course, cannot be analyzed or studied as one would a novel because there is no single guiding intelligence or artistic intention. Beginning with an outline and a script, soon the talents and visions of numerous people are involved, each of whom leaves a decided impression on the final product—the director, the producers, the actors, the cinematographer, the film editor, and numerous others whose names fill the credit lists at the end, not to mention the limitations of financial backing and the market potential for films of its genre. It is purely a product of collaboration and cannot easily be done any other way.

Efforts to develop the concept of the "auteur" on the part of film critics—that is, the belief that the director is the primary creative force and therefore the actual author of a film—are but misguided efforts to treat motion pictures as one would products of the solitary artist. Rather than accept film on its own terms, it is forced to fit a preconceived notion that the only worthwhile art is that produced by the individual.

Another form of popular culture where collaboration has been the order of the day almost from the start has been the comics. The very first comic strips were drawn by single artists, such as Richard Felton Outcault, Frederick Burr Opper, Rudolph Dirks, and Carl Schultze, but when their characters proved to be enormously popular with the public—the Yellow Kid, Happy Hooligan, the Katzenjammer Kids, and Foxy Grandpa—the newspapers for which they worked promptly claimed ownership of their creations on the work-for-hire principle, and considered the creator unnecessary to the promotion and survival of the property. Legal battles in two cases, over ownership of the Yellow Kid and the Katzenjammer Kids, resulted in a situation in which the same characters drawn by different artists were appearing in competing newspapers simultaneously.

Whether or not they retained control of their creations, it soon became evident to the successful cartoonists that the grueling schedule of producing daily comic strips could be alleviated by taking on assistants, to help at first with incidental details and eventually with the entire strip itself, with the creator writing, supervising, or doing some detail himself. It was not uncommon for a cartoonist to use a writer for the gags or continuity, a letterer for the dialogue and narrative, and an assistant either to do preliminary sketches or ink the finished version. One cartoonist, Ham Fisher, creator of Joe Palooka, became notorious for his use of talented assistants who were paid very little for their contributions, among whom was Al Capp before he created his own strip, *Li'l Abner*. When Fisher accused Capp of having stolen characters from his strip for *Li'l Abner*, he began a lifetime battle of mutual character assassination and acrimony which took no prisoners and became legendary in the comics community. For the public, it served to reveal the fact that most cartoonists hired others to do what readers thought they were doing on their own. A further irony was that Capp ran his own sweatshop during *Li'l Abner*'s most successful years, and among his many assistants was the future master of fantasy poster painting, Frank Frazetta. Capp claimed at least to draw the faces of the characters at first, though others handled the rest while he chased after talk show appearances, the lecture circuit, and college coeds.

It is true, however, that some cartoonists have insisted on being entirely responsible for their features. Charles Schulz, for example, has for a record of over forty years written, drawn, inked, and lettered *Peanuts* every day without missing a single deadline. This is a remarkable achievement which gives the body of his work a special integrity that other strips lack, but it does not guarantee consistency in quality, and he has found it necessary to turn over to teams of collaborators the *Peanuts* merchandising—animated films, greeting cards, toys, dolls, napkins, comic books, and the thousands of other items that have flooded the market and made him a multi-billionaire.

Among comic book artists, Will Eisner has always demonstrated a full mastery of all elements of the medium—plotting, writing, drawing, lettering, and inking—as demonstrated in his recent book-length graphic narratives such as *A Contract with God* and *The Heart of the Storm*. But he has just as often collaborated with other artists and writers as in the days of his weekly feature *The Spirit*, and he established one of the early shops which hired teams of creative people to produce comic book pages to order for publishers on a mass scale. Schulz and Eisner are often cited as the ideal independent comic artists, and some artists like Bill Watterson in *Calvin and Hobbes* and Art Spiegelman in *Maus* have followed in their footsteps, but they remain the exceptions rather than the rule.

All of this simply serves to underline the fact that most comic strip and comic book features have been collaborations. It was writer Jerry Siegel and artist Joe Shuster who teamed up to give us Superman, the most successful and popular superhero in American culture since Davy Crockett and Daniel Boone. It was Joe Simon and Jack Kirby together who created that quintessentially American comic book warrior Captain America, as well as other popular features such as the Young Allies, the Boy Commandos, and the Newsboy Legion which allowed young readers to have heroes their own age. It was editor Stan Lee and artist Steve Ditko who produced Spider-Man, the anti-hero with personality problems, especially suited for the alienated readers of the 1960s.

A glance at the credits on the title page of a contemporary comic book suggests that at a minimum, at least seven people are involved in its creation: a general editor, a project editor, a script writer, a penciler who does the rough sketches, an inker who finishes the art, a letterer who does the dialogue and narration, and a colorist who brings the project to full-color completion. It is not unusual for further names to be added—idea people, assistants, original creators, and various associates. It is clearly not possible to identify in much comic book publishing a single guiding hand or author.

In the area of animation, one need only mention the dominant figure of Walt Disney, who had a genius for drawing into his cartoon assembly line some of the brightest talents of his generation and stamping the stunning products of their imaginations with the Disney corporate name. Disney was perhaps the most successful collaborator of this century, although it was Ub Iwerks who gave us the image of Mickey Mouse and Floyd Gottfredson and Carl Barks who made Mickey and Donald Duck into fully developed and extremely popular comic strip and comic book characters. The genuine genius of Iwerks, Gottfredson, and Barks aside, where would they have been without the inexhaustible inventive talent of Disney and his insistent concern for the quality of all products bearing his name? As another form of film-making, animation is necessarily a collective endeavor.

It is not only in the so-called "lowbrow" and popular arts, however, that collaboration has been commonplace. Among the "highbrow" arts, literature has witnessed any number of successful group efforts, especially in this century. In London before and after World War I a group of writers and artists gathered to form the Bloomsbury Group to provide mutual support for their unconventional life-styles and aesthetic theories. Several collaborative projects came out of the group, and without such support, we might not have had the remarkable novels by Virginia Woolf which helped establish modern fiction. After the war the salons and cafés of Paris witnessed the gathering of many bright and promising writers who, under the tutelage of Gertrude Stein and James Joyce, would move to the forefront of American fiction, Ernest Hemingway and F. Scott Fitzgerald among them. How much Hemingway's famous style owes to Stein and how much Fitzgerald and Hemingway owe each other are still matters of scholarly debate. Even Faulkner, who stayed away from the cafés when he was in Paris, could not escape the profound influence of Joyce and the stimulating conversations of the Lost Generation about Freud, society, art, and literature, even if it reached him indirectly through Sherwood Anderson, Phil Stone, and others.

A major collaboration to come out of this same intellectual milieu was that between expatriates T.S. Eliot and Ezra Pound. The older Pound helped get "The Love Song of J. Alfred Prufrock" into print and even took a directly shaping editorial hand in the final form of Eliot's "The Waste Land," arguably the most influential and certainly the most discussed poem in modern English letters. Without Pound, "The Waste Land" would not be the poem as we know it—the brilliant product of two exceptional talents.

On this side of the Atlantic, after World War I, a group of young students and aspiring writers began to meet in 1922 in the home of a Jewish mystic in Nashville, Tennessee, and decided to publish a magazine, *The Fugitive*. Here the early efforts of John Crowe Ransom, Allen Tate, Robert Penn Warren, Hart Crane, and Laura Riding, among others, appeared—all to become distinguished voices in American poetry. In the first issue, they didn't even sign their names to the poems, and their collaborative method of discussing and critiquing each other's poems at group meetings would inspire a system of analysis which would become known as the New Criticism and shape the teaching of and writing about literature for several generations. Four members of the Fugitive group would later become central to another Southern collaborative effort, the writing of an Agrarian manifesto called *I'll Take My Stand* in 1930. Without the impetus of the Fugitive and Agrarian movements, the shape of the Southern Literary Renaissance might have been considerably different or not have taken place at all.

Thomas Wolfe, a major writer in that Renaissance, might not have seen print had not a patient editor, Maxwell Perkins, been willing to extract and organize from Wolfe's mountain of disorganized manuscripts the novels that brought him fame and fortune. Perkins had already nursed Hemingway and Fitzgerald into print with his skillful editorial collaboration, but in the case of Wolfe, Perkins' name might appropriately have appeared on the title page. This would be even more clearly the case with regard to his later editor, Edward C. Aswell, who carved two novels and a collection of stories out of an eight-foot pile of manuscript left behind after Wolfe's untimely death and for which he even created new text when necessary. The Wolfe we know is purely the product of collaboration. There are any number of other examples that can be offered of the power of group effort in American letters, from the Hartford Wits and New England Transcendentalists to the Imagist poetry movement, the Beat Generation, the Group Theatre, and the Black Mountain Poets.

In Europe, the history of art beginning in the 1870s was punctuated by one group movement and aesthetic philosophy after another, including impressionism, expressionism, futurism, cubism, dadaism, and surrealism. In a burst of creative collaboration, the impressionists Claude Monet and Auguste Renoir once set up their easels together on the banks of the Seine River and began furiously to talk and paint. They began to influence each other so profoundly that some of their paintings are remarkably similar. While involved in the development of cubism, Pablo Picasso and Georges Braque worked so closely together that each began to think like the other and they even refused to sign their names to their work. Said Picasso, reminiscing later, "People didn't understand very well at the time why very often we didn't sign our canvasses.... It was because we felt the temptation, the hope of an anonymous art, not in its expression but in its point of departure" (Gilot 75). They sought an anonymous personality in pursuit of originality. Even that violent individualist, Vincent Van Gogh, once tried to live and work with that other classic loner Paul Gauguin, but the tensions soon terminated the experiment despite the admiration they held for each other's paintings. Obviously, the community of artists has had a strong appeal for a great many painters and sculptors and has provided them with a creative energy and sympathetic inspiration difficult to attain on one's own.

Some of the recent efforts in textual scholarship to rescue the writer's primary intentions reflect, I think, a misconception of how literature has been produced in the late nineteenth and twentieth centuries. The writer is clearly the originator of the manuscript, but he or she does not stand in any direct relationship to the reader. Generally speaking, between the creator and the receiver there stand several influential people—the author's agent, the acquisitions editor, the primary reader who evaluates the manuscript, the copy editor who prepares it for the printer, the typesetter, the proof-reader, the promotion editor, the marketing manager and sales staff, the book reviewer, the wholesaler, and finally the bookstore retailer. The whole structure is a complex series of negotiations and compromises dedicated to producing the best book possible for the given market and thereby making a living if not enriching each participant in the process. Sometimes the process works to the detriment of a book and no one benefits, but most often it succeeds. Otherwise, it would have been abandoned long ago. This is not to say that this is necessarily the best possible process and that good literature inevitably results. But it is the way literature has been done in this century, and to pretend that we live in a society where the artist is totally free to address the patrons and exercise full control over the creation is not realistic. The concept of the artist as complete individualist is a romantic notion whose day has passed and perhaps never really existed anyway except in our imaginations.

Yet much of modern textual criticism and scholarship is determined to bring us back as readers to the author's original impulse, as if the whole process described above has been a corruption of some noble ideal. We are asked to give primacy to a version of a novel that was never meant really to exist outside the archive. The Pennsylvania edition of Theodore Dreiser's *Sister Carrie* is a case in point. Four textual critics have meticulously restored in all its massive length the author's original version using the manuscript and the typescript of the text. In the preface, they note:

> Dreiser's wife and his friend Arthur Henry cut and revised the manuscript and the typescript. The typists and the publisher's house editors made further changes. The *Sister Carrie* that was published in November 1900 was marred by this editorial interference and censorship and has been the basis of American editions and foreign translations until the present. (Dreiser ix)

As they go on to admit in the historical commentary at the end of the edition, these were considered by Dreiser as welcome intrusions or "interference." Both Dreiser and Henry were beginning writers who decided to write their first novels simultaneously so "they could share the experience" (Dreiser 505), and they swapped portions of their work, providing advice and editorial suggestions to each other as they proceeded. Always happy to have all the help he could get, especially with spelling and grammar, Dreiser enlisted the aid of his schoolteacher wife Sara, nicknamed "Jug," to offer corrections and criticism:

> Throughout the composition of the manuscript, in fact, Dreiser offered his drafts to Jug and Henry for revision and editing. This practice was by now habitual: during his apprentice years as a newspaper reporter, Dreiser had become accustomed to working with copy-editors and rewrite men, and he had never developed much sensitivity about his prose. He had always been a poor speller and an indifferent grammarian; Jug, who knew the mechanics of the language from her teaching days, could correct demonstrable errors in his drafts. Henry's function was different; he was a published author with some feeling for the style and rhythm of English prose, and Dreiser allowed him to identify and revise awkward spots in the drafts. The manuscript of *Sister Car-*

rie therefore exhibits, in nearly every chapter, markings by both
Jug and Henry. (Dreiser 506–7)

The typists also added punctuation and corrected spelling errors,
but sometimes misread his difficult handwriting or skipped over
sentences in the manuscript. Except for these latter changes, which
Dreiser himself allowed to stand, all the other alterations were accepted or approved by the author. When the publisher required
that 30,000 words be excised from the lengthy novel, Dreiser, unable to face the task himself, asked Henry to do the job. The textual
critics admit that "almost without exception his cuts quicken narrative pace and tone down sexual passages" (Dreiser 520). In other
words, Henry made the novel more readable and suitable for the
turn-of-the-century marketplace.

If ever an author benefited from editing and excising, it was, in
my opinion, Dreiser. He was given to rambling Germanic sentences, difficult syntax, overwhelming detail, and endless digres-
sion, not to mention a poor grasp of the rules of spelling and punctuation; we wouldn't want to read him at the manuscript stage.
Dreiser was gifted when it came to characterization, narrative development, realistic detail, research into social milieu, and thematic
power. As had Walt Whitman earlier, Dreiser gave voice to the
enormous economic, political, and ethical struggles that were the
birth throes of a major new world-class nation. He is an influential
and unavoidable presence on the American literary scene, but a
polished prose stylist he was not. To my mind, he is the perfect example of the kind of writer who needed the guidance and refinement offered by the American publishing system. Dreiser seems to
have known this, too. I find it ironic that the textual editors note in
their preface, "The Pennsylvania Edition of *Sister Carrie* has been,
since its inception, a collaborative effort" (Dreiser ix). They would
rescue Dreiser from the very process essential to their own work.

The new edition of *The Great Gatsby*, in the Cambridge Edition
of the Works of F. Scott Fitzgerald, is another case in point.
Fitzgerald relied heavily on Maxwell Perkins to help with technical
and structural problems in the manuscript, which took him almost
three years to see through to publication. He would write his editor three months after the book appeared, "Max, it amuses me
when praise comes in on the 'structure' of the book—because it
was you who fixed up the structure, not me" (Fitzgerald xviii).

One of the most effective features of *The Great Gatsby*, then, was attributable to Perkins.

Apparently Fitzgerald used a minimum of punctuation, and what he did use was inconsistent and idiosyncratic, especially commas. While removing most of the punctuation inserted by the house editors at Scribners does not for the most part impede our understanding, in a few instances this is not the case. Take, for example, the restored version of the first sentence of Chapter IV:

> On Sunday morning while church bells rang in the village along shore the world and its mistress returned to Gatsby's house and twinkled hilariously on his lawn. (Fitzgerald 49)

I had to read this sentence three times before I understood it clearly because of the uncertainty as to the subject of the verbs of the main clause. How much better is the version with the house-supplied punctuation in the 1925 text:

> On Sunday morning while church bells rang in the village along-shore, the world and its mistress returned to Gatsby's house and twinkled hilariously on his lawn.

There is an openness and fluidity in the "lite," punctuation-free *Gatsby*, but I cannot say I prefer it to the original comma-ridden text. I'd rather risk the calories. The textual critic in this case, Matthew J. Bruccoli, who is noted for his intelligent and common-sense textual practices, did resist following Fitzgerald all the way in returning to authorial intentions. Fitzgerald had various titles in mind as the novel progressed: "Among the Ash Heaps and Millionaires," "Tramalchio in West Egg," "The High-bouncing Lover," and "Gold-hatted Gatsby" among them. Fortunately, both Perkins and Bruccoli had the wisdom to resist Fitzgerald's final, desperate plea in a telegram: "CRAZY ABOUT TITLE UNDER THE RED WHITE AND BLUE STOP" (Fitzgerald 207). *The Great Gatsby*, the title Fitzgerald placed on the manuscript, was clearly the best choice, and authorial intention was contrary to the best interests of the novel. Bruccoli notes, "it is too late now to retitle a classic novel" (Fitzgerald 180). I am also wondering if it isn't too late to be re-editing a classic novel.

The texts of Faulkner's novels have also been under similar reconstruction by another astute textual critic, Noel Polk, who has returned in each case to the typescript of the work after Faulkner did his final revisions and corrections and before the copy editors

at Random House began their process of regularization and alter-
ation. This itself is a compromise since everyone agrees that
Faulkner's final intentions, if he had any, cannot be determined.
Sanctuary presents a particularly thorny dilemma. When his publisher registered shock upon seeing the original text of *Sanctuary* in
proof stage, Faulkner broke the galleys down, reorganized, and
rewrote the novel. In the afterword to his edition of the restored
text, Polk admits that "the revised *Sanctuary* is a smoother, faster-
paced, and more dramatic novel than its heretofore unpublished
predecessor" (Faulkner 304). Polk goes on to say that had Faulkner
decided to rewrite *The Sound and the Fury*, the revised version
"would almost certainly have been a different book from the early
one, although not necessarily superior to it" (Faulkner 305). The
business of determining what text at what stage should be the au-
thoritative one is unresolvable, and the author's final intention
may seldom be the best guiding principle, if it matters at all.

All of these versions of standard American novels—*Sister Carrie*, *The Great Gatsby*, and *Sanctuary*—are books which really have
no place in American literary history. They are anomalies and belong, if anywhere, on the shelves of research libraries and the
desks of specialists interested in the working habits of our major
writers and the textual histories of their novels. They are treasure
houses of information about the ways of creativity and genius and
the sources of fiction that lays claim to greatness. Buy they are *not*
the novels that were issued in their respective historic periods;
they are *not* the books that were reviewed, read, and discussed by
generations of critics and teachers; they are *not* the novels which,
despite the tamperings of market-place publishing in America,
have emerged as books of lasting value; and they should *not* serve
to replace them among general readers or in the classroom. The
original texts remain impressive monuments to the abiding power
and ability of writers able effectively to deal with the compromises
of a largely collaborative industrial society and emerge victorious.

There are numerous other examples of the importance of collaboration in all types of modern culture that I can mention only
briefly. In comedy, one might take note of Laurel and Hardy, the
Marx Brothers, Abbott and Costello, Monty Python, and *Saturday
Night Live*; in popular music, Lerner and Lowe, Rogers and Ham-
merstein, the Beatles, and the Rolling Stones; in comic opera,
Gilbert and Sullivan; in popular philosophy and history Will and

Ariel Durant; in sexual research, Masters and Johnson; etc. Such a list can be continued indefinitely.

My conclusion, of course, is clear by now, and my statement is a simple one. We must begin to find ways to address and evaluate the influence of collaboration in cultural studies, whatever our areas of specialization and the disciplinary bases from which we work. In the study of cultural products, it is important to recognize that in many, if not most, cases we are talking about things which came into being by cooperation and delicate negotiation between creators, producers, and consumers. Individualism as an ideal will remain important in the hearts and minds of those who will sustain the American democratic experiment, but it can only obscure the visions of those who insist on seeing it as the primary source of creativity and place a premium on its cultural value. We must make allowance for the dynamics and the vital power of the art of collaboration.

Works Cited

Dreiser, Theodore. *Sister Carrie*. The Pennsylvania Edition. Ed. John C. Berkey, Alice M. Winters, James L.W. West III, and Neda M. Westlake. Philadelphia: U of Pennsylvania P, 1981.

Faulkner, William. *Sanctuary: The Original Text*. Ed. Noel Polk. New York: Random House, 1981.

Fitzgerald, F. Scott. *The Great Gatsby*. The Cambridge Edition. Ed. Matthew J. Bruccoli. Cambridge: Cambridge UP, 1991.

Gilot, Françoise, and Carlton Lake. *Life with Picasso*. New York: McGraw Hill, 1964.

Writing to Collaborate: Collaborating to Write

Michael Schrage

Several essays in this anthology examine the myth of the lonely "auteur," while others explore the role technology can play in augmenting the creative writing process. This essay argues that collaboration is as much a creative medium as it is a human relationship. What's more, the medium of collaboration is shaped by the media of collaboration—the tools and techniques that collaborative writers and editors use. While it is far from clear how the evolution of collaborative media will transform the medium of collaboration, it is certain that this co-evolution of medium and media will fundamentally change the way readers, writers and critics view the creation of texts. Indeed, the role of collaboration and collaborative media, I argue, will be essential to any meaningful discussion of creativity in writing.

Just as paper, film, and video provide both opportunities and constraints for expression, so too for a collaboration. In fact, viewing collaboration—particularly collaborative writing—as a medium gives us important new ways to examine the processes both of creating and of interpreting texts. The collaborative medium incorporates both the technical and the personal.

The properties of the collaboration will strongly influence the quality of the text. The various tools and techniques that go into the collaborative process may ultimately prove as revealing and important as the authors' intent. The goal of this essay is to offer the reader new insights into creative expression through the medium of collaboration.

For the purpose of clarity, collaborative writing is here defined as an act of "shared creation": two or more individuals with complementary skills interacting to craft a text that neither could have created on his/her own.

I am not talking about a de minimis "collaboration" where a copy editor crosses T's and dots I's; I'm referring to texts that are unambiguously the product of shared minds—texts that the authors acknowledge literally could not have been created without an effective collaboration with the other.

These textual collaborations can take unusual forms. As a journalist, I remember the qualitative differences in my interviews with sources when I sought simply to extract information from them versus the times I tried to prod them into using creative metaphors and analogies to explain themselves. The process of straightforward interrogations was scarcely collaborative; no shared understanding was created. I simply took the information and plugged it into my story. By contrast, getting people to express their ideas with metaphors proved quite a provocative collaborative exercise. I certainly couldn't have come up with the explanatory metaphors on my own and my sources were unlikely to come up with them without my questions and follow-ups. In other words, we collaborated around these metaphors and analogies to create shared understandings that we couldn't have come to separately. The people who read my newspaper stories were (I hope) the ultimate beneficiaries. Similarly, because my newspaper (*The Washington Post*) didn't have enough word processors to go around, reporters often had to share keyboards. When I was required to write a story with another reporter because the topic cut across two beats—for example, my own high-technology beat and a colleague's international trade beat—we soon discovered that the best way to collaborate on a story was not to exchange drafts but to sit shoulder to shoulder and take turns at the keyboard. What happened was that the screen and keyboard became the medium of "shared space" through which we collaboratively wrote our story. There was an undeniably qualitative difference between stories that were written side-by-side in an interactive way and those that were exchanged as files on a computer system. In effect, the collaborative tools we used turned two individuals into a single collaboration.

That is what makes collaboration as much medium as relationship. Collaborative writings have two audiences—the ultimate reader and the collaboration itself. The collaboration itself is interposed between the writers and the readers. In other words, the collaboration transcends the individual authors. The collaborators negotiate meaning and determine what expressions will be appropriate. Just as the quality of paper can determine the crispness and legibility of print, the quality of the collaborative medium affects the crispness and comprehensiveness of expression.

This is beautifully articulated by sociologists Lionel Tiger and Robin Fox in their work *The Imperial Animal* (New York: Holt, Rinehart and Winston, 1971)—a book exploring the biological boundaries of human culture and relationships. The book was written as a collaboration, and indeed, it was the nature of that collaboration, the authors say, that provoked inordinate curiosity: "... what appears to cause more people more puzzlement," the authors write,

is how two people could actually write a book together. Did X write one chapter and Y the next? Did bold X really write it while surly Y wielded a fierce editorial pen? Did X do the recitative about monkeys and Y the aria on newborns?

No. We both had one sacred rule. Every single sentence had to be written with both perpetrators present.... No taking home of manuscripts, no dividing up of chapters. Either one could rewrite anything or rewrite everything, so much so that eventually we forgot totally who started and finished what, whose idea was this and whose caveat that. In the end what occurred was a kind of improvisation rather like jazz. A theme would be announced, worked over, run through, and worked over again, to the point where the separate instruments blend into one sound. While the separateness is there, it is submerged in the joint product—which becomes the only thing that matters. We had fun writing it; we hope you have fun reading it. We also learned more through writing it together than we could ever have through solitary research. There is probably a moral in this about the biology of social behavior; a moral for the reader to draw.

While the analogy to improvisational jazz is somewhat pedestrian, there is no ignoring just how compelling, appropriate and media-wise the musical analogy is. The notion of seamlessness—the idea that a successful collaboration represents a holistic blending of personalities and expression—should force us to reevaluate just what we mean by "writing." In effect, writing becomes not a medium for the expression of individual styles and ideas but a vehicle to integrate them.

Texts that are collaboratively designed and written to integrate perspectives can't help but be qualitatively different from texts designed to express individual perspectives. A dialogue is not the same as a soliloquy even if the words express the same ideas. Obviously, a duet or a trio represents a different musical medium than a solo performance. The way musicians "collaborate" to interpret a score unquestionably affects the quality of the music.

Unfortunately, in literature—and most of creative writing—a rich and complex semantic ritual has sprung up to minimize the importance of collaboration in the creative task of writing. As a young editor at Charles Scribner's, Maxwell Perkins transformed American literature with his unerring knack for finding fresh talent. Perkins discovered and launched F. Scott Fitzgerald and Thomas Wolfe. Both his literary and his commercial judgments were astute. His biographer noted that

> he was famous for his ability to inspire an author to produce the best that was in him or her. More a friend to his authors than a taskmaster, he aided them in every way. He helped them structure their books, if help was needed; thought up titles, invented plots; he served as psychoanalyst, adviser to the lovelorn, marriage counselor, career manager, moneylender. Few editors before him had ever done so much work on manuscripts, yet he was always faithful to his credo, "The book belongs to the author."

Perkins surely didn't coauthor his writers' books, but he was indispensable in shaping *The Great Gatsby* and *Look Homeward, Angel*. Not merely a catalyst, Perkins offered a compelling intellect and sure counsel that sculpted and refined his authors' prose. No, not a co-author—but just an editor?

Consider Ezra Pound's intimate working relationship with T.S. Eliot, arguably the finest English-language poet of this century. Pound relentlessly pushed and prodded Eliot. "Pound persuaded his fellow poet that his future lay in literature, not philosophy; in London, not the United States—a future to which Eliot then and there committed himself," one critic writes; "And the poem that afterward brought him fame and fortune, *The Waste Land*, was—as we have known for fifteen years—almost as much Pound's work as it was Eliot's." There's no concealing the lyrical brilliance of *The Waste Land* or other works by Eliot such as *Four Quartets*, but could Eliot have been quite so much the genius without Pound? Or does the real genius of the poetry lie within the collaborative intersection of Eliot's writing and Pound's editing? What does genius mean if it takes two?

Indeed, far too many critics are too quick to review the texts of "authors" when they should really be reviewing the texts of "collaborations." I hasten to point out that I'm not calling for a variant of deconstructionism—which seeks to crack texts into their seemingly component parts; rather, I'm arguing that analyzing certain texts independent of the relationships that produced them is like trying to analyze a child's motivations by chatting with only one parent. You produce an analysis that may be factually accurate but fundamentally incomplete.

Similarly, writers who collaborate aren't just exchanging ideas on a sheet of paper; they're struggling to create shared understandings and shared expressions. Their collaboration is an interpersonal medium to produce an intelligible and coherent text. To the extent they succeed, the writing enjoys the quality of integrative seamlessness that a reader should find intriguing. If they fail, the result is a porridge of twice-examined half-baked paragraphs that have meaning but only lumpy connections. To retreat again to the musical analogy, simply imagine a duet with each member singing in a different key. Without shared creation and shared expression, the medium generates discord and cacophony.

In other words, creating a shared experience is different from sharing an experience. The former is an attempt to converge towards meaning; the latter is parallel processing. A "group" is not a "team."

The Perkins example becomes especially useful here. Perkins was a common denominator for authors who certainly represented radically different styles. Perkins became a dynamic, highly interactive, participative tool to elicit and amplify the original author's expressions. Perkins didn't do this by any algorithm or formula; he did it, both personally and professionally, by building a web of shared contexts with his authors.

Like a medium, Perkins became a vehicle for his writers to refine, reshape, and reinvent their thoughts. That's not to say that

Perkins became a human typewriter or interpersonal vellum for his authors. He didn't. But, quite clearly, texts crafted with Perkins were qualitatively (and in Thomas Wolfe's case, quantitatively) different than without him. Working successfully with Perkins meant that both Perkins and the author came to a new, shared understanding of the direction of plot and the shape of characters. Perkins was not like a conductor interpreting a score, he was like a fellow improvisational musician expressing concerns about rhythm, phrasing, and tone. He didn't merely sculpt the material; he actually changed, in collaboration with the author, the nature of the material itself.

These were successful collaborations; indeed, their success is the stuff of modern legend. But putting aside the legendary aspects and looking at the collaborations in the cold light of writing's real exigencies, we can see that the co-laborers sweated under what we now must regard as primitive writing conditions—conditions that favored, and in most cases perpetuated, individualism vis-à-vis collective effort. Writing was pursued as a process internal to the individual—a miracle of the human mind to which community and technology were equally irrelevant. We have subsequently found new ways for writing to become "civilized" and socialized— a product of community. Would the landscapes of T.S. Eliot's *The Waste Land* read differently if Pound had edited with Post-It notes? (For that matter, would Eliot have felt the barren isolation that the poem describes if he had been engaged in an active, fruitful collaboration of a more immediate sort?) Suppose Max Perkins had edited Tom Wolfe on-line?

Today collaborative writing possibilities are increasingly facilitated by the new collaboration-friendly technologies that create shared space within which co-workers of the world can unite freely. Two bodies still can't occupy the same space at the same time; but collaborative technologies have redefined textual space to make it multiply accessible, and in the process created a multitude of collaborative potentialities.

Section II

What Does It Mean to Collaborate?

Breaking the Silence:
Collaboration and the Isolationist Paradigm

James S. Leonard and Christine E. Wharton

Contemporary literary criticism, under the influence of Jacques Derrida, has made much of the supposed secondariness (actually tertiariness) of writing, which, like the Platonic experiential bed/table, is said to be multiply removed from the truth. Pure thought tries to image reality, speech tries to reproduce thought, and writing—an impoverished, because highly figurative, representation of the eidos/logos which it struggles to signify—stands in for speech. With each step in this triple mediacy, the dream of truth's immediate presence recedes, replaced by a progressive drift toward the epistemological nightmare of pure figuration.

But writing has an immediacy myth of its own, fostered especially by English and American Romanticism: writing is the tool with which the poet tries to capture (or recapture) the elusive glimpse into the good and beautiful truth of things lying at the heart of silence. The silent locus/nature of truth calls for solitude, mirroring the truth itself as transcendently unitary. Socrates, who, with his nearly interminable dialogical explorations, stands at the center of Derrida's logos myth, can also be found losing himself in moments of the obverse. Subverting dialogue, he stands on a neighbor's porch for an indefinite time *before* attending a symposium at the house of Agathon (Plato, *The Symposium*). Socrates' construction may be that noetic intuition is altogether incommunicable—as indicated by his noticeable silence (in the face of Agathon's queries) regarding the substance of his solitary meditation, and perhaps more generally suggested (despite Derrida's alternate analysis in "Plato's Pharmacy"[1]), by his apparent non-interest in producing writings.[2] On the other hand, the Romantic nineteenth century, in the spirit of Hegelian comprehension (and adding a corollary to the Socratic "doctrine of recollection"), reviews its excursions in the subsequent tranquility of the poem.

Wordsworth, in spite of his fondness for the company of friend Coleridge and sister Dorothy, prefers in his mental adventurings to "wander lonely as a cloud," enjoying the companionship of flowers and trees in whose "jocund [but quiet] company" "a poet could not but be gay." And better still,

> ... oft, when on [his] couch [he] lie[s]
> In vacant or in pensive mood,
> They flash upon that inward eye
> Which is the bliss of *solitude*.
>
> (191; our emphasis)

Wordsworth's English Romantic successor Keats, enjoying the pleasures of urn, nightingale, psyche, melancholy, or autumn, or just savoring the poetic quality of sleep, looks always toward that solitary entrancement by which he will be transported away from human society and into the poetic realm of silence. The eminently American Emerson defines the poet as "he whose eye can integrate all the parts" of the horizon (23 [*Nature*]), carrying forward the emphasis on a singular vision, while his friend Thoreau, in the "Solitude" chapter of *Walden*, states flatly that he has "never found the companion that was so companionable as solitude.... A man thinking or working is always alone, let him be where he will" (386).

All these are familiar passages, and the Romantic devaluation of society in favor of silent communion with the natural (which proves finally equivalent to one's own musing) is obvious in each. But we should not overlook the subtext of implication within Romanticism's association between solitary meditation and writing. Here speech is bypassed (despite Wordsworth's identification of the poet as "a man speaking to men" [453]), and the writing of poetry, while not wholly immediate, stands in close relation to an unfallen experience of Truth. The poet's craft is ideally, as Dylan Thomas says, "Exercised in the still night / When only the moon rages" (196 ["In my craft or sullen art"]): a Coleridge hastens to write upon returning from his opium dream, a Milton to dictate (aloud but monologically) upon waking from his muse-haunted sleep. To write, in this myth of poetizing, is to emerge, but only partly, from a trance of unhindered vision; writing, in its silent solitariness, is the nearest approach to recapturing the originative inspiration. Its efficacy lies in its closeness not to the unalloyed reason of logocentrism but to the immaculate vision of transcendental experience. This romance with the transcendental, as Richard Rorty says, "hope[s] for a language which can receive no gloss, requires no interpretation, cannot be distanced, cannot be sneered at by later generations. It is the hope for a vocabulary which is intrinsically and self-evidently final" (89). This sort of vocabulary would be the language to transcend all languages; that is, it would be indistinguishable from direct, non-linguistic intuition of Truth. The ostensible silence and solitude of writing are necessary adjuncts to the worldless wordlessness of Romantic transcendence; and the conversion into mute symbols on the written page, while not a precise replication of the wordless transcendent moment, at least avoids the noisy divagations of actual conversation. It strives toward, to borrow an expression from Wallace Stevens, "pure rhetoric of a language without words" (*Collected Poems* 374 ["Credences of Summer"]) or as Thomas puts it, the "movement from an overclothed blindness to a naked vision" (quoted in Fitzgibbon 142).[3] The value of writing's monologue, at least as it applies to Romantic poetry, is that it evades the untidiness of a discursive exchange in which the alien intelligence/psyche injects discordant, therefore unwanted, elements—postulating instead a single, closely held understanding.

This may seem like excessive attention to Romantic poetry in an essay supposedly on the matter of collaboration. But the point has to do with a tenacious tendency, however inexplicit, to fit writing, including critical/theoretical writing, to the Romantic mold, as if the written were most essentially "palpable and mute as a globed fruit."[4] With that tendency, its companion piece, the paradigmatic writer/critic-as-lone-genius, materializes as a withdrawn, distant figure powered by unearthly inspiration (divinity, opium dream, etc.) whose solitary soul is more sensitive than those of ordinary mortals—endowed, as Wordsworth says, "with more lively sensibility, more enthusiasm and tenderness, ... a greater knowledge of human nature, and a more comprehensive soul, than are supposed to be common among mankind" (453). Wordsworth is speaking expressly of the poet, but it has been until recently a commonplace (as Pope, Eliot, and others testify) that only poets were fully qualified as critics.

In an article on the collaborations of W.H. Auden and Christopher Isherwood, Edward Mendelson, citing the greater pervasiveness of collaboration in the seventeenth and eighteenth centuries, explains the Romantic preference for singularity in terms of our usual sense of "public" vs. "private": "On the whole, collaboration is a public act in a public context, and it occurs when writers address an audience that is wide but well-defined, when literature enjoys the responsibility of a public role.... Romantic vision is private" (276). Mendelson's attention to public perception of the act of writing suggests that willingness or unwillingness (or from another point of view, ability or inability) to collaborate is determined not only by the "private" vision of particular individuals but by the character of the era as a whole. In the hybridized (or perhaps schizoid) twentieth century, the proposition that a "literary work" is a "public object" has been widely accepted, but for the most part, the *production* of that "work," or of most other types of writing, has continued to be viewed as a private act, pointing to the carryover (or reprise) of early nineteenth-century romanticism's denial of credible collaboration. It remains true that, as Jack Stillinger says, "critical appreciation of a masterwork requires it to be the production of a single organizing mind" (138).

The critic-as-Romantic-poet model was, ironically, smuggled into the twentieth century (more specifically, the New Criticism) in part by Eliot's influential characterization of the poetic mind as catalyst. Despite his disavowal of "emotion recollected in tranquility" and despite the superficially scientific nature of his mind-as-catalyst analogy, that analogy characterizes writing more as passion than action. With the New Criticism some notable collaborations emerged (Brooks and Warren, Wellek and the other Warren, Wimsatt and Beardsley) at the same time that criticism itself was emerging as a separately respectable vocation. But in spite of these, a romantic nostalgia projected/enforced the image of the critic-as-virtuoso: a new sort of isolationist relying on skills that, though somewhat different from those of the poet, are nevertheless "Exercised in the still night / When only the moon rages."

More recently, stylistic strategies (devised precisely to contest/undercut Romantic assumptions) generating the difficult differentiations of structuralism, flamboyant enigmas of deconstruction, or artful idiosyncrasies of reader response, have, again ironically, effectively re-moved the individual critic (merged with the singular critique) toward a status not so unlike that of the Romantic poet. Stanley Fish banters with students and colleagues about whether there is a text in the class; but when the time comes to seriously collect his thoughts on the subject of "interpretive communities," he removes, we imagine, to a place seemingly secure from the intrusions of the interpretive communities he discusses. Norman Holland gathers his reader-response data, then, one would suppose, retreats to the apparent solitude of home or office to compose his "lima bean theory" without the cacophonous distraction of all those readers responding. While the active engagement of the text by the various forms of poststructuralist critical endeavor has effectively converted the reading activity into a form of writing (as re-writing), the practice of writing even in this context remains, to a surprising degree, an ideal form of reading, seemingly attentive to the singular text of one's inspiration.

The privileged status of radically individualized productivity/sensibility has been sustained philosophically in recent decades by continuing literary-philosophical pursuit of, for example, Heidegger's singularizing "authenticity" or the individuating effect of his later "poetic listening," and (despite Nietzsche's importantly contrary influence) of the extravagantly prophetic Nietzsche of *Thus Spoke Zarathustra*. Heidegger's *Being and Time* discloses the significance of "understanding one's *ownmost* and uttermost potentiality-for-Being—that is to say, the possibility of *authentic existence*" (307; Heidegger's emphasis); "Dasein *is authentically itself* in the primordial individualization of ... reticent resoluteness.... *As something that keeps silent*, authentic *Being*-one's-Self ... 'is' that thrown entity as which it can authentically be" (369–70; his emphasis). As Christopher Fynsk has argued, Heidegger's "analysis of Dasein in *Being and Time* leads back insistently to the solitary self" (28). Rorty broadens the point: "What is common to early Heidegger on authenticity and to the early Wittgenstein on the sense of the world as a limited whole is the urge to see social practice as *merely* social practice, thereby rising above it. This is the urge to *distance* the social practice to which one has been accustomed ... by seeing it as [merely] contingent" (61). This effect is extended as Heidegger's later work meditates on the primordial relation between "Saying" and silence, and authentic existence modulates toward "the poetic"—"the gentle force of the singular [and, arguably, singularizing] and innocent capacity to hear" (*OWL* 100–1 ["The Nature of Language"])—that path by which the word lets "the poet become who he can be" (*OWL* 141 ["Words"]).[5] And for Nietzsche (at least in moments of his thought), as Kathleen Higgins contends,

> The suspension of ... dependence [on familiar interpretations and terminology] requires that the individual take leave of the community in some fashion. Nietzsche observes that the individuals who [spend] all their time in conversation with others will continually attune the formulation of their thoughts to those with whom they attempt to communicate. An individual can hear the most profound insights that arise from within only if there are occasions when both the linguistic conventions of the community and the stylistic considerations relevant to his or her particular audience are not demanding the individual's attention. (116)

Zarathustra's "closure" promises a singularly (or singularized) "new" beginning: "Zarathustra has ripened, my hour has come: this is *my* morning, *my* day is breaking" (*Zarathustra* 439; Nietzsche's emphasis).[6]

The philosophical rhetoric couples with popular images of the men themselves, underwriting the writer's separateness: Heidegger in pastoral retreat in the Black Forest, Nietzsche in Sils Maria have emerged as somewhat otherworldly lonely-genius figures in the contemporary mythology of writing. Hannah Arendt speaks of the strangeness and mesmerizing power of Heidegger's early fame: Heidegger's early lectures at Freiburg "dealt with texts that were generally familiar; they contained no doctrine that could have been learned, reproduced, and handed on. There was hardly more than a name, but the name traveled all over Germany like the rumor of the hidden king" (294).[7] And Werner Brock describes Heidegger's later secludedness as follows:

> On both occasions when I met Professor Heidegger ... I had to drive for an hour to the small town of Todtnau in the Black Forest Mountains, then to climb still further until the road became a path and all human habitation scattered and invisible. There on top of a mountain, with the valley deep down below, with nothing but space and wilderness all around, in that small skiing hut, I spoke to the philosopher.... His living conditions were primitive; his books were few, and his only relationship to the world

was a stack of writing paper. His whole life revolved within those white sheets and it seemed to me that he wanted nothing else but to be left in peace to cover those white sheets with his writing. The atmosphere of silence all around provided a faithful setting for Heidegger's philosophy. (ix–x)

Stevens, in his essay "Imagination as Value," visualizes Nietzsche, "walk[ing] in the Alps in the caresses of reality," as the antithesis of the humdrum existence of modern socialized men and women who "crawl out of ... offices and classrooms and become alert at the opera" (*Necessary Angel* 150; with respect to contemporary mythologies, it may be significant that Stevens, a non-academic, resorts to "classrooms" as one of the two loci of the quotidian).

These nineteenth-turned-twentieth-century sketches of the philosopher's art help to perpetuate a literary-critical investment in rhetoric comfortably close to that of Emerson's poet as Adamic "Namer or Language-maker":

The poets made all the words, and therefore language is the archives of history, and, if we must say it, a sort of tomb of the muses. For though the origin of most of our words is forgotten, each word was at first a stroke of genius, and obtained currency because for the moment it symbolized the world to the first speaker and to the hearer. The etymologist finds the deadest word to have been once a brilliant picture. Language is fossil poetry. (231 ["The Poet"])[8]

We have been drawn to the same trope in its Nietzschean extension: "What is originality? To *see* something that has no name as yet and hence cannot be mentioned although it stares us all in the face.... Those with originality have for the most part also assigned names" (*Gay Science*, 218 [#261]; Nietzsche's emphasis). And Heidegger reinscribes the circle: "Language itself is poetry in the essential sense.... Poesy—or poetry in the narrower sense—... takes place in language because language preserves the original nature of poetry.... Art, as the setting-into-work of truth, is poetry.... Art lets truth originate.... To originate something by a leap, to bring something into being from out of the source of its nature in a founding leap—this is what the word origin (German *Ursprung*, literally, primal leap) means" (*PLT* 74–78 ["The Origin of the Work of Art"]). This path leads toward the sort of metaphysical nostalgia that Derrida has exposed in Heidegger's "Anaximander Fragment" and elsewhere: "the quest for the proper word and the unique name" (Derrida, *Margins* 27). Yet even such substantially counter-vailing voices as Derrida, Michel Foucault, and Roland Barthes find themselves and their works wrapped/rapt in a singular mystique (or mystical singularity).

In comparison, science, which like literature has a history (and mythology) of lone-genius orientation (da Vinci, Galileo, Newton, Einstein, etc.), has, in face of twentieth-century complexity and the fragile limits of even the most agile minds, inclined more and more toward group undertakings and joint publication. We can note, for example, the celebrated physicist Stephen Hawking's thoroughly collaborative efforts and publications as not simply a matter of overcoming his physical handicap. He promotes a "collaborative understanding" of scientific questions/work, emphasized by the pervasive and generalized "we" in his writings (e.g.: "At the start of the 1970s, then, we were forced to turn our search for an understanding of the universe from our theory of the extraordinarily vast to our theory of the extraordinarily tiny" [51]).[9] And Werner Heisenberg, in *Physics and Beyond: Encounters and Conversations*, expresses his intention "to demonstrate that science is rooted in conversations" (quoted in Schrage 84). One (or more, if collaborating) could say that science is ironically, if unknowingly, surpassing the humanities with a stronger sense of human community, of the communicatory, of the fundamentally shared nature of language/experience.

Joint effort disrupts the seductive illusion that an individual can privately (in relation to some absolute) achieve a distinctively original voice to the extent that he/she is (or is at) the primordial source of language. In other words, collaboration testifies to the pre-existence of the language context and the illusive/delusional character of an utterly "new beginning" or an absolute beginning point. The act of collaborational writing, however dangerous—joining up with an "other" in contexts in which, it has been thought, every other may be the enemy—openly critiques the isolationist paradigm. In collaborative writing, original singleness of vision is neither possible nor sought. A certain achievement of "unitary thought" is worked out: a relatively seamless fabric of textual logic, the effect of a single voice speaking. But significantly, here the effect is a self-confessed illusion; the voice is professedly a simulated one. It cannot be imagined otherwise without denying the collaborative process altogether. Voice and logical structure are

experienced as products of negotiation within an essentially interactive language context. Romanticism's paradigmatic conversion
of a single, wordless insight to the inevitably disappointing secondariness of words is displaced by a multiplicity of proposals and
counterproposals laid on the table as intellectual coin to be
bartered in a market place of collaborative endeavor. Here the dis-
sonances and solutions of collaborative exchange re-place the ad-
versarial impulse. Collaboration is the bargaining process—strategy, play, gamesmanship—by which a multiplicity becomes
"coherent." And while all are enriched, the "singleness" of the result belongs to no one individual.

The play of strategies within collaborative activity experiences
the schisms suggested for the general problematic of language by
deconstruction's "différance," as the name given to "the 'active,'
moving discord of different forces, and of differences of forces"
necessarily at work in any utterance (Derrida, *Margins* 18). By this,
collaborative texts offer readier inroads into postmodern terrain
than individual elaborations can manage. Not accidentally, the experiments of Derrida and others with the "multiple text" format
(*Glas*, etc.), which visually and thematically unsettles ideal-
ist/realist assumptions about the originalness and unitariness of
meaning/language, try to force joint venture. But at least two difficulties inhere in these Derridian multiples, neither of which afflicts
what could be called the paradigmatic form of collaboration: a single text multiply authored from onset to finish. On the one hand,
"deconstructive" tinkering with format may not sufficiently reori-
ent (disorient) the text. When components of a multiple text, however cleverly juxtaposed, are produced by different authors, they
remain in constant danger of retaining ordinary authorial separateness. Or in the more obvious case, if the texts are written by a
single individual, the split text is easily "read through" in terms of
a unitary purpose originating in authorial "single-mindedness";
the format becomes mostly cosmetic. Collaboration, however, in-
verts the "schismatic." The split is "originary"; the text *appears* unitary. On the other hand, deconstructive theory perhaps overshoots
the mark. As Christopher Norris notes, the central question contra
Derrida (et al.) asks, "Is it possible to go so far toward eliminating
voice, presence, origin, and the whole 'logocentric' tradition of
Western discourse, without in the process giving up the claim to
communicate intelligible meaning?" ("Derrida at Yale" 255). In

contrast, viable collaboration derails Romantic logocentrism without forfeiting the essential community of discourse.

In this light collaborational writing can be seen to advance the structuralist and poststructuralist program for writing in general, practiced, as Barthes says, "in order to rediscover the crucial problems involved in every utterance, once it is no longer wrapped in the beneficent cloud of strictly *realist* [including idealist] illusions, which see language simply as a medium of thought" ("Science versus Literature" 413). More subtly for all writing, more obviously, as seen, for collaborational writing, this means that the "pure thought" paradigm is replaced by "collective bargaining," spontaneous invention by a publicly editorial process (an exposition of the disposition of language possibilities); and "revision," most commonly miscast as the unfortunate aftermath of writing, now plainly becomes its vitally dominant activity. This is the demise of the unedited solitary genius for whom, as Shelley remarks, "when composition begins, inspiration is already on the decline" and who substantiates that it is "an error to assert that the finest passages ... are produced by labour and study" (331). The Shakespeare who "never blotted a line" now remains only as mythical figure.

Nietzsche—collaborating with Derrida, Foucault, etc.—asks, "Finally, is it necessary to posit an interpreter behind the interpretation? Even this is invention, hypothesis" (*Will to Power* 267 [aph. 481]). Foucault and his followers have forcefully argued that the function of the author figure is to reduce the circulation of meaning and, therefore, to limit uses of the text to those sanctioned within the convention of the author figure:

> the author is not an indefinite source of significations which fill a work; the author does not precede the works, he is a certain functional principle by which, in our culture, one limits, excludes, and chooses; in short, by which one impedes the free circulation, the free manipulation, the free composition, decomposition, and recomposition of fiction.... The author is ... the ideological figure by which one marks the manner in which we fear the proliferation of meaning. (988)

While not discounting the meaningfulness of discourse, collaboration re-turns toward anonymous text. A recent collaborative article in *Newsweek* by political luminaries Henry Kissinger and Cyrus Vance provides a good example. The most remarkable aspect of the essay may be that it was written at all, since it would seem unlikely for two such strong personalities with such different political allegiances and vocabularies to collaborate on a political essay.[10] Either one voice could dominate completely (whether thoroughly or alternately), or both could be resolved into a third, openly hypothetical voice. That they collaborated effectively means that they chose the latter option, sacrificing individual personae for the sake of a more complicate third. But that third does not deny disagreement. Rather than a narrow dogmatizing interested in incontestable ground (however small the plot), it recognizes the importance of taking a spectrum of opinion into account. Collaboration itself, in other words, becomes the center of attention, culminating in the essay's final paragraph with the recommendation that "we adopt more selective and *collaborative* international strategies based on new realities" (34 [our emphasis]). The immersion/submersion of the individual in the larger enterprise leaves behind the conclusion in which one side "wins" and the other "loses." While the individual writer strives against others to be *first* to achieve a particular insight, to articulate the insight *more* fully and *more* clearly, to guard her or his own territory against intrusion, and by success in these endeavors to gain individual recognition and its concomitant rewards (at the expense, of course, of those "beaten" in the contest), collaboration abandons, at least in its internal workings (i.e., the relations among collaborators) and in its example, the competitive in favor of something more cooperative. Again, the editorial model, with its mutual interdependence, is the relevant one— whether assignment of respective roles is consistently maintained or each collaborator takes her/his turn as editor and edited.

Our purpose is not to suggest that enough collaboration may save the world from nuclear destruction (although, if writ large enough, as Kissinger and Vance imply, it might), but to point out the way in which the act of collaboration moves opinion to the fore expressly/expressedly *as opinion*—and correlatively, thinking/writing to the fore as language activity. Collaboration is a recognition, an admission, of the non-transcendental character of writing—writing as action, and a function of interaction. This model of collaborative effort differs from the Socratic pseudo-dialogical model by which we, finally, attend not to the speaker but to a vision of the palpably mute Truth.[11] Though it shares with that model an interest in interrogating relations between public and private, internal and external, and what has come to be thought as

subject and object, the most significant form of Socratic (or Hera-
clitean) externality is intended to be "pre-subjective" and "extra-
linguistic"; the collaborative, though decisively "a-subjective," is
inevitably linguistic. Like David Bleich's pedagogical model for
collective reader response, collaboration seems to begin with "sub-
jectivities" and move toward "objectivity." But that objectivity is
always virtual (as, we would argue, is conventional "subjectiv-
ity"[12]), the reflection of some "coherent" agreement/disagreement
among perspectives, and not of an arrival at the pre-existing Logos
within which seeming discordances are always already resolved.
The collaborative is evidence of what we might now call the communal quality of writing/discourse/thinking. Again, collaboration
is, and makes plain, a virtual and thoroughly linguistic singularity
spoken by a laboriously fabricated voice—in Stevens' phrase, "As
if the language suddenly, with ease, / Said things it had laboriously spoken" (*Collected Poems* 387 ["Notes toward a Supreme Fiction"]).

Explicit collaboration counters what Barthes has called "the
myth of Einstein": "There is a single secret to the world, and this
secret is held in one word; the universe is a safe of which humanity
seeks the combination" (*Mythologies* 69), and the brain of the individual genius (Einstein, for instance) is "a mythical object" (*Mythologies* 68) directed toward discovering that combination.[13] In place
of "the myth of Einstein," collaboration substitutes a fabric of con-
ventional/contractual understanding for which the "under-
pinning" (underpenning) or "substructure" is immediately only
the mediately human. Collaboration's aggressive disclosure of
these workings joins with the currently circulating proposition that
all textuality is intertextual—which, in effect, tells us that any
writing is essentially collaborative. This is a postmodern "subtext"
of any particular critical dismantling: effective exposure/dis-
ruption of the idealist/realist bias "built into" language.[14]

This amounts to saying that resistance to collaborating may be,
among other things, a matter of reluctance regarding the mod-
ern/postmodern argument with the notion of self-evident, un-
mediated, and absolute grounding. (Even the infamous anti-meta-
physicians Nietzsche—despite Heidegger's interested view of
Nietzsche as the last metaphysician—and Heidegger retain this
reluctance although they expose, or try to expose, the unavoidable
problematics of idealist/rationalist systems.) In which case, un-

easiness about collaboration reflects our generalized contemporary uneasiness with the complications of cultural (and cross-cultural) convention/conviction (or in literary terms, intertextuality) as high court of appeals.

Notes

1. Derrida's view depends, in part, on reading Plato's Socrates as Plato's spokesman, or even "Plato's master and guide in the ways of dialectical argument" (Norris, *Derrida* 32). But as Stanley Rosen says, "Nothing about Plato's relation to the Socrates of his dialogues is self-evident, except perhaps that Socrates did not write dialogues" (37).

2. For additional discussion of Socratic silence and "noesis" in the context of Plato's *Symposium*, see Rosen 268–77.

3. Thomas says about his own writing, "My poetry is, or should be, useful to me for one reason: it is the record of my individual struggle from darkness towards some measure of light, and what of the individual struggle is still to come benefits by the sight and knowledge of the faults and fewer merits in that concrete record. My poetry is, or should be, useful to others for its individual recording of that struggle with which they are necessarily acquainted." Note the way in which the Platonic image of spiritual struggle from darkness to light couples with the original "privacy" of the written record, which may then be shared, post-struggle/post-writing, with others.

4. Notice the extent of interchangeability between the mute/muted globed-fruit image of poetry (from Archibald MacLeish's "Ars Poetica") and Heidegger's "the essential being of language is Saying as Showing" (*OWL* 123 ["The Way to Language"]).

5. Our view, in brief, regarding the issue of "continuity" from early to later Heidegger sees *Being and Time's* "authenticity" as expanded, not deleted, by the later work. In other words, the destiny of Heidegger's initial concern with authentic selfhood played itself out in terms of "authentic" (i.e., poetical/primordial) relation to Being.

6. For Nietzsche, the fuller picture is, happily, more complex than this emphasis on autonomy suggests, since, for example, in *The Gay Science* we can find "one must be able to lose oneself occasionally if one wants to learn something from things different from oneself" (245 [aph. 305]) and in a Zarathustran vein, "anyone who manages to experience the history of humanity as a whole as *his own history* will ... [be] a person whose horizon

encompasses thousands of years past and future, being the heir of all the nobility of all past spirit ... and at the same time the first of a new nobility ... if one could burden one's soul with all of this ... ; if one could finally contain all this in one soul and crowd it into a single feeling—this would surely have to result in a happiness that humanity has not known so far" (268 [aph. 337]). In other words, the most profoundly realized/realizing individual would be (and see himself as) the most thorough participant in the human community. But our point in this essay has to do with a particular aspect of Nietzsche's influence on subsequent thinking, and not the richest possible readings of Nietzsche.

7. That Heidegger may have become invested in that rumor is suggested by Rorty's "the reification of language in the later Heidegger is simply a stage in the hypostatization of Heidegger himself—in the transfiguration of Martin Heidegger from one more creature of his time, one more self constituted by the social practices of his day, one more reactor to the work of others, into a world-historical figure, the first postmetaphysical thinker" (64).

8. Wordsworth's "The earliest poets of all nations generally wrote from passion excited by real events; they wrote naturally, and as men: feeling powerfully as they did, their language was daring, and figurative" (465), though less radical, likewise ties linguistic potency to origination.

9. See Hawking 50ff. for further examples.

10. Actually, Kissinger and Vance, in an ecstasy of collaborative enthusiasm, published three essays together in the summer and fall of 1988. The other two were "Bipartisan Objectives for American Foreign Policy," *Foreign Affairs* 66 (Summer 1988): 899–921 and "American Foreign Policy: A Bipartisan View," *Current* (Washington, D.C.) 307 (November 1988): 30–40.

11. Cf. Plato's *Symposium*: "But tell me, what would happen if one of you had the fortune to look upon essential beauty entire, pure and unalloyed; not infected with the flesh and colour of humanity...? What if he could behold the divine beauty itself, in its unique form?" (Plato 207 [211e]).

12. Nietzsche, for example, offers: "'Everything is subjective,' you say; but even this is interpretation. The 'subject' is not something given, it is something added and invented and projected behind what there is" (*Will to Power* 267 [aph. 481]).

13. Einstein himself contributes to the view of his work as non-dialogical (or at least non-conversational) by asserting, "The words or the language, as they are written or spoken, do not seem to play any role in my mechanisms of thought" (Schrage 86).

14. Cf. Derrida, *Margins* 12–14.

Works Cited

Arendt, Hannah. "Martin Heidegger at Eighty." In *Heidegger & Modern Philosophy*. Ed. Michael Murray. New Haven: Yale UP, 1978. 293–303.

Barthes, Roland. *Mythologies*. Trans. Annette Lavers. New York: Hill and Wang, 1972.

———. "Science versus Literature." In *Introduction to Structuralism*. Ed. Michael Lane. New York: Basic Books, 1970.

Brock, Werner. Foreword to *Existence and Being*. By Martin Heidegger. Chicago: Henry Regnery, 1949. ix–x.

Derrida, Jacques. *Glas*. Trans. John P. Leavey, Jr., and Richard Rand. Lincoln: U of Nebraska P, 1986.

———. *Margins of Philosophy*. Trans. Alan Bass. Chicago: U of Chicago P, 1982.

Emerson, Ralph Waldo. *Selections from Ralph Waldo Emerson: An Organic Anthology*. Ed. Stephen E. Whicher. Boston: Houghton Mifflin, 1957.

Fitzgibbon, Constantine. *The Life of Dylan Thomas*. Boston: Little, Brown, 1965.

Fynsk, Christopher. *Heidegger: Thought and Historicity*. Ithaca: Cornell UP, 1986.

Hawking, Stephen W. *A Brief History of Time: From the Big Bang to Black Holes*. New York, Bantam, 1988.

Heidegger, Martin. *Being and Time*. Trans. John Macquarrie and Edward Robinson. New York: Harper and Row, 1962.

———. *On the Way to Language*. Trans. Peter D. Hertz. New York: Harper and Row, 1971.

———. *Poetry, Language, Thought*. Trans. Albert Hofstadter. New York: Harper and Row, 1971.

Higgins, Kathleen Marie. *Nietzsche's "Zarathustra."* Philadelphia: Temple UP, 1987.

Kissinger, Henry, and Cyrus Vance. "An Agenda for 1989." *Newsweek* 111 (June 6, 1988): 31–34.

Nietzsche, Friedrich. *The Gay Science*. Trans. Walter Kaufmann. New York: Vintage, 1974.

———. *Thus Spoke Zarathustra*. In *The Portable Nietzsche*. Ed. and trans. Walter Kaufmann. New York: Viking, 1954. 112–439.

———. *The Will to Power*. Ed. Walter Kaufmann. Trans. Walter Kaufmann and R.J. Hollingdale. New York: Vintage, 1968.

Norris, Christopher. *Derrida.* Cambridge, Mass.: Harvard UP, 1987.

———. "Derrida at Yale: The 'Deconstructionist Moment' in Modernist Poetics." *Philosophy and Literature* 4 (Fall 1980): 242–55.

Plato. *Lysis, Symposium, Gorgias.* Trans. W.R.M. Lamb. Vol. 3 of the Loeb Classical Library edition of *Plato.* Ed. G.P. Goold. Cambridge, Mass.: Harvard UP, 1925.

Rorty, Richard. *Essays on Heidegger and Others.* Cambridge, Eng.: Cambridge UP, 1991.

Rosen, Stanley. *Plato's "Symposium."* New Haven: Yale UP, 1968.

Schrage, Michael. *Shared Minds: The New Technologies of Collaboration.* New York: Random House, 1990.

Shelley, Percy Bysshe. *A Defence of Poetry.* In *Criticism: The Major Statements.* Ed. Charles Kaplan. 2nd ed. New York: St. Martin's, 1986. 309–35.

Stevens, Wallace. *The Collected Poems of Wallace Stevens.* New York: Knopf, 1954.

———. *The Necessary Angel: Essays on Reality and the Imagination.* New York: Knopf, 1951.

Stillinger, Jack. *Multiple Authorship and the Myth of Solitary Genius.* New York: Oxford UP, 1991.

Thomas, Dylan. *The Poems of Dylan Thomas.* Ed. Daniel Jones. New York: New Directions, 1971.

Thoreau, Henry David. *Walden.* In *The Portable Thoreau.* Ed. Carl Bode. New York: Penguin, 1977. 258–572.

Wordsworth, William. *Selected Poems and Prefaces.* Ed. Jack Stillinger. Boston: Houghton Mifflin, 1965.

Union and Reunion:
Collaborative Authorship

Linda K. Hughes and Michael Lund

A friend of ours reports that she went, a couple of years ago, to her twenty-fifth high school reunion. Having gone away to college, farther away to graduate school, and farther away still to academic positions, she had not been back to her small home town in years; and she was apprehensive about whether she would remember everyone, whether anyone would remember her, whether there would be a reunion of the class of 196–.

Several weeks ahead of time, she dug out her high school yearbook and, like a true academic, began to study up for the event. But it was a disaster: she stared at pictures in which no face seemed familiar; she read names but could not recall people to go with them; events described and commemorated seemed never to have happened in her past. She asked herself, who were these people? When did these things take place? Was there ever a Class of 196– anyway, a union for which there could be a reunion, a whole in which individuals existed as discrete, integral parts?

This crisis inspired by the high school reunion parallels questions about authorship that have recently occupied the profession of English, particularly insofar as collaborative writing offers a challenge to conventional models. That is, who is the author of a literary work? Who is, for example, the author of a high school yearbook? As a member of the Class of 196–, our friend felt that she and her classmates had to have written the yearbook. It was their lives that made up its text, they who posed for and took the pictures, they who took action and penned the words to capture them for memory. Yet reading that work twenty-five years later, our friend did not see herself as subject or author.

The simple concept that an author is a person who writes a text can no longer be taken at face value. The author—a real, living person—is more than would be contained in any text. Even an autobiography does not inscribe the author completely, since some experiences have been omitted, others given brief treatment so that selected key moments can be dealt with at length. An author, then, is always more than any text.

Ironically, however, an author is also less than any text. Writers are always surprised by what some people find in their work. Responses absolutely unforeseen during the process of composition occur as regularly as some students' exam answers seem unconnected to the lectures and discussions through which their professors thought to prepare and shape their responses. So, in this sense, the author is always less than the text.

This is as true of yearbooks by multiple authors as it is of single texts composed by individuals. More is perceived in a yearbook than the staff ever anticipated, especially after twenty-five years have passed. And yet the class that put together the yearbook is larger and more complex than the text it left behind. Where did the yearbook come from, then?

This question is only a step or two away from the Foucaultian answer, that the discourse within which all exist is the author of any text. It is not hard at first to see that discourse as the author of a high school yearbook. Produced by a staff of many individuals, influenced by their friends not on the staff, by teachers who had impressed them, school officials they knew they must respect, parents they hoped to please, and existing conventions for reporting they did not even recognize as governing their actions, the yearbook is a product of multiple and interrelated forces, a composite of units from many sources, the expression of individuals and a culture. Only the whole thing, the yearbook, exists as a product of that discourse, the author of itself.

But, wait a minute.... Most hate to give up their "selves" so easily. Discourse can exist only when there are authors and audiences; discourse may precede, but it also follows individuals. This fact was made clearer to the two of us during the two years we collaborated on a study of major nineteenth-century literary texts. In the collaborative process, we learned, each individual is in turn—and at times simultaneously—an author and a reader, with indistinct boundaries between the two. In any collaborative or individual composition, in fact, the writer is always an author and an audience. Author and audience must collaborate in any creative effort; when a text is read, audience and author come together in a form of union.

II

Unlike the class of our friend, we did not undertake to write a yearbook. We did, however, envision from the beginning a book with both text and illustrations. This was *The Victorian Serial*, a study of serialization's effect on the initial reception and interpretation of sixteen major novels and poems. Our very subject entailed multiple forms of collaboration, or at least literary works whose meanings derived from more than individual texts directly identified with single authors. Because serials are continuing stories over extended time with enforced interruptions, reading audiences and contexts play an unusually large role in this literary process. Suspense and anticipation are the most frequently cited factors in serials' appeal and effect (associated with the cliff-hanger, a literary and economic inducement for readers to purchase succeeding installments). But our interest lay also in the extended middle of any serial work. Because a serial lacked closure for weeks, months, or even years, readers had the opportunity to assess, discuss, interpret, and speculate about a novel or poem, alone or with other readers, while the work was still in progress.

Not only did enforced interruptions, or time, play a role in creating meaning, then, but so also did audiences' interactions with the text. Some authors even invited conventional assumptions or expectations from readers in early installments so that their reversal in a later part could challenge and move reading audiences. Though any text demands or at least implies a reader, serial readers collaborated with an author and text to a greater degree than in other publication formats to create essential elements of the literary experience.

Moreover, because serial readers were repeatedly forced to turn away from the text during the reading process (often at regular intervals), their literary experience was characterized by a deliberate breaking of literary illusion and a return to other activities. Reading did not occur in an enclosed realm of contemplation possible with a single-volume text; rather, Victorian literature, because of its parts structure, was engaged much more within the busy, continuous context of everyday life. In that space between readings, the Victorian world continued to direct a barrage of new information and intense experience at readers; and that context complicated and enriched the imagined world when the literary work was resumed. Again, readers' comprehension of a work's meaning and texture was influenced by a kind of partnership between an author's text and a number of nonliterary forces, as well as between writer and real (as opposed to imagined or hypothetical) readers.

But other literary, or at least textual, elements also collaborated with readers, authors, and texts to shape interpretation of Victorian serial works. Because serialization was so prevalent a mode, readers often engaged multiple texts at once, reading in a given month several parts of prospectively whole stories rather than a single sustained work. The reviewing industry also played an important role. Especially in monthly and weekly periodicals, serial literature was reviewed a part at a time, as each installment was published, rather than as a whole work with a clearly discernible pattern and intent. These reviews, of course, were essential to our own work, since they allowed us to assess actual (not ideal or implied) readers' responses and the effect of serialization on literary interpretation. But for Victorian audiences these reviews would themselves have become part of the original reading of a serial work, another set of voices and texts interwoven with the author's text and vision. Insofar as these reviews both reflected and shaped readers' own interpretations, the printed reviews also collaborated in the serial literary process, becoming part of a larger union.

And, finally, an essential element of many serial novels was the part's illustration. (Though less frequently, illustrations could also play a significant role in the reception of poetry.) Indeed, the paper covers of the monthly shilling parts issued by Dickens and others helped spur expectation and interpretation with their suggestions of cycles, mood, tone, and even plot. Many studies of the collaboration between author and illustrator, pen and pencil, have already appeared; and these indicate yet again that Victorian serials can in many ways be said to have been collaborative, though few were ascribed in their own day to more than one author. Samples of these illustrations appear in our own text, *The Victorian Serial*, and help us to identify, as well as to replicate by analogy, the interplay between the verbal and visual in the works we discuss.

III

We have written the preceding paragraphs from the endpoint of our work, from the far side of collaboration; and we need to retrace our steps to explain our collaborative method before we go on to explore in a conclusion the implications of collaboration for concepts of authorship and texts. Like many scholars, we had been exchanging ideas over the years in the kind of de facto collaboration so pervasive and vital to our profession that it is difficult to pinpoint, assess, or even acknowledge (cf. Bleich 16, 36–37). We began collaboration in the narrower sense of the term—the production of a single text by two or more acknowledged authors—when we began applying for grant support that would give us the opportunity to work full-time on writing.

We should explain that throughout our work together we have been at separate institutions over a thousand miles apart (ironically, as we neared completion of *The Victorian Serial*, our geographical distance expanded). To insure that we were able to do concentrated work at the same time, we considered grant support essential from the beginning. Individual ACLS grants-in-aid allowed us to study contemporary reviews of parts of serial literary works at the British Newspaper Library. But these individual grants also allowed us to collaborate on the invention phase of our project: we arranged to do research at the same time and discussed what we were finding during coffee and lunch breaks. Though each of us looked at different materials and took notes separately, then, our collaborative discussions shaped both what we looked for and what we saw in our individual research. On one hand, each anticipated the other as audience, and hence assumed the roles of writer and reader necessary to individual composers. On the other hand, because we anticipated shared authorship of a single text, we also pursued inquiry cooperatively through a series of mutual suggestions and observations. We did not share the same method of notetaking (one of us used notecards, the other yellow pads, with different organizing headings and symbols). Yet we knew that hovering behind or around work of an individual hand was the influence of another mind. We produced multiple texts (two sets of notes), but each text was in a significant way collaborative.

After completing our first phase of research, we began to apply for grants to support the writing of our book.[1] Doing so required us to produce a twenty-five-page narrative of our approach, methods, goals, preliminary findings, and so forth. In our initial drafting we wrote letters to each other, called on the telephone, and exchanged computer disks. Here, as in most of the writing of *The Victorian Serial*, our method was to assign sections to each of us for drafting after we first discussed our approach. We then composed sections individually, sent drafts to each other, critiqued each other's work, revised again, and produced, in the end, a version we were both happy with. And our work on the grant application led us to collaborate on other texts related to our larger project, especially conference papers.

When we received an NEH Interpretive Research award, we were ready to begin collaboration in earnest. We had sixteen months to complete our project and funding for four trips to do face-to-face collaboration. Our previous experience shaped the work plans we made at the outset and allowed us to begin work directly, but by the end of the project our collaboration techniques had changed and developed in new ways.

We continued to adopt a format that mediated between collaboration and individual effort. Though our work was grounded in shared assumptions and approaches, one of us had primary responsibility for the research, analysis, and drafting related to serial poetry, the other primary responsibility for the same activities related to serial fiction. We both read all literary texts discussed in our project, but we did not read each other's research notes from contemporary reviews.

It is important to acknowledge here as well that our approach to nineteenth-century serial literature fostered our collaboration. Traditionally, serial novels and poems have been read as if they were the whole texts they became when issued in single volumes— that is, as if publication format did not affect the "meaning" of a work. Our argument was that the way in which a work was read affected the original audience's perception of its meaning. It was, then, relatively easy for each of us to work individually, following this very precise, focused thesis: reading each work as a serial affected its reception among Victorians. Other collaborative projects without a single, governing principle of approach might not proceed so smoothly.

Before we began writing chapters, we undertook sustained background reading for four months. We both read critical works that seemed essential to our project, but otherwise each undertook a separate list of works, took notes on the computer, printed duplicate sets of notecards from the reading, and then shared these notes. At the end of our reading program, then, we had identical sets of communal notecards, though we had done much of the reading individually. As we composed drafts of chapters, we drew upon this common fund of notes, short fragments of text we may or may not have directly produced as individuals. Looking back on this phase of our collaboration, in fact, we could not say where individual effort began or ended; the boundaries between individual self and the texts we used and produced had dissolved into a larger union.

The same could be said of the actual writing phase that followed, an enterprise punctuated by a series of reunions for the original grant-writing class of two people. Our general practice was to meet face-to-face at the outset of writing a chapter, discussing what we were trying to say, sharing—and debating—the essential points and framework until we had a controlling thesis for the entire chapter. With a collaborative intellectual framework in place, each of us then went to work for a month or so individually.

Each chapter was devoted to several serial works assessed in relation to a central Victorian preoccupation (home, history, empire, doubt, and, at the century's end, the unraveling of central assumptions). Once we had a complete draft of a chapter, notes, and works cited, we printed copies of the chapter and were ready to meet for a revision session (one that generally ended with a discussion of the succeeding chapter).

Before we met face-to-face, each of us went over the chapter individually, proofing and marking any points of disagreement in the argument. Each played the roles of audience and author, then, for his or her own prose and that of the collaborator. If either of us had questions or reservations about the other's draft during the composition process, we shared them in general terms over the phone. But we deliberately avoided highly detailed or extended discussion of differences at a thousand-mile distance. Drafting had not yet been completed at this stage, after all, and sustained dispute over a chapter's section would have been premature and inefficient. We also felt that pursuing disagreements at a distance might render the collaboration itself fragile, and that our overriding project, the larger collaboration, should take precedence over a minor difference of opinion. (We consider agreement upon major assumptions and principles a necessary precondition for successful collaboration.)

We saved all detailed discussions of the draft for face-to-face meetings, when we had enough time for detail but also constraints on time that forced us to resolve conflicts before the meeting was over. Our method of revising was to take turns reading the draft aloud, each person reading the sections for which he or she had had primary responsibility. When either had a suggested change or question, reading stopped, we discussed the merits of a change, and we made a decision. This arrangement allowed us to keep the shape and substance of the entire chapter before us as we considered revisions, something we could not have done had we merely directed attention to passages involving proposed changes. This format, in fact, also allowed us to affirm and endorse what we had produced, not just query or challenge it.

Sometimes, of course, we did disagree. On one chapter's conclusion, for example, we disagreed so fundamentally that we had to leave it for some six months, coming back to it only after we had drafted the rest of the book (at which point relatively minor changes in wording suddenly left us both satisfied). Usually we resolved any conflicts within a two-day work session, and in fact disagreement was infrequent; because we began with a collaborative intellectual framework, a chapter thesis we had cowritten face-to-face, the work which appeared to be done individually was already in fact a collaborative enterprise. One person touched the keyboard as the words appeared on the screen, but more than one mind was directing the single pair of hands.

As the collaboration continued over the months, we sometimes found ourselves forgetting, when we read our chapters aloud, who had written what, and one of us might interrupt reading aloud with, "Did I write that, or did you?" Our dissolving sense of proprietorship over words might partly have resulted from the mechanics of revision; since one of us might add a sentence or reword an extant one in text the other had drafted, the end result was an interlace of two authors' words, not juxtaposed sections of individually-composed text. But the more important cause of our confusion over a passage's source was the nature of collaboration itself.

The real answer to the question, "Did I write that, or did you?" is "*We* wrote that," a "we" not strictly identified with either one of us, yet not a simple aggregate of two identities either—rather a union that is greater than the two parts that composed it. This "we" resists simple definition but can at least be approached by its effect, which was to allow two "I's" to meet, interact, and somehow produce a single text. This "we" blurred individual identities, but the result was not a sense of diminished autonomy and selfhood but an extended sense of community.

By the end of the project, in fact, "we" literally wrote text. The two of us had saved the introduction for last, knowing that only then would we have a full sense of what our study articulated, and its significance. This section was also, of course, one of the most difficult to write. Each of us wrote separate sections, as before, but this time our sections overlapped and even strained against each other. With the grant period rapidly drawing to a close, we had two parts of a chapter that insisted on remaining divergent parts, the antithesis of what collaboration seeks to achieve.

We waited to resolve this problem at our last face-to-face meeting. Here we kept some of the initial pages from the earlier drafts, threw out the rest, and started composing together on the spot, one person at the keyboard, but now two voices calling out the words that should be evoked from the keys. This final collaboration—the hardest (and perhaps least practical) to carry out—was thus also a collaboration of production media, since we composed via computer *and* conversation. One of us might start saying a sentence only to have the other complete or revise it, so that in this case the resulting text was collaborative at every point.

IV

Through the years of collaboration on research, note-taking, invention, background reading, drafting, and revision, then, we had produced a text in which the relation of author to text became extremely complicated; though each of us knows what each did during the stages of work on *The Victorian Serial*, neither of us can say simply of any part, "That is mine." *The Victorian Serial* was written by an entity that might be called "HughesLund," which might aptly be troped as "whose land?" For the boundaries, the territories of authorship, dissolved and faded away in the union of collaboration.

This complicated relation of individual to text makes collaboration an interesting framework within which to view contemporary critical theory. Nineteenth-century celebrations of a literary text as the direct inspiration and outpouring of an author have given way to the influence of deconstruction and new historicism, which acknowledge the role of historical persons in producing texts but identify those texts as, ultimately, the product of systems of language (ecriture) or cultural discourse.[2] Few today are likely to write in the vein of the January 15, 1870 *Saturday Review*, whose reviewer responded to Tennyson's *Holy Grail and Other Poems* (1869): "To study what must have formed the chief material for those poems is to recognise with greater clearness than before the genius which has been at work upon them, the intuitive delicacy in selection, the power and the beauty, which will render them immortal" ("Character" 75). Nor would contemporary scholars declare as simply as a reviewer for the *Academy* on October 22, 1870, "Dickens is to the Briton what a story from the *Arabian Nights* is to the Oriental; it is the invention of a single man against the memory of a generation of grandmothers" (3).

Collaboration on one hand shores up the arguments lodged against traditional notions of authorship and authorial intention. This is so not only because collaboration entails the dual roles of author and audience that characterize all writing, but also because collaboration highlights the blurred boundaries of authorship. Steven Knapp and Walter Benn Michaels are, among more recent commentators, two of the most important to uphold traditional notions of authorship. They dispute the contentions of hermeneutics that "a text means what its author intends but also necessarily means more, acquiring new meanings as readers apply it to new situations," and the tenet of deconstruction that "an author can never succeed in determining the meaning of a text; every text participates in a code that necessarily eludes authorial control" ("Against Theory 2," 50). In contrast to these positions, Knapp and Michaels maintain that "a text has only one meaning" and that "its meaning is whatever its author intends" (68).

In our view the collaborative process blurs the outlines of individual identity on which traditional assumptions about a text's relation to its author rests. And for us this feature is common to all writing.[3] To write even a private diary, an author must project an audience as well as an authorial self, and both concepts will be shaped by an individual's previous experience of texts. A single author has a greater degree of control over what words appear on the page than does an individual collaborating with another, but all authors participate in a social network in order to write.

Indeed, a single author who desires to publish a work perforce collaborates with an audience, since the author's conceptions and intentions are constrained by what the publishing industry and purchasing readers will understand, tolerate, and respond to. This feature of authorship is, again, particularly visible in nineteenth-century serialization, where writers were told by editors and publishers about the restrictions they would have to accept if they wanted to appear in print. For instance, the editors of *Harper's New Monthly Magazine*, through their regular persona as the "Easy Chair," wrote to a disgruntled younger author in January 1855 about the nature of literary careers. The "Chair" admitted that it had "long ago renounced the writing of books, not because it believed in the dishonesty of publishers, because it saw too plainly the dismal chances of a book-making career. A man who lives by the pen must make up his mind to compromise, and submit, and suffer, as in all other pursuits" (266).

The collaborative process challenges the capitalist assumptions underlying the elevation of authorship and the inauguration of copyright laws in the nineteenth century (cf. Foucault 115, 124–25), as well as modern efforts to retain concepts of authorial control over meaning. But collaboration, in our view, also suggests a more human-centered and communal view of writing than is usually proffered among contemporary theorists. Derrida argues that what was previously considered to be an author's presence in the text is an artifact of writing; after the words remain on a page but are removed from a living author through publication or the passing of time, the text cannot be said to inscribe the author.[4] Rather, the sense of an author is an artifact of written language and codes. But for those who have collaborated, this seems an incomplete description of the writing process.[5] Peggy Kamuf, refuting the claims of Knapp and Michaels, conflates their identities into what she calls "KaM," sometimes calling KaM a "he," sometimes a "they." Insofar as one focuses on KaM as a "he" whose text is subject to the processes Derrida identifies, both Derrida's and Kamuf's arguments seem compelling.

But insofar as we focus on KaM as the "they" who produced the text, the relation between language and self seems to be pried open once again. For if collaboration undermines a direct identity between author and text, it also undermines (or at least opens up) the notion of textuality as part of a language system that is antecedent to the living individual who momentarily interacts with linguistic codes to produce a text. In collaboration, the text becomes a site where two or more individuals meet, interact, communicate, and sustain cooperative work. It is in some ways like a class reunion.

Perhaps it can even be said that texts *do* inscribe this intersubjective presence where collaboration is involved, since the very absence of boundaries between author and author and text is a sign of two persons' interaction by and through language. That is, the text's very inability to delineate which words are more closely allied to one collaborator than another or to suggest how two minds have integrated their thoughts to produce a single text becomes an indication that communication between two human beings has occurred, even if the path of that transference can never be traced. A yearbook, similarly, exists and asserts a community of class and potential later reunions, though what individuals inspired what part of that text can never be exactly determined.[6]

And given the implicit collaboration in any scholarly or literary enterprise, the necessary interaction of one mind with others' texts and spoken words—a process particularly visible in nineteenth-century serial texts—it may be necessary to find ways of articulating yet again the implicit function of language to create, perpetuate, and extend community. It may be necessary to see any text, that is, not only as the artifact of a language system or discourse but also as a site of encoded community, where traces of human interaction remain even if they cannot be traced directly to single authors, only to a variety of communities. Walter Ong has argued that all authors write for an audience they imagine reading their work. We would add that all audiences imagine an author writing the texts they read. In the crossing of those lines from author to audience, audience to author, lies a community.

V

When our friend got to her high school reunion several summers ago, she began to discover that she had been part of the Class of 196– after all. The subjects of the pictures and narratives in her high school yearbook were herself and her peers. Although the memories had faded, almost to nothing in many cases, the past began to come back in the special atmosphere of the gathering, stimulated by voices, faces, talk. Just as, earlier, class members had been authors of the yearbook, now they also became active audiences of it, the yearbook's text taking on new meaning, including the possibility of reunion.

That communities are as necessary to literature as are individual authors is visible in the way Oliver Wendell Holmes affirmed a social group similar to the Class of 196–, his Harvard class of 1829. Beginning in 1854 this prolific nineteenth-century man of letters celebrated a body of individuals through the publication of *Songs of the Class of 1829.* These poems often appeared in other contexts, such as in his regular pieces for the *Atlantic Monthly.* At one point in *The New Portfolio* (January 1885–July 1886 in *Atlantic*), we can see how authors and audience are necessary to the creation of literary texts, how together they shape the discourse which in turn shapes them. Holmes appeals to fellowship in a single community, to a sharing in the human condition:

> If one could have before him a set of photographs taken annually, representing the same person as he or she appeared for thirty or forty or fifty years, it would be interesting to watch the gradual changes of aspect from the age of twenty, or even of thirty or forty, to that of threescore and ten. The face might be an uninteresting one; still, as sharing the inevitable changes wrought by

> time, it would be worth looking at as it passed through the curve
> of life,—the vital parabola, which betrays itself in the symbolic
> changes of the features. (524)

The human interest in the patterns emerging from experience
("curve of life," the "vital parabola") belongs both to the aging author and to the aging audience.

> The same kind of interest, without any assumption of merit to be
> found in [such records of time's passing], I would claim for a se-
> ries of annual poems, beginning in middle life and continued to
> what many of my correspondents are pleased to remind me—as
> if I required to have the fact brought to my knowledge—is no
> longer youth. (524)

According to Holmes, these essays in the *Atlantic* require readers,
"correspondents" who "remind" the author, in order to become
literature. Although it appears at first to be only Holmes continuing his text here, the subjects (his audience) are essential to this literary experience.

> Here is the latest of a series of annual poems read during the last
> thirty-four years. There seems to have been one interruption, but
> there may have been other poems not recorded or remembered.
> This, the latest poem of the series, was listened to by the scanty
> remnant of what was a large and brilliant circle of classmates and
> friends when the first of the long series was read before them,
> then in the flush of ardent manhood:— (524)

Then follows Holmes's poem presented to his Harvard classmates
in Cambridge, in which authors and audience merge into a larger
whole: "Our heads with frosted locks are white, / Our roofs are
thatched with snow, / But red, in chilling winter's spite, / Our
hearts and hearthstones glow" (524). Holmes's writing in the *Atlantic* binds together audience and author into one community
(though an exclusive one), represented here by the poet and his
classmates. Together they make use of and extend their discourse.

VI

We do not mean to suggest that there are no differences at all
between a writing situation such as Holmes's and one involving
two or more authors of a single text. A single author may be con-

strained by audience expectations, publishers, and the author's own grounding in a literary and social community. But a single author may more easily project and "totalize" an audience than one who must actively work with a collaborator to create a text. The difference is one of degree rather than kind, since no author can work except as part of a textual community; still, the pragmatic realities of collaboration are more likely to require active negotiation and entail the pitfalls of personality clashes than are single-author writing situations. Thus history records instances of several authors who could work fleetingly or not at all in collaboration with another, but flourished as single authors. Pound and Eliot collaborated on *The Waste Land*, Dickens and Collins collaborated on *The Frozen Deep*; but these writers generally worked as single authors. Stephen Gill's biography of Wordsworth makes it clear that although Wordsworth and Coleridge, during the year preceding publication of *Lyrical Ballads*, may have worked even more closely than Holmes did with his audience, the two British poets could not succeed at direct collaboration: "The two poets were engaged in such a subtle dialogue that poems such as *Frost at Midnight* and *Tintern Abbey* seem almost the creation of not one but two minds. Attempts at real collaboration [on *The Ancient Mariner*], however, failed completely" (131). As Wordsworth wrote later, "'Our respective manners proved so widely different that it would have been quite presumptuous in me to do anything but separate from an undertaking upon which I could only have been a clog'"; and as Gill concludes, Wordsworth had such definite ideas about what he wanted to achieve in his poems that he "proved incapable of writing to order or to another man's plan" (132).

Accommodating two active wills and personalities to a single text can be tricky. As noted earlier, we were careful to postpone discussions of deep disagreements until face-to-face sessions so that we could keep the collaboration intact. Even David Bleich, who advocates collaborative learning and writing for political as well as intellectual reasons, avoids dual authorship: "Two people might either agree or disagree on what matters in any one person's work. Double perspectives would develop in agreed-upon items, but they would be much harder to develop for disputed points" (281). But that collaboration remains possible despite the difficulties posed by clashing wills or disputes suggests how profoundly social the writing process is—a medium through which distinct individuals can transfer and negotiate ideas.[7] The writing process, that is, fosters unions and reunions among those who might customarily define themselves as individuals.

But if collaborative authorship more dramatically reveals the evidence that language follows as well as precedes human beings who can interact with each other, the same can ultimately be said of all writing, which is always implicitly collaborative.[8] Holmes, penning his column to influence readers, was also influenced by them, not only through imagined responses but also through letters or even, perhaps, family members or friends commenting that what he was about to write would not be as easily accepted by his readers as he might assume. Single authorship, then, entails willed involvement and negotiation, though the processes may be less direct than in explicit collaboration. And in this sense every instance of a published text represents a trace of some mutual cooperation and understanding that occurred in and through language, or the text would never have been produced in the first place.

Notes

1. The most important agency here, not surprisingly, was the National Endowment for the Humanities. NEH is the only agency we know of supporting literary scholarship with grants explicitly offered for collaborative projects. Most humanities scholars are aware of programs to support collaborative editing of texts; fewer are aware of the program that supports collaborative interpretation, perhaps because collaborative interpretation is a less frequent practice in our discipline than in others. The program we refer to is the Interpretive Research program, which funds "coordinated or collaborative research" in "biographies; historical and analytical studies in literature and the arts; research in history, philosophy, and other humanities; research in political science, sociology, and cultural anthropology; and other major collaborative or cooperative undertakings" (NEH 2).

2. Nineteenth-century notions of the relation between author and text, however, linger in the academy, itself largely a nineteenth-century creation. Many eagerly follow the outpouring of academic articles from the best-known theoreticians or critics, and that late twentieth-century readers identify these authors with their texts is indicated by the practice of bringing them to conferences and institutions as keynote or guest speakers, and by students' seeking them out to study with them.

3. This view of all writing and reading as implicitly collaborative does not originate with us. Several decades ago Kenneth Burke presented the following in *A Rhetoric of Motives*:

> Longinus refers to that kind of elation wherein the audience feels as though it were not merely receiving, but were itself creatively participating in the poet's or speaker's assertion. Could we not say that, in such cases, the audience is exalted by the assertion because it has the feel of collaborating in the assertion? (57–58)

As Don M. Burks asserts, the implication is that "Poets, playwrights, performers, and speakers all are trying to bring about collaboration, trying to induce audiences to work together with them, to collaborate" (256). Proponents of reader-response and reception theory also, of course, urge a collaborative view of the literary process.

4. As Derrida says in "Signature Event Context," "For a writing to be a writing it must continue to 'act' and to be readable even when what is called the author of the writing no longer answers for what he has written, for what he seems to have signed, be it because of a temporary absence, because he is dead or, more generally, because he has not employed his absolutely actual and present intention or attention, the plenitude of his desire to say what he means, in order to sustain what seems to be written 'in his name'" (181).

5. Derrida, of course, focuses on the product of writing, not the process. As we argue below, the product of collaboration forms evidence that a process of interaction has taken place.

6. Cf. David Bleich: "Historically, literature (including its more general reference to any sort of text) has been an enterprise which temporarily fixes a culture's uses of language.... With written literature, even though the text remains more or less the same over long periods, each new reading, or set of readings that develops historically, is equivalent to a new performance of oral literature. In this way, there is always an inevitable sameness to each new literary event and there is always an inevitable uniqueness; the literary event, oral or written, is always social and always entails some sort of 'language fixing,' as each reader remembers the reading experience by fixing it. By understanding literary events (literature) in this social and collective sense, its relation to language and writing seems to be more visible" (114).

7. Cf. Derrida, who asserts (via a rhetorical question) that "To say that writing *extends* the field and the powers of locutory or gestural communication presupposes, does it not, a sort of *homogeneous* space of communication?" (175). We would answer yes, and no. Our "union" perhaps corresponds to Derrida's "homogeneous space," but we see that "space" as the

result, in many cases, of interaction and negotiation among heterogeneous parties.

8. Foucault argues that any writing manifests a "plurality of egos," since, for example, the author who writes a preface to a mathematical treatise is not identical with the author who worked out a new theorem (130). But Foucault is far more skeptical of the possibility of community than we are. If he proposes a typology of discourses that would "reveal the manner in which discourse is articulated on the basis of social relationships" (137), he also asserts that "the subject (and its substitutes) must be stripped of its creative role and analysed as a complex and variable function of discourse" (138).

Works Cited

Bleich, David. *The Double Perspective: Language, Literacy, and Social Relations*. New York: Oxford UP, 1988.

Burke, Kenneth. *A Rhetoric of Motives*. 1950; rpt. Berkeley: U of California P, 1969.

Burks, Don M. "Dramatic Irony, Collaboration, and Kenneth Burke's Theory of Form." *Pre/Text* 6.3–4 (1985): 255–73.

"The Character of Lancelot." *Saturday Review* 29 (January 15, 1870): 75–76.

Derrida, Jacques. "Signature Event Context." *Glyph* 1 (1977): 172–97.

Foucault, Michel. "What Is an Author?" *Language, Memory, Practice: Selected Essays and Interviews*. Ed. Donald F. Bouchard. Trans. Donald F. Bouchard and Sherry Simon. Ithaca: Cornell UP, 1977. 113–38.

Gill, Stephen. *William Wordsworth: A Life*. Oxford: Clarendon P, 1989.

Holmes, Oliver Wendell. "*The New Portfolio*." *Atlantic Monthly* 55 (April 1885): 523–24.

Kamuf, Peggy. "Floating Authorship." *Diacritics* 16 (1986): 3–13.

Knapp, Steven, and Walter Benn Michaels. "Against Theory." *Critical Inquiry* 8 (Summer 1982): 723–42. Rpt. *Against Theory: Literary Studies and the New Pragmatism*. Ed. W.J.T. Mitchell. Chicago: U of Chicago P, 1985. 11–30.

———. "Against Theory 2: Hermeneutics and Deconstruction." *Critical Inquiry* 14 (1987): 49–68.

National Endowment for the Humanities. *Interpretive Research: Projects.* [Application Instructions and Forms.] OMB No. 3136–0120. Exp. 06/30/89.

Ong, Walter. "The Writer's Audience Is Always a Fiction." *PMLA* 90 (1975): 9–21.

Rev. of *Edwin Drood. Academy* October 22, 1870: 3.

Common Ground and Collaboration in T.S. Eliot

Jewel Spears Brooker

> The working man who went to the music-hall and
> saw Marie Lloyd and joined in the chorus was him-
> self performing part of the act; he was engaged in
> that collaboration of the audience with the artist
> which is necessary in all art.

Eliot, Selected Essays 407 (cited as SE)

I

T.S. Eliot is generally regarded as an elitist. Long associated
with intellectual coteries, he flaunted in the early poems such poly-
syllabic monstrosities as "polyphiloprogenitive." Complex poems
like "Gerontion" and *The Waste Land*, though providing fodder for
generations of voracious critics, seemed inaccessible to ordinary
readers. Not surprisingly, Eliot has often been accused of a deliberate attempt to outrage common readers by cultivating complexity for its own sake. The conspicuous cerebration in his poetry, the
sometimes pontifical tone of his literary and social criticism, his
distrust for majoritarism and modern democracy, his identification
with the Anglican church, even (or especially) his ubiquitous um-
brella and his elegant weariness—all these and more went into the
elitist image of this connoisseur of Stilton cheese and Cheshire cats.

Eliot's reputation as an elitist has obscured one of the most
significant features of his thought. At the bottom of everything he
wrote, including his greatest poems, is a search for common
ground. The word "common" is repeated over and over again in
his essays. As Eliot uses it, "common" has no pejorative connota-
tions; it carries, rather, the standard dictionary meaning of

61

"shared" or of "belonging to several or many." Eliot's influential critical doctrines—e.g., tradition, classicism, impersonality, wholeness, orthodoxy—are without exception a celebration of commonness; his great poems, from "The Love Song of J. Alfred Prufrock" to *Four Quartets*, constitute a pursuit of commonness. His innovations in poetic form are integrally related to a desperate attempt to secure common ground. Many other aspects of his life—e.g., his attraction to the theatre, his affiliation with the Church of England—are explicable in terms of his appreciation for what can be meaningfully shared with human beings of every class in his culture. The 1929 essay on Dante, pivotal in Eliot's career as thinker and artist, is a good starting point for exploring his insistence on commonness.

Eliot's deep esteem for Dante is based on his conviction that the Florentine "is the most *universal* of poets" (*SE* 200; Eliot's emphasis). While the concept of universality is too complex to be captured in a synonym, or even in an essay, there can be no doubt that the simple idea of commonness is the core of Eliot's meaning. Dante's achievement was possible because his poetic medium, medieval Italian, was extremely close to "universal Latin," and thus, for practical purposes, a common language throughout Europe. "The language of each great English poet is his own language; the language of Dante is the perfection of a common language" (*SE* 213). The common—or universal (Eliot interchanges the adjectives)—language made possible a common mind. Dante "thought in a way in which every man of his culture in the whole of Europe then thought" (*SE* 203). This common mind greatly diluted national and/or racial mentalities because it "tended to concentrate on what men of various races and lands could think together" (*SE* 201). Inseparable from this common language and common mind was a common culture. "The culture of Dante was not of one European country but of Europe" (*SE* 201).

In reference to literary form, Dante benefited from access to a "method which was common and commonly understood throughout Europe" (*SE* 203). This method is allegory, "not a local Italian custom, but a universal European method" (*SE* 205). Allegory, of course, is contingent on the poet and his reader sharing certain unstated knowledge. The association of Dante's genius with his appropriation of common ground continues in Eliot's discussion of Dante's visual imagination. The surface level of Dante's poetry is consistently an appeal to what human beings have in common—i.e., the senses. This makes Dante more universal because, in Eliot's words, "our eyes are all the same" (*SE* 205). The sense behind the nonsense in Eliot's often ridiculed view that "Genuine poetry can communicate before it is understood" (*SE* 200) is related to the universality of the senses. "We can see and feel the situation of the two lost lovers [Paolo and Francesca], though we do not yet understand the meaning which Dante gives it" (*SE* 206). Appealing to this universal common ground, Dante quickly establishes contact with his readers and then easily sustains that communion until the ideas on which the allegory has been built are understood.

The most important common ground connecting Dante and his international audience was the Christian religion, particularly the Catholic ideational system which culminated in St. Thomas Aquinas's synthesis of Aristotle, St. Paul, and the church fathers. Eliot's principal position on the relation of art and belief is that although readers need not endorse the beliefs embodied in a poem, they must at least "understand" them. Less than belief, but more than knowledge, understanding is an acceptance of the ideas in a poem as coherent and as possible.

> When I speak of understanding, I do not mean merely knowledge of books or words, any more than I mean belief; I mean a state of mind in which one sees certain beliefs, as the order of the deadly sins, in which treachery and pride are greater than lust, and despair the greatest, as possible. (*SE* 220)

Dante's incomparable advantage was that his audience went beyond understanding; like the poet himself, they believed firmly in the central doctrines of Christianity.

The importance of common ground in Eliot's thought can also be illustrated from "What Is a Classic?"—his 1944 Presidential Address to the Virgil Society. Eliot begins by trying to reclaim the word "classic" from the semantic quagmire created by centuries of cultural politics.

> If there is any one word on which we can fix, which will suggest the maximum of what I mean by the term "a classic," it is the word *maturity*.... A classic can only occur when a civilization is mature, when a language and a literature are mature; and it must be the work of a mature mind. (*On Poetry and Poets* 54; cited as *OPP*)

Eliot refuses to say just what he means by "maturity," rationalizing that mature readers already know the definition, and immature ones are incapable of understanding it. In spite of this evasion, he deigns to give a criterion. The measure of maturity is the extent to which it consists of what is common. At bottom, the maturity of Virgil, like the universality of Dante, contains as semantic core the simple idea of commonness.

The Virgil essay, like the Dante essay, features one of Eliot's perennial contrasts, that between what is merely personal and what is common. It is not Virgil's originality that makes him a classic, but the harmonious marriage of that originality with collective achievement. The common resources that made Virgil's greatness possible were, first of all, linguistic. He inherited a mature language, characterized by "a common standard, a common vocabulary, and a common sentence structure" (*OPP* 56). Even style, the slippery concept usually related to individual genius, is measured by its inclusion of the common. The development of classic literature, Eliot maintains, "is the development toward a *common* style" (*OPP* 57). A common style cannot be adequately illustrated from English literature, especially not from the greatest poets, Milton and Shakespeare, because in reading these poets, one is bound to be distracted by individual style.

> In modern European literature, the closest approximations to the idea of a common style, are probably to be found in Dante and Racine; the nearest we have to it in English poetry is Pope, and Pope's is a common style which, in comparison, is of a very narrow range. A common style is one which makes us exclaim not "this is a man of genius using the language," but "this realizes the genius of the language." (*OPP* 65)

Eliot goes on to suggest that the rise and fall of a civilization can be charted by observing the style of its literature: "The age in which we find a common style, will be an age when society has achieved a moment of order and stability, of equilibrium and harmony; as the age which manifests the greatest extremes of individual style will be an age of immaturity or of senility" (*OPP* 57). To review more of Eliot's address on Virgil would be to repeat in different words his analysis of the universality of Dante. His conclusion is that the perfect classic will be popular with the general public because it will have sprung from a community of taste, a community of ideas.

Eliot's emphasis on the importance of common ground is a constant in his prose writings from 1917 to the early sixties. The argument he makes is less interesting than the fact that he seems compelled continually to make it. His obsession is related to a crisis in history. All of Eliot's essays on the importance of common ground, such as those on Dante and Virgil, are based on an analysis of the relation of art to conditions of history. Consistently, his analyses involve a contrast between the past and the present—not the glorious past and the sordid present, but a past when art was possible and a present when it is impossible. The situation in thirteenth-century Florence or in pre-Christian Rome, then, is only a pretext in those essays. Eliot's real subject is the situation in twentieth-century London, in what he refers to in his 1923 review of Joyce's *Ulysses* as "the immense panorama of futility and anarchy which is contemporary history" (*Selected Prose* 177; cited as *SP*). In describing the common ground connecting Dante to his audience, Eliot is lamenting the absence of common ground between the modern poet and his audience. He is saying how "easy" art was then in order to underscore how difficult it is now. His amazement at "just how *little* each poet had to do" is a form of astonishment at just how *much* he and his contemporaries would have to do. His great predecessors had received the common ground they needed as a gift from history. But for the modern poet, history had no such gratuities. The generous mother, in the language of "Gerontion," had become a parsimonious whore who

> ... deceives with whispering ambitions,
> Guides us by vanities. Think now
> She gives when our attention is distracted
> And what she gives, gives with such supple confusions
> That the giving famishes the craving. Gives too late
> What's not believed in, or is still believed,
> In memory only, reconsidered passion ...

This lamentable metamorphosis in the character of history is crucial in understanding Eliot and his contemporaries. In their time, the basic assumptions of reality which had supported Western thought for some three hundred years were swept away, producing the epistemological limbo in which the modern mind still lingers.

The enormity of the crisis faced by modern artists can be understood in terms of a concept of historical progression outlined by

José Ortega y Gasset in *Man and Crisis*. Ortega suggests that when the world as it is known by one generation is succeeded by a different world, when the way of knowing that world is succeeded by a different way of knowing, the usual situation is that the skeleton of the old world remains intact, leaving a structure for measuring one's losses and for interpreting the new world. But occasionally, Ortega argues, there is a very different type of succession of worlds in which, to extend his metaphor, the backbone of the universe collapses, producing a catastrophe which he calls a "historical crisis." Basic longstanding and widely diffused systems of thought which have served as the skeleton of the world are totally fractured, producing an epistemological void and creating in people a sense of disorientation and panic as they stand on the *terra incognito* dividing two worlds. The crises associated with the Enlightenment and with the Romantic or Revolutionary period do not qualify as historical crises. In both periods, the world retained its epistemological skeleton and could be interpreted in terms established by Newton and Descartes. The distinguishing feature of being in historical crisis is that one is tossed violently into an epistemological vacuum. The only imbroglios of the last two millennia which satisfy Ortega's criteria are the Copernican revolution of the early Renaissance and the Einsteinian of the early twentieth century.

That the early twentieth century was a time of historical crisis is perhaps now a commonplace in the history of ideas. Ortega y Gasset's famous essays on art and culture (e.g., "The Dehumanization of Art") are based to some extent on this notion of crisis. Karl Jaspers' classic of existentialist theology, *Man in the Modern Age*, proceeds from a similar idea of the modern situation. A.O. Lovejoy's *Revolt Against Dualism* shows that the early twentieth-century dethronement of Descartes constituted a historical crisis in philosophy. The analogous crisis in physics, discussed in such books as Jacob Bronowski's *The Common Sense of Science*, was the dethronement of Newton. Even literary critics—Nathan Scott, for example—have discussed the early part of this century as a time when the progress of knowledge seemed to cancel the possibility of knowing. In "Hölderlin and the Essence of Poetry," Heidegger calls this time of epistemological crisis a great "Between." It is the age of need between the era of the gods who have fled and the gods who are coming, the "No-More" of Newton's God and the

"Not-Yet" of his successor (*Existence and Being* 289). Eliot puts it this way: "The present situation is radically different from any in which poetry has been produced in the past; namely ... now there is nothing in which to believe.... Belief itself is dead" (*The Use of Poetry and the Use of Criticism* 130; cited as *UPUC*).

II

The collapse of common ground in history, then, is behind Eliot's obsession with the idea of common ground. But why is common ground so important for an artist? Why does its presence make Dante a beneficiary of history, and its absence make Eliot a victim of history? The answer is not, as may be supposed, that Eliot thought of art as communication. This ancient idea, advocated in the twentieth century by such eminent voices as the anti-formalist Tolstoy and the formalist I.A. Richards, has a limited importance in Eliot's aesthetic. Eliot required common ground because he thought of art as collaboration, and collaboration is contingent upon common ground.

Eliot's definition of collaboration, like his definition of commonness, may be found in the most ordinary dictionary. To collaborate means simply "to labor together" or "to cooperate willingly in a project." Collaboration is the doing of one job by more than one person. At the center of Eliot's theory of art is the view that the greatest art can only be achieved through collaboration, and that the greatest artists are not necessarily the most brilliant or energetic, but the most willing and most able to collaborate.

The greater artists, according to Eliot, realize at least three types of collaboration. Giants such as Dante and Virgil realize all three types at once. The first is collaboration with the auditor or reader of the poem. The audience contemporary with Dante, say, joined in creating *The Divine Comedy*; each future audience in turn participates in its creation. The second type of collaboration is philosophic or ideational. Great artists do not use their own private ideas, but collaborate with philosophers, theologians, etc. Dante did not think up original material; in building the intellectual structure of his poem, he collaborated with Aquinas and others. The third type of collaboration involves the poet with other artists, both living and dead, in the production of a "really new" work of art. Dryden, for example, did not perfect his particular forms as much through invention as through collaboration with other poets.

The collaboration of an artist with his immediate audience is discussed by Eliot in his 1923 memorial essay on Marie Lloyd. Eliot's admiration of this music-hall comedienne, sometimes seen as an affectation, is entirely consistent with his admiration of Virgil and Dante. The superiority of each derives from the fact that he/she did not work alone, as a mere individual talent, but collaborated with his/her audience. "The working man who went to the music-hall and saw Marie Lloyd and joined in the chorus was himself performing part of the act; he was engaged in that collaboration of the audience with the artist which is necessary in all art" (*SE* 407). Miss Lloyd's work of art, her act, was not what she did alone on stage, but what she and her audience did together. Like Virgil and Dante, she avoided gestures which would have attracted attention to her individuality. "There was nothing about her of the grotesque; none of her comic appeal was due to exaggeration" (*SE* 406). She was a "representative" of the British lower classes, in collaboration with whom she raised both her life and theirs to a kind of art. Like all great dramatic art, her performance was a cunning exploitation of what she and her audience had in common. Her ability to control them, to convert even hostile responses into part of the show, was gained by suspending self in a cooperative enterprise.

The collaboration of an artist with philosophers is discussed in Eliot's 1920 essay on William Blake. Eliot contrasts Blake, "only a poet of genius," to Dante, "a classic." The main difference is that Dante "borrowed" ideas, whereas Blake "fabricated" them.

> His philosophy, like his insight, like his technique, was his own ... this is what makes him eccentric; and makes him inclined to formlessness.... The borrowed philosophy of Dante and Lucretius is perhaps not so interesting, but it injures their form less. (*The Sacred Wood* 155–56; cited as *SW*)

Blake's poetry illustrates "the crankiness, the eccentricity" of the artist who is unwilling or unable to collaborate. "What his genius required, and what it sadly lacked, was a framework of accepted and traditional ideas which would have prevented him from indulging in a philosophy of his own" (*SW* 157). Eliot's assessment of Blake includes the conviction, centrally expressed in the Dante and Virgil essays, that the common ground a poet needs for collaboration must be given by history. "The fault is perhaps not with Blake himself, but with the environment which failed to provide what such a poet needed; perhaps the circumstances compelled him to fabricate" (*SW* 158). Forced to be philosopher and poet at once, Blake was bound to fail, in Eliot's view, as philosopher or as poet or as both. This is the principle behind Eliot's ostensibly outrageous response to critics who discuss Dante's "philosophy": "I can see no reason for believing that either Dante or Shakespeare did any thinking on their own" (*SE* 116).

The third type of collaboration is collaboration with other artists. Over and over again, Eliot attributes his admiration of poets to their "capacity for assimilation" (*SE* 271). In what must seem like an odd compliment, Eliot says that "Dante had the benefit of years of practice in forms employed and altered by numbers of contemporaries and predecessors, ... and when he came to the *Commedia*, he knew how to pillage right and left" (*SW* 63). Eliot is even more explicit in a 1927 essay on the Jacobean dramatist, Thomas Middleton. This rather obscure writer is praised for "collaborating shamelessly" with Dekker, Rowley, and others. Admitting that Middleton is not the equal of Shakespeare or Webster, Eliot insists that in one way he is their superior. "Of all the Elizabethan dramatists, Middleton seems the most impersonal, the most indifferent to personal fame or perpetuity, the readiest, except Rowley, to accept collaboration" (*SE* 140). The art of Jonson, Chapman, Donne, and Webster is vitiated by intrusion of personality, but the art of Middleton, "who collaborated shamelessly, who is hardly separated from Rowley," is impersonal: "Middleton remains merely a collective name for a number of plays" (*SE* 140). "His greatness is not that of a peculiar personality, but of a great artist or artisan of the Elizabethan epoch" (*SE* 141). This is Eliot's criterion for the classic, to be stated again some twenty years later in his address on Virgil.

Crucial to Eliot's view of art as collaboration is the idea that collaboration must not be limited by time. A poet must actively collaborate not only with present, but with future audiences. Also, a poet must collaborate not only with present philosophers and artists, but with past ones. Extra-temporal collaboration is the subject of Eliot's celebrated early essay "Tradition and the Individual Talent." The first, perhaps the fundamental, point is contained in the title. Ordinarily, tradition and individual talents are opposite concepts in criticism. Most critics measure value in art either by the extent to which a work is traditional or the extent to which it is original. Eliot says that tradition and individual talent are not opposites, but complements, not two concepts, but two parts of one. He equally deprecates the tendency to praise an artist for conformity to past models and the tendency to praise him for "those aspects of his work in which he least resembles anyone else" (*SE* 4). There are a number other antitheses, more or less parallel to that between tradition and individual talent, which Eliot abrogates in this famous essay—e.g., mind of Europe versus private mind; timeless versus temporal; past versus present; ideal order of monuments versus new work; mind of poet versus ordinary mind. Central to his meaning in each instance is a contrast between what is or should be common and what is private or individual. In each case, Eliot replaces the "or" with "and"; that is, he replaces the antithetical relationship with a complementary, interdependent one.

In a later essay, Eliot defines tradition as "the collective personality, so to speak, realized in the literature of the past" (*OPP* 58). In the 1919 essay, he tries to clarify tradition by associating it with the "historical sense." The historical sense is the living presence of other artist-collaborators, dead ones included, within individual artists. It is an internalization, an organic assimilation of the common ground which unites them to all other artists, living and dead:

> The historical sense involves a perception, not only of the pastness of the past, but of its presence; the historical sense compels a man to write not merely with his own generation in his bones, but with a feeling that the whole of the literature of Europe from Homer and within it the whole of the literature of his own country has a simultaneous existence and composes a simultaneous order. (*SE* 4)

Putting Homer, Virgil, Dante, and Shakespeare into one's bones, wherefrom they cannot be removed even by surgery, is possible, Eliot admits, only through great labor. Nevertheless, this labor is indispensable for individuals because it insures that their work will be achieved in collaboration with those great dead ones living in their bones. It protects their work against narrowness and eccentricity. To artists who take the pains to acquire this historical sense, collaboration will be "compelled"—i.e., unconscious and impersonal. Automatically, the new work will be a development and modification of the art of predecessors.

Eliot's longing for collaboration with his audience accounts for his lifelong interest in drama. Many of his early essays—for example, "A Dialogue on Dramatic Poetry"—argue that the possibilities for collaboration are maximal in the theatre. And one of his most striking attempts to bring his audience into his art is found in *Murder in the Cathedral*. In no uncertain way, he forces his audience to take a part in the play. Beckett's sermon, for example, is not addressed to any of the characters on the stage, but to the spectators. This transforms Eliot's audience in the theatre into Beckett's congregation in the cathedral. Again, after the murder, the guilty knights harangue members of the audience, forcing them to play the role of the judge who has superior perspective. Eliot also works in a temptation of the audience, and he manages to implicate the spectators as accomplices in the murder. Eliot's ability to gain collaboration through form is evident here. He initiates the collaboration by including a role for the audience, a role it cannot possibly refuse. Simply by being members of the audience, the spectators are automatically involved as collaborators. Each new audience encounters *Murder in the Cathedral* only partially written; unconsciously, each new audience completes it. Each new audience encounters a play with players missing from principal roles; seduced by form, each new audience performs its part, making the play a reality.

Eliot's view that great art is based on collaboration has analogues in his views on most subjects. Great religion, for example, is based on collaboration. Eliot especially disliked the performer-spectator service prevailing in American Protestantism, in which the pulpit is often used to harangue a congregation with eccentric and divisive views. On the other hand, he deeply appreciated the Anglican service in which the priest does not dominate or dictate, but joins in common prayer and Holy Communion with the congregation. Eliot's appreciation of the Mass, "the consummation of the drama, the perfect and ideal drama" (*SE* 35), is related to the fact that the audience at Mass becomes part of the drama through collaboration. Theology also must be constructed collaboratively:

> No religion can survive the judgment of history unless the best minds of its time have collaborated in its construction; if the Church of Elizabeth is worthy of the age of Shakespeare and Jon-

son, that is because of the work of Hooker and Andrewes. (*SE* 301)

The spirit of Anglicanism, the *via media* where Puritanism and Catholicism meet on common ground, was attractive to Eliot. The Calvinists and the Jesuits, both of the essence in understanding Donne, were little more to Eliot than sects. They were eccentric concerning matters of faith; they refused to collaborate. In other areas, too, from public education to political science, Eliot measured value by the presence or absence of collaboration.

Much that has been considered merely iconoclastic about form in Eliot's poetry (and in the modern arts generally) can be explained in terms of the incongruity between a fundamental in art, i.e., that art requires collaboration, and a condition in history, i.e., a dissolution of common ground. He and many others who endured the same deprivation tried to bypass the epistemological crisis by gaining collaboration entirely through form. Many aspects of form in Eliot's poetry (and in the modern arts generally)—e.g., allusiveness, juxtaposition, fragmentation, multi-perspectivism, deliberately unfinished surfaces—are comprehensible as stratagems for forcing collaboration from readers. And Eliot's collaborators include, in addition to readers, artists and philosophers. His collaboration with other artists, such as Dante and Ezra Pound, is undisputed. His collaboration with philosophers, such as Bradley and Russell, is less obvious than that with other artists, but it is just as important.

Eliot's obsession with common ground in culture and his emphasis on the necessity of collaboration in art lend themselves to generalizations regarding one of the great watersheds in the history of aesthetic form. Particularly suggestive is his contrast between the art produced in times of cultural unity and that produced in times of cultural chaos. When the members of a culture share basic beliefs and basic ways of organizing ideas, artists can use these common assumptions not only as reference points in their art, but perhaps of even greater importance, they can use these common ways of ordering experience as a guide to form. Collaboration with contemporaries, especially with an audience, is possible on many levels—for example, religious, philosophic, nationalistic. Collaboration with artists and with thinkers of other periods is also possible, or at least is unimpeded by any traumatic repudiation of the past. With common ground to endow it, collaboration is spontaneous and unproblematic; it does not become a conscious aim in aesthetics. The art produced in such periods of grace will tend to be an extension of life into art, blurring the boundaries between life and art.

But when the members of a culture share no basic intellectual assumptions and no framework for interpreting experience, artists must purge art of ideas and construct their own mental frameworks. Collaboration with contemporaries, especially with an audience, seems to be at once required and precluded. Collaboration with earlier thinkers and artists is also forbidden because of a repudiation of the past. To return to Ortega y Gasset's description of a historical crisis, the backbone of a world collapses, requiring artists to create, if at all, *ex nihilo*. With no valid reference points in the external world, art becomes ingrown, referring only to itself. And artists, for the same reason, tend to become solipsistic. Collaboration, without common ground to support it, demands conscious attention from artists. If they are to gain collaborators, they must gain them by force or by stealth, using techniques which circumvent the epistemological crisis by displacing the grounds of collaboration from life to art itself. In such periods, art and life will be separated by a great gulf. Purified of ideas, out of harm's way, art will be abstract and nonrepresentational.

Eliot once said that Yeats was part of the consciousness of an age which could not be understood without him (*OPP* 308). This statement, certainly, is true of Eliot himself. He rebuked those who called him the voice of their generation, and he once remarked that *The Waste Land* "was only the relief of a personal and wholly insignificant grouse against life" (*The Waste Land Facsimile* 1). From his own point of view, then, his poems from "The Love Song of J. Alfred Prufrock" to *The Waste Land* may have have been primarily a form of rhythmical grumbling. But from the point of view of cultural historians, these poems constitute an invaluable document on a major crisis in the history of aesthetic form and in the history of Western civilization. When read with the assumption that Eliot was an elitist, they are bound to be misinterpreted. And to misunderstand poems like "Gerontion" and *The Waste Land* is to misunderstand to some extent both our century and ourselves.

Works Cited

Eliot, T.S. *The Complete Poems and Plays 1909–1950*. New York: Harcourt, 1952.

————. *On Poetry and Poets*. London: Faber, 1957.

————. *The Sacred Wood*. New York: Knopf, 1921.

————. *Selected Essays*. New York: Harcourt, 1950.

————. *Selected Prose of T.S. Eliot*. Ed. Frank Kermode. New York: Harcourt, 1975.

————. *The Use of Poetry and the Use of Criticism*. London: Faber, 133.

————. *The Waste Land: A Facsimile and Transcript of the Original Drafts Including the Annotations of Ezra Pound*. Ed. Valerie Eliot. New York: Harcourt, 1971.

Heidegger, Martin. "Hölderlin and the Essence of Poetry." Trans. Douglas Scott. *Existence and Being*. Chicago: Henry Regnery, 1949.

Ortega y Gasset, José. *Man and Crisis*. Trans. Mildred Adams. New York: Norton, 1958.

Section III

How Does Collaboration Work?

Toward a Working Definition of Collaborative Writing

Jeanette Harris

Awareness and acceptance of writing as a collaborative act are clearly growing. Although *PMLA* and its imitators continue to publish single-authored articles almost exclusively, it is increasingly common for even these authors to confess that they relied extensively on assistance from friends or colleagues. These admissions, unlike similar acknowledgments in the past, suggest more than polite gratitude for minor suggestions or obligation to a devoted spouse for typing the manuscript or at least putting up with the author while the text was being written. They suggest our growing realization that in one sense, all writing is collaborative.

However, this new, more realistic attitude toward writing as a collaborative act has not resulted in a satisfactory definition of collaborative writing, which we continue to define primarily by what it is not—as the opposite of writing that is individual and independent. As Kenneth Burke points out, definition by negation, defining something "in terms of what it is not" (25), is perfectly legitimate. But in attempting to understand collaborative writing, it is not particularly instructive to think of it only as the opposite of solitary writing. In this essay I want to formulate a working definition of the concept of collaborative writing, one that reflects accurately our basic assumptions about how texts are constructed by both writers and readers.

In order to define collaborative writing, we must first consider the possibility that all writing is collaborative, an assertion that cannot be dismissed lightly and that, if true, solves our problem by eliminating the need to distinguish between individual and collaborative writing. The argument that all writing is collaborative most often derives from the following assumptions:

1. Since we generally assume that writing evolved from speaking and since oral language is always inherently social, then writing too must be viewed as basically a social phenomenon and thus a collaborative act.

2. Since, as Walter Ong (among others) reminds us, "every text builds on pretext" (162), then everything that is written is essentially a revision of a "prior text."

3. Since, according to social constructionists, both language and knowledge are social constructs, then all texts are obviously also social rather than individual constructs.

4. Since, as the deconstructionists and reader-response theorists assert, all texts are completed in the act of reading, then a writer never functions alone to create a text.

I believe that all of these assertions are perfectly valid and that they argue convincingly for the assumption that all writing is collaborative in a very real sense of that term. However, I don't think we can dismiss the problem of defining collaborative writing on the basis of this assumption. For we still need to distinguish among different degrees of collaboration. That is, even if all writing is ultimately collaborative, some writing is immediately more collaborative than other writing.

In the past, collaborative writing was often referred to as plagiarism if we were talking about students; if we were discussing professional writers or ourselves, it was editing. Although technical writers and scientists have traditionally dealt with the issue of collaborative writing openly and directly, most academic humanists and professional writers have carefully nourished the illusion that truly respectable writing was something that a single, solitary author created on her or, most often, his own.

In general, the views about collaborative writing divided along aesthetic/pragmatic lines. That is, if one were engaged in writing that was primarily intended for pragmatic purposes, then collaboration was permissible. If, on the other hand, one were writing for aesthetic purposes, collaboration was concealed or considered a lesser accomplishment. Therefore, when writers whose purposes were aesthetic involved others in their writing, they often concealed it, referred to it as editing, or rationalized that it wasn't really collaboration because no one else physically performed the act of writing the words. As a result, the illusion existed that writing for aesthetic purposes was a solitary act—a writer working alone to create art. In spite of the obvious collaborations of playwrights since the time of Shakespeare and the less obvious but no less real collaborations of novelists such as Joseph Conrad and Ford Madox Ford and poets such as Ezra Pound and T.S. Eliot, we have generally accepted the idea that the creative act is inevitably solitary.

The idea that artists work alone, guided only by their own genius or some inspirational muse, is not limited to literature. It informs every artistic discipline. Like a poem or a novel, a symphony or a painting has traditionally been perceived as the result of an individual endeavor. Recently, however, the myth of the solitary artist has begun to crumble. For example, the 1989 exhibit entitled "Picasso and Braque: Pioneering Cubism" focused on the "remarkable collaboration" between Picasso and Braque (Kies). The exhibit firmly established the very real collaboration that occurred between these two artists even though they did not work together on the same canvases. Their early Cubist paintings were clearly the result of something more than one artist merely influencing another. As Emily Bardack Kies notes in the brochure she wrote for the exhibit at the Museum of Modern Art in New York, "It is unlikely that Cubism as we know it could have developed without the interaction that arose between the two artists."

One reason why it was possible to sustain the myth of the solitary artist in literature for so long is that, until recently, collaborative writing was defined very narrowly. Only if two or more people actually joined forces to construct a physical text did we use the term collaboration. As a result, the equally real collaborations that frequently occur before a written text exists or after it is supposedly "finished" were ignored or discounted as insignificant. If we analyze the process of text construction, we see that collaboration can occur throughout text regardless of whether a writer has pragmatic or aesthetic purposes. Thus, to define collaborative writing accurately, we must broaden our view to include what happens during the entire process of text construction.

A text exists first in the mind of a writer. James Moffett refers to this unwritten form of a text as *interior dialogue*, Linda Flower and John Hayes describe it as a *mental representation* of a text, and

Stephen Witte uses the term *pretext*. I prefer the terms *interior text* or *mental text* because they reinforce the idea that this preliminary, unwritten discourse is, nevertheless, a form of the text. The interior text is the dynamic, evolving mental representation that a text assumes as it is constructed by both writer and reader. It is the version of the text that exists in the mind of the writer initially and in the mind of the reader ultimately—what the writer anticipates and the reader remembers. In the words of Wolfgang Iser, it is the "virtual dimension of the text" (279).

Interior texts vary, of course, depending on the length of the text, the purpose(s) of the writer, the audience for whom the text is intended, and the subject that is being addressed. In the case of a poem, an interior text may begin as a single image or even a rhythm. Even novelists often begin the process of constructing a text with little more than a vague sense of what they plan to write or their purposes for writing. Virginia Woolf, for example, writing in her diary of her plans to begin *Jacob's Room*, states simply, "It's the spring I have in my mind to describe" (34). And Henry James comments in one of his notebook entries, "I heard an allusion yesterday ... which suggested the germ of a story" (16). Other writers begin with a question or a problem and may construct elaborate, detailed interior texts before they commit any words to paper.

An interior text is constantly evolving and changing even after the physical text is completed—or even if the physical text is never completed. An interior text expands, growing from a single idea or image to a complex network of related ideas and images. The finished product may, in fact, bear little resemblance to the original conception. Just as a proposition that exists in deep structure may be transformed, combined, and modified until it assumes a quite different written or spoken form, an interior text may undergo countless modifications as it is shaped into a physical text.

However brief or lengthy, fragmentary or complete an interior text may be, it determines to a great extent both form and content of the final text. The interior text continues to evolve throughout the construction of a text, interacting recursively and incrementally with the physical text once it exists. Thus, at any time during the construction of a text, a modification in the interior text may affect the written text. If a writer discusses the text with someone else and, as a result modifies the interior text that is guiding the process of text construction, then that writer has, in effect, collaborated. Picasso and Braque probably collaborated in just this way—not working on each other's canvases but modifying their paintings significantly through discussions and comments both before the works existed as physical entities and during the painting of them.

Of course, with writers, this kind of thing happens all the time in a very casual, informal way. We nearly always discuss our writing with others, and frequently something they say or something we say as a result of something they say leads us to a new insight. I cannot imagine writing any type of academic discourse that I have not first explored in a dialogue with someone who knows enough about the subject to provide me with some responses. Just as the act of writing seems to enable me to see relationships, make connections, and organize my thoughts, the act of talking seems to help me figure out what I really want to say. Discussing my ideas with another person continues and externalizes the dialogue that has begun in my mind. This essay, for example, evolved out of discussions with a friend who is much more knowledgeable about literature than I am, was modified by my experience of reading it as part of a CCCC panel on collaborative writing, and was further shaped by suggestions by the editors of this collection. That only my name appears on it merely reflects the fact that I was the one who physically wrote the essay.

We need not, of course, term collaborative all writing that is indirectly shaped by casual conversations with friends. But we need to be aware that a very real collaboration can occur even if only one person physically writes the text. If a writer consciously and deliberately engages with another person in ways that affect the interior text, then that writer has collaborated as surely as if he or she shared the physical writing task with another.

Collaboration often occurs even more explicitly and directly once a text assumes a form that I term the *generative text*. The *generative text* is most easily understood as writing-in-progress, what Walter Beale would term "discourse performance *in potentia*" (83). When we write, we are not merely transcribing or translating an interior text; the process of constructing a generative text also enables us to construct new meaning. As we search for words, we find new ideas by making connections, seeing possibilities and recovering information from long-term memory. Writers often produce various forms of a generative text—notes, diagrams, outlines, and, of course, rough drafts—as they transform their interior texts into completed written texts. A generative text may assume literally a thousand different forms, layers and layers of text built one upon the other. Like the interior text, the generative text is used by the writer to shape the final version. It is, in fact, the interaction between the interior and generative texts that produces the final text. We cannot modify one without modifying the other.

In the past, collaborative writing has usually meant a shared production of a generative text. In other words, if two or more people engage in the construction of a generative text, then the writing is deemed collaborative. However, we cannot limit our definition of collaborative writing to those cases in which two or more writers share the production of text.

Any substantive modification of the interior or generative or even the completed text that occurs as a result of one writer's conscious and deliberate interaction with another can be defined as collaborative writing. If we use this comprehensive definition, we can see that collaboration is not limited to technical writers. Writing for both aesthetic and pragmatic purposes often can be most accurately described as collaborative.

However, as long as the solitary production of a text is privileged over collaboration, most people, at least those associated with departments of English, will continue to claim individual authorship when possible. Since tenure and promotion, not to mention merit raises, often hinge on such distinctions, who can blame them?

It is also likely that many writers in the arts and humanities, those who write primarily for aesthetic purposes, will continue to write as individuals—scrupulously and proudly working in near-isolation, keeping their ideas to themselves, refusing assistance of any kind, resenting even the few changes that a copy-editor may impose on their text. Such writers often believe that even discussing their ideas with someone else is detrimental to their process. Others fear that their ideas will be "stolen." Because the tradition of viewing aesthetic writing as an individual rather than a social construct is a lengthy one and because some writers really do prefer to work as much as possible in isolation, there is no danger that individual authorship will disappear, but it is likely that collaborative writing will increasingly be a legitimate alternative.

For political as well as philosophical reasons, it is unfortunate that we do not have a term other than collaborative writing to apply to a shared act of text production. When two people talk together, we have words such as *conversation, dialogue, dialectic,* or even *chat* or *rap.* But when two people write together, we can only qualify the term *writing* itself. Because until recently the "solitary writer, arrested in the moment of transcription" has been what Linda Brodkey calls the "official view of writing" (399), there was no need for terms to designate the concept of collaborative writing or the different forms it assumes.

In fact, at present, we use the term *collaborative writing* not only to mean sharing the production of a text but also to refer to the process of text interaction that has been made possible by new computer technology. Increasingly, composition is taught in computer-based classrooms in which each student works at a computer that is networked to the other computers in the room. As a result, students have access to all the other students' texts and are encouraged to read and comment on those texts as often as possible. Thus each individual student's text is shaped directly by the comments of his or her fellow students and indirectly by the ideas that the student encounters in reading and responding to the texts of the other students. Even when computers are not networked, they invite intervention and encourage collaboration. It is simply much easier to write collaboratively if the writing is being done on a computer. Whether writers are working at a single computer or each has his or her own, a computer-generated text can be easily manipulated to accommodate the contributions of multiple authors.

As our understanding of collaborative writing expands, we may well find that we need not only to define and redefine the term but also to find other terms that distinguish among different types of collaborative writing. The type of collaboration that occurs between an editor and a writer is not the same as that between coauthors or among students working at networked computers. But until such terms evolve, we must be content with the idea that collaborative writing is a very broad term that encompasses many different ways of sharing responsibility for the construction of a text.

The time is past when we all viewed writing romantically and unrealistically as a solitary act of creation. We are now aware of the social nature of all writing and have recognized that collaborative writing cannot be defined narrowly and literally to mean a process in which two people physically engage in the production of a single text. As I have argued in this essay, sharing in the act of constructing a text involves cognitive as well as physical collaboration. Writers may collaborate before they have begun to write, while the text exists only as a mental phenomenon, or after they think they have finished writing, when an editor or friend or colleague offers suggestions that result in substantive modification of the text. Once we have accepted collaboration as a legitimate form of authorship for all types of discourse, we can turn our attention to even more interesting questions about the results of collaborative writing—a subject that has only begun to be explored.

Works Cited

Beale, Walter H. *A Pragmatic Theory of Rhetoric*. Carbondale: Southern Illinois UP, 1987.

Brodkey, Linda. "Modernism and the Scene(s) of Writing." *College English* 49 (1987): 396–418.

Burke, Kenneth. *A Grammar of Motives*. Berkeley: U of California P, 1969.

Flower, Linda and John R. Hayes. "Images, Plans, and Prose: The Representation of Meaning in Writing." *Written Communication* 1 (1984): 120–60.

Iser, Wolfgang. *The Implied Reader*. Baltimore: Johns Hopkins UP, 1974.

James, Henry. *The Complete Notebooks of Henry James*. Ed. Leon Edel and Lyall H. Powers. New York: Oxford UP, 1987.

Kies, Emily Bardack. *Picasso and Braque: Pioneering Cubism*. New York: The Museum of Modern Art, 1989.

Moffet, James. *Teaching the Universe of Discourse*. 1968; rpt. Boston: Houghton Mifflin, 1983.

Ong, Walter J. *Orality and Literacy: The Technologizing of the Word*. New York: Methuen, 1982.

Witte, Stephen P. "Pre-Text and Composing." *College Composition and Communication* 38 (1987): 397–425.

Woolf, Virginia. *A Writer's Diary*. Ed. Leonard Woolf. New York: Harcourt, 1953.

Toward a Revision Decision
Model of Collaboration

Shirley K Rose

Scenario #1

Alicia, an assistant professor at University A, and Bradford, an assistant professor at University B, have coauthored a scholarly article which has been published in their discipline's leading journal. Alicia and Bradford both feel they have contributed equally to researching and composing the article and revising it according to the journal editor's suggestions.

When Alicia prepares her dossier for her tenure review, she will list the article along with publications she has authored alone. Her university and her department have explicit policies recognizing coauthorship as equal in merit to single authorship. But when Bradford prepares his dossier, he will list their article in a separate category from others he has authored alone, as his university's tenure procedures and policies require. In addition, he must compose a brief explanation of his contribution to the article and provide copies of correspondence between Alicia and himself and between the two of them and the journal editor.

Scenario #2

Andrea often asks her executive secretary, Barry, to draft memos and reports which are distributed under Andrea's own name. After Andrea briefs him on the purpose of the documents, Barry is usually able to proceed without further instructions. Andrea wants to recognize and reward Barry's work by recommending his promotion to executive assistant. To do so she must find a way to make the significance of Barry's contributions clear to her own boss without suggesting that she has abdicated to him the key responsibilities of her own position.

Scenario #3

Alonzo is a technical writer at a relatively small new company which develops computer software for biomedical applications. He is responsible for preparing user manuals for the software. Alonzo must work closely with both the software engineers who are developing the software and the company's marketing department, which has contact with the biomedical professionals who use the software. In order to avoid interdepartmental conflicts and misunderstandings, Alonzo has been trying to formally specify the review process for composing the user manuals.

Scenario #4

Amanda, Betty, Carlotta, and Dorothy have formed a writing group. They meet regularly to read their works in progress and give one another encouragement and advice for revisions. Over several months, they have experimented with various strategies and processes for conducting their group sessions and now are trying to identify which procedures are the most useful and comfortable for them.

* * *

Each of these scenarios describes a collaborative writing situation. The involvement and responsibilities of the participants vary according to the role each has assumed in the act of collaborative composing. What they share is a need to describe those roles. All of these participants in collaborative composing need some way to identify and analyze their roles in the decision-making and their part in the evolution of the text. They must find some way to account not only for the quantity of their individual contributions, but also for the quality or nature of those contributions—that is, how their roles may differ from the roles of other collaborators.

The needs of our fictional collaborators are not unique. Collaborating writers in a variety of contexts—academic, business, and technical communication are only a few—encounter this same need to identify, analyze, and describe their interaction in order to understand their individual roles and the procedures which have contributed to their relative success and satisfaction with collaborative efforts. For as Stephen Doheny-Farina observed in his study of how a small computer software company wrote its business plan, "the writing process not only influenced the substance of what was written, but also influenced the organization" (167). Geoffrey Cross, in his Bakhtinian analysis of a failed process of collaboratively composing an annual business report, concurs:

> ... group writing is a political process involving power and conflict stemming both from the nature of groups and from the nature of language. The better their techniques of collaboration, the better the odds that power and conflict will be channeled toward constructive ends. (200)

The model of collaboration proposed below attempts to account for the differences in negotiation and decision-making strategies involved in a variety of collaborative writing interactions. The model describes these interactions as a series of decisions about the text as it evolves toward the "final" draft—the version to be presented to the intended audience. In *Singular Texts/ Plural Authors* Ede and Lunsford raise a question about the "ethics" of coauthorship: "... in cases of group authorship, where does the responsibility lie? Who stands behind the words of a report written by fifteen people?" (156). By representing collaborative writing as a decision-making process, the model described below identifies who is responsible for making critical decisions as well as who is responsible for suggesting ideas and contributing text segments as the text evolves.

Design of the Model

Based on a conception of all discourse as socially constructed and thus essentially collaborative, the model accounts for, yet differentiates between, the negotiation and decision-making enacted by an individual author and that enacted by two or more collaborating writers. The model is capable of further discriminating among a variety of kinds of interaction between collaborating writers, such as (1) coauthorship, (2) cooperative writing (where more than one writer or group of writers is involved in planning, drafting, and revising, but authorship is not credited to all involved or is credited to a corporate entity), and (3) peer response.

The model describes a sequence of actions which, if followed, replicate a variety of collaborative writing efforts. That is, while the model is not a systematic representation or codification of empirically observed data, it is capable of generating a sequence of actions and outcomes which resemble those which can be observed in collaborating writers. The elements of the model are *participants*, *propositions*, and *writing decisions*. The participants are the collaborating writers engaged in action for the purpose of producing a written text for an intended audience. Alicia, Brad, Alonzo, Amanda, Betty, and the others in our opening scenarios are, then, *participants*, whom I will designate as "A," "B," "C," etc.

Propositions are articulations of purpose or goal, plans or strategies, or stretches of actual text—sentences, paragraphs, or longer units of discourse. Because invention processes often begin with and continue to involve face-to-face dialogue, formal and informal meetings, brainstorming sessions, phone calls, and other "social" interactions, as Bazerman, Selzer, and Odell have observed, the model's design includes these interactions as well as the drafting of written text. The nature of a specific "P"—whether sentence, paragraph, or longer stretch of discourse—depends upon how far the collaboration has progressed.

Writing decisions regarding these propositions include the following:

1. *Proposing*—articulating a goal, plan, or possible text. Proposing includes both the original generation and the subsequent repetitions of a goal, plan, or written text.

2. *Reviewing*—reading or listening to a proposition.

3. *Responding*—taking action upon reviewing a proposition; response takes one of four forms:

    a. rejecting—wholly dismissing the proposition;

    b. accepting—approving the proposition as articulated;

    c. modifying—changing the proposition by addition, deletion, substitution, rearrangement, or paraphrase, and thereby creating a new proposition; and

    d. querying—asking questions about the proposition, requesting elaboration or explanation.

4. *Canceling*—ending the process of collaboration. To cancel the proposition is to ignore it, to fail to further negotiate or make decisions about the proposition.

5. *Asserting*—presenting a proposition to its intended audience.

The model is designed to represent the participants negotiating and making a series of decisions about propositions. Each decision is represented as a choice from among a set of alternatives. These alternatives are the available strategies for negotiation which will lead to the next decision. Participants enact a series of negotiations and decisions which culminate in a final decision regarding a proposition. The decision-making process is initiated by the action of proposing and is terminated either by the decision to "assert"— that is, to present the proposition to the intended audience—or the decision to cancel the proposition. Though there are a finite number of decision types, the model allows for an infinite number of decisions and negotiations for an infinitely revised proposition.

In Figure 1 (p. 90), a diagram of this model of collaborative writing, participants are designated by the letters "A" and "B." Propositions are designated as "$P_{1a}, P_{1b},.... P_{1z}$" for a series of modifications of a proposition or as "$P_{1a}, P_{2a},.... P_{nz}$" for a series of different propositions. Decision points are indicated by arrows ($\rightarrow$); alternatives among which choices can be made at these decision points are indicated by braces ({}); and a cancellation—that is, a decision to leave a text unfinished—is indicated by "0."

Operating and Testing the Model

The model is set into operation when a participant "A" proposes a proposition "P_{1a}." The outcome is determined by the choices participants make among negotiation alternatives at each decision point.

For this model of collaborative writing to be sufficient, it must be adequate to generate each kind of collaborative interaction which can be observed among collaborating writers. Further, the model should distinguish between varieties of collaborative interaction; that is, each type of collaborative writing interaction should be represented by the model as a different sequence of negotiation

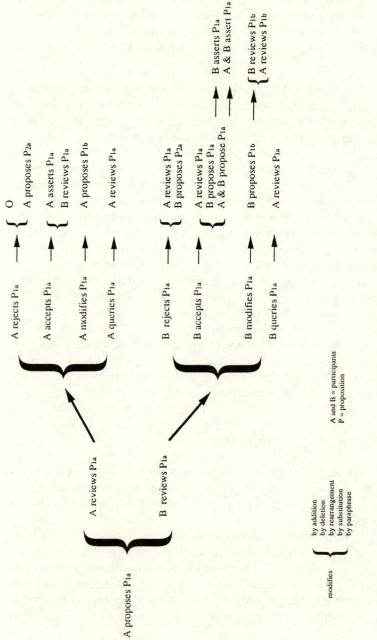

Figure 1: Model of Collaboration

and decision-making actions. In the section which follows I will explain how this model meets these requirements by demonstrating how it would generate a sequence of negotiations and decisions which resemble the interactions of writers engaged in coauthorship, "ghost writing," cooperative writing, and peer response groups.

The model allows for a careful, precise differentiation among dozens of possible patterns for collaboration. In *Singular Texts/ Plural Authors*, Ede and Lunsford identify the following "seven patterns of organization":

1. Team or group plans and outlines. Each member drafts a part. Team or group compiles the parts and revises the whole. (63)

2. Team or group plans and outlines. One member writes the entire draft. Team or group revises.

3. One member plans and writes draft. Group or team revises.

4. One person plans and writes draft. This draft is submitted to one or more persons who revise the draft without consulting the writer of the first draft.

5. Team or group plans and writes draft. This draft is submitted to one or more persons who revise the draft without consulting the writers of the first draft.

6. One member assigns writing tasks. Each member carries out individual tasks. One member compiles the parts and revises the whole.

7. One person dictates. Another person transcribes and revises. (64)

The collaborative writing model described here allows for more distinctions to be made among the many possible patterns for collaboration. For example, the four patterns followed by the collaborators in my opening scenarios could be characterized as follows.

Coauthorship involves two or more writers who share responsibility for decision-making from planning stage through presentation to the intended audience. The model can generate the following sequence of negotiations and decisions within such an interaction: one writer proposes a proposition; another writer reviews the proposition and responds by modifying the proposition and proposing the resulting new proposition; the first writer reviews this new proposition, accepts it, and joins the second writer in proposing the new proposition, reviewing it, accepting it, and finally asserting it, or presenting it to its intended audience. This sequence has involved both writers in the decisions to propose, review, and accept the proposition; thus both are qualified to assert the proposition, or claim authorship. The collaborative interaction between Alicia and Bradford described in the opening scenario resembles that suggested by the diagram in Figure 2.

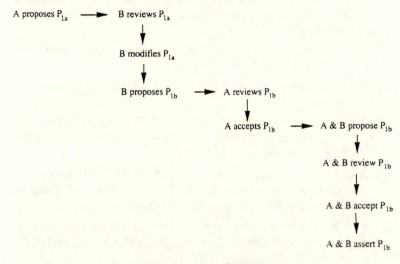

Figure 2: Co-authorship

This description has been oversimplified, but it demonstrates that, as coauthors, Alicia and Bradford are both involved in making decisions about revisions and both commit themselves to ideas and wording by joining one another in asserting P_{1b}—that is, presenting their proposition to its intended audience.

The model can also accommodate collaborative practices of shared authorship based on individual contributions of separate portions if all the authors had the opportunity for revision of all portions. Coauthorship might, thus, be defined as a collaborative writing interaction in which all authors have had the opportunity or the power to revise or approve the final draft of a proposition that has been asserted.

Ghost writing involves two or more writers in one or more of the decisions required to accomplish goal-setting, planning, drafting, and revising, but excludes one or more of these writers from the final decision to present a particular written text to its intended audience. One possible sequence which can be generated by the model results in a similar outcome: one writer proposes a proposition; another writer reviews the proposition and modifies it; the first writer reviews the modified proposition and responds by accepting it, proposing it, and asserting it. This sequence eliminates the second writer's opportunity (or responsibility) to review, accept, and assert the final version of the proposition, so the second writer cannot claim authorship. The collaborative interaction between Andrea and Barry, executive and secretary in Scenario #2, resembles such a sequence. Figure 3 represents this "ghost-writing" collaborative sequence.

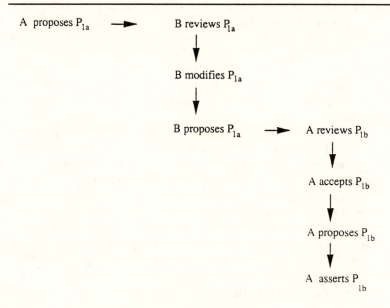

Figure 3: Ghost Writing

Cooperative writing involves a number of collaborators with a variety of expertise to contribute toward achieving a shared purpose. In a not atypical technical communication situation, one person will draft a document based on purposes and plans decided upon by other members of the collaborating group. The draft is submitted to each of the others, who request changes. The drafter attempts to make revisions which either incorporate all of the requested changes or resolve differences raised by conflicting instructions, then submits the document for further review. The process is repeated until all members of the group are satisfied. Alonzo, of Scenario #3, is involved in a similar collaborative process. In Figure 4, "A" could designate Alonzo, "B" could designate the software engineers, and "C" the marketing department.

Peer-response groups constitute still another type of collaborative writing interaction. As Ede and Lunsford have taken pains to argue in *Singular Texts/Plural Authors,* much of the peer-response interaction that occurs as part of peer-editing group work in composition classrooms is actually based on a pedagogy which views the writer as a solitary, isolated individual; nonetheless, the collaborative writing model described here includes peer writing groups as one of several types of collaboration. In a typical peer response interaction, a writer presents a draft to one or more peers, who may suggest revisions. The writer considers these suggestions, perhaps revises the draft, and presents a final draft to the intended audience.

This is the pattern suggested in the interactions between Amanda, Betty, Carlotta, and Dorothy in Scenario #4. The model can generate a similar sequence: Participant A proposes P_{1a}, Participant B reviews P_{1a} and responds by modifying the proposition, thus creating P_{1b}. Then Participant C, after reviewing both A's original proposition and B's modification, modifies both and proposes P_{1c}. In turn, participant D reviews all of the versions and queries A about some aspect of the original proposition. Finally, A reviews her original proposition as well as the suggested modifications and proposes yet another version, P_{1d}, which she reviews, accepts, and asserts as final draft without consulting her peers again.

Because participants B, C, and D have not been involved in reviewing the new proposition (even though they have contributed to its evolution), they have not been involved in the decision step

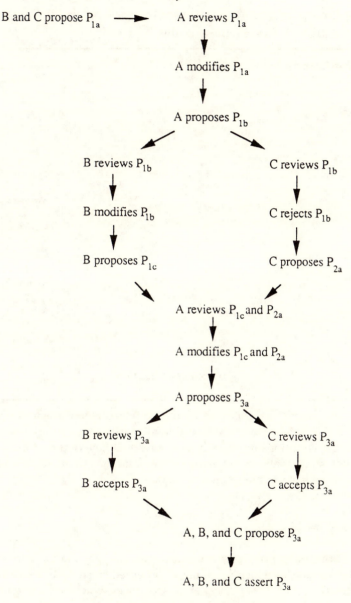

Figure 4: Cooperative Writing

which leads to acceptance and assertion and are thus not considered authors. Figure 5 represents this sequence.

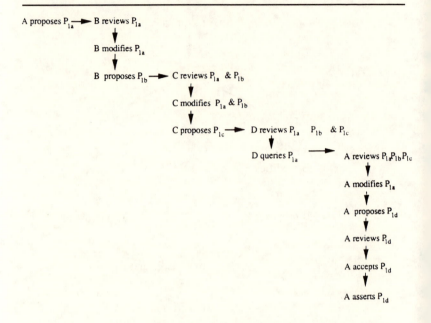

Figure 5: Peer Response

The procedures followed by the participants in these four collaborative interactions are but a small portion of a multitude of possible variations in procedures. One advantage of the proposed model is that it allows for precise differentiation among these various possible patterns of collaboration.

Uses of the Model

If this model proves sufficient to generate negotiation and decision sequences which resemble all observed collaborative writing interaction, and does not generate sequences which would be unrecognizable as a form of collaborative writing, then it will serve as a possible description of collaborative writing interaction. Employed by the characters in the opening scenarios, for example, the model would help describe their respective contributions and procedures for collaboration.

The model could aid in understanding microcosmic collaboration by analyzing several aspects of group-writing interactions. The quality of contributions of various participants in collaborative writing efforts could be analyzed by focusing on decision-making points, which would help to identify the relevant choices writers make in the composing process. By focusing on the decisions to *use* text as well as on the generation of text, the model accounts for the contribution that "boilerplate texts" and discourse chunks from data bases make to the construction of a successful document. Generation of text segments assumes less importance than the decisions to use and modify them.

The quantity of contributions can also be accounted for, using the number of turns in an emerging dialectic to code both talk and written text. Likewise, turn-taking analysis could help in understanding the sequences of contributions which make up serial communication chains.

Further, the model promises to aid in accounting for collaborating writers' satisfaction with their process. Ede and Lunsford have identified eight factors related to the amount of satisfaction collaborating writers feel:

1. the degree to which goals are clearly articulated and shared;

2. the degree of openness and mutual respect characteristic of group members;

*3. the degree of control the writers have over the text;

*4. the degree to which writers can respond to others who may modify the text;

*5. the way credit (either direct or indirect) is realized;

*6. an agreed upon procedure for resolving disputes among group members;

7. the number and kind of bureaucratic constraints (deadlines, technical or legal requirements, etc.) imposed on the writers;

8. the status of the project within the organization (65).

The four asterisked factors are directly addressed by the collaborative model. Each of these kinds of analysis would help us to understand why one collaborative effort seems more efficient, more productive, or even more enjoyable than another.

Finally, the model allows a degree of analysis which would make it possible to eventually write "rules" for types of collaboration. For example, one such rule might be: "Status as a participant in cooperative writing requires that one has both modified another participant's proposal and made a proposal which has been reviewed and modified or accepted by all other participants." Or, "Status as a participant in coauthorship requires that one have available all four options of response (reject, accept, query, modify) to every proposal offered by another participant."

The model serves also to aid our understanding of discourse as macrocosmic collaboration, for the model can be extended to include the discursive interactions of a community. As Roen and Mittan have argued, "scholars do not work alone, even when they think they do, because they are always affected by heteroglossia" (289). Collette Daiute's research has demonstrated that collaborative writing experience is useful for developing individual writing skills. Daiute cites Vygotsky's notion that individual thinking and communication skills are modeled on social interactions—that social interactions are valuable for what we usually think of as "autonomous" thought.

Using the model described here, writing collaboratively can be said to require sharing responsibility for decision-making. For example, an academic discipline or other discourse community might be better understood through an analysis of its citation practices. For such an analysis, the cited author would be designated as Participant A and the citing author as Participant B. This interaction could then be represented as Figure 6 suggests.

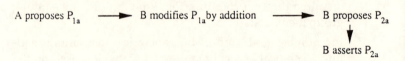

A proposes P_{1a} $\longrightarrow$ B modifies P_{1a} by addition $\longrightarrow$ B proposes P_{2a}
$\downarrow$
B asserts P_{2a}

Figure 6: Citation as Collaboration

Examining the process of collaboration on a single text may help us to recognize the collaborative nature of discourse in general and to discover the actual sources of influence and patterns of development of a community's discourse. Perhaps the most important contribution this model of collaborative writing has to make to our own community's ongoing conversation is that it allows us to recognize "authorship" as a willingness to make decisions about and assume responsibility for what one contributes to and accepts within that conversation.

Works Cited

Bazerman, Charles. "Scientific Writing as a Social Act: A Review of the Literature of the Sociology of Science." *New Essays in Technical and Scientific Communication: Research, Theory, Practice.* Ed. Paul V. Anderson, R. John Brockman, and Carolyn R. Miller. Farmingdale, NY: Baywood, 1983.

Cross, Geoffrey A. "A Bakhtinian Exploration of Factors Affecting the Collaborative Writing of an Executive Letter of an Annual Report." *Research in the Teaching of English* 24.2 (1990): 173–203.

Daiute, Colette. "Do 1 and 1 Make 2? Patterns of Influence by Collaborative Authors." *Written Communication* 3.3 (1986): 382–408.

Doheny-Farina, Steven. "Writing in an Emergent Organization: An Ethnographic Study." *Written Communication* 3.2 (1984):158–85.

Ede, Lisa, and Andrea Lunsford. *Singular Texts/ Plural Authors: Perspectives on Collaborative Writing.* Carbondale: Southern Illinois UP, 1990.

Odell, Lee. "Beyond the Text: Relations Between Writing and Social Context." *Writing in Nonacademic Settings.* Ed. Lee Odell and Dixie Goswami. New York: Guilford, 1985.

O'Donnell, Angela M., Donald F. Dansereau, Thomas Rocklin, Judith G. Lambiotte, Velma I. Hythecker, and Celia O. Larson. "Cooperative Writing: Direct Effects and Transfer." *Written Communication* 2.3 (1985): 307–15.

Roen, Duane H., and Robert K. Mittan. "Collaborative Scholarship in Composition Studies: Some Issues." *Methods and Methodology in Composition Research.* Ed. Gesa Kirsch and Patricia A. Sullivan. Carbondale: Southern Illinois UP, 1992.

Selzer, Jack. "The Composing Process of an Engineer." *College Composition and Communication* 34 (1983): 178–87.

Ethical Research in Computer-Based Writing Instruction

Fred Kemp

Good learning is not easy on the learner. Modern cultural and linguistic comprehensions suggest that good learning isn't simply the result of greater and greater acquisition of information, a stretching of some internal database, but rather that it involves seismic shifts in the way the learner views the universe. Obviously, some disciplines in this sense rock the boat more than others, but all disciplines, to some extent, require that the learner challenge previously held beliefs and values and accommodate personal codes to a necessarily shifting sense of what makes the universe tick and how one fits into the clockwork.

Teachers, therefore, perform a kind of violence upon their students, forcing a re-evaluation of comfortable assumptions and encouraging a continuing intellectual skepticism. "Codes of ethics" for teachers and especially researchers presume that this professional violence has limits. In most classes, a basis for a code of ethics would consist, it seems to me, of two concerns: the first would address the kind of material the teacher is pressing upon students, which I term here the "ethics of content," and the second would address the nature of teacher/student authority and a possible exploitation of students, which I call the "ethics of exploitation." In computer-based collaborative writing classes there are two further ethical concerns, which I call the "ethics of privacy" and the "ethics of technology." Since in my research I require what might be considered unusual classroom actions, ethical concerns for what occurs in the classroom are for me an important part of overall ethical concerns in the research itself.

The Ethics of Privacy

I teach writing using networked computers, and I research computer-based writing pedagogy at a large research institution. My particular pedagogical emphasis is on collaborative instruction, which I define as students writing to students using a variety of formats and for a variety of purposes and employing networked microcomputers as text distributing devices (CMC, or "Computer Mediated Communication"). In the classrooms I supervise, students write as individuals, but they electronically distribute their prewriting or drafts to other students in various combinations (pairs, groups, the class as a whole), who then comment on the writers' efforts and return critiques. This form of writing instruction is effective because it invigorates the writing process by introducing a writer-reader relationship more like that outside academia, and it powerfully emphasizes critical reading as the essential element in revising.

The glaring ethical concern in such a pedagogy centers upon the notion of privacy and whether students have a right to control the readership of their own assigned writing. There has evolved in traditional writing instruction the feeling that students write only to teachers, that there exists a client relationship between student and teacher which entails a form of privileged communication. In some classes, essays are folded lengthwise when they are passed to the front of the room in order to keep other students from reading from them even at a glance. Teachers often write comments on the last page of an essay to keep such comments secure for the writer alone. It is presumed that "good" papers can be read to the class or used as classroom models, since the writers should feel privileged to be so singled out, but examples of weak writing shouldn't be read aloud, even when the writer's identity is hidden, for that constitutes suspiciously intrusive behavior.

The problem with "privacy" in a writing classroom is that writing itself is not primarily a private act. However complexly one would delve into writing and language theory, it seems incontrovertible that writing is essentially a public act and that the effectiveness or authority of a piece of text depends upon some sort of collusion or complicity between writer and reader. Major social questions concerning ownership of text—relating back to the invention of the printing press, the institution of copyright laws, traditional attitudes toward intellectual property rights, and aesthetic and romantic notions of authorship—continue to be debated among journalists, publishers, academicians, and writers. Obviously, a great deal of correspondence is indeed private, but the kind of writing I believe academia seeks to promote constitutes clear, informative, and effective public expression of ideas, not the sort of thing found in love letters or secret government memoranda.

I therefore believe that any classroom ethic which considers assigned writing to be a private communication between student and teacher subverts the act of writing itself and certainly writing instruction. Assigning the teacher to be the sole reader of student text is instructionally debilitating. It severely limits the amount of writing-to-be-read that the students generate, the range of readership any student writer encounters, and the student's ability to deal with the rhetorical concerns of audience, purpose, and tone. What drives the writing act itself and infuses writing with its necessary creative fears and tensions is the requirement to present ideas publicly.

Once student writing is considered a part of the classroom domain, there is no need for permission slips allowing classroom use of student writing. Nor do classroom databases need to be particularly secured. It becomes the student's responsibility to ensure that what he or she writes can enter the classroom domain without embarrassment or compromising privileged information. The students in my classrooms write to each other from the first day on, beginning with informal and ungraded autobiographies. Obviously, a number of students are nervous about publicly exposing what they see as their personal writing deficiencies, but once a fair amount of ungraded student text has been distributed electronically and read, this nervousness, like most initial timidity in any situation, disappears. People are essentially interested in other people. The networked computers provide the right touch of comforting initial anonymity, even when students use their own names (which I require), while encouraging a very human curiosity about one's classmates.

There are methods which I use in class which quickly dissipate any concerns students may have about the privacy of text within the classroom. The "groupware" (software designed for group actions on a network) which I use is The Daedalus Instructional System, which includes within its features synchronous and asynchronous messaging. Simply put, short messages can be written and "sent" among students in a variety of formats. From the very first moments of class, students are sending "e-mail" or quickly typed comments to each other. Since these comments are written without revising and are not the threatening academic "essay," the students soon get used to writing to each other for the purpose of communicating ideas, not demonstrating formal skills. The initial drafts that they distribute and critique are intentionally assigned to be crude and ill-formed documents. Accordingly, almost all distributed text for the first four weeks of class is ungraded, constantly redrafted, and therefore "non-traumatic." Any crisis in sharing student writing is avoided by a swift and painless immersion into the process of ungraded classroom publication.

Since I feel that assuming public responsibility for one's own writing is an important motivational ingredient in good writing, I allow students to use pseudonyms only infrequently. There are assignments for which pseudonyms are quite appropriate, such as assignments in which students assume fictitious roles or attempt to position themselves rhetorically along gender-neutral or race-neutral lines, and these can be good mind-expanding exercises. Generally, however, I see little psychological reason, and no pedagogical reason, for disguising a classroom author once (and as I indicated above, this doesn't take long) the students have grown accustomed to classroom publication.

The Ethics of Content

Ordinarily, one would consider improper classroom materials to consist of lectures or assigned readings which extend beyond the usual norms of taste or relevancy. In the networked computer-based collaborative writing class, however, the general "text" of any class is not delivered through lecture or assigned readings, but rather through student writing itself. Networked computers allow students to study the accumulated writing of their classmates.

In this regard, it is important that instructors promote guidelines restricting certain kinds of expression, particularly those which slur groups or beliefs. The instructor in the networked collaborative classroom has a much tougher job than the instructor in the teacher-centered traditional classroom. The latter needs only to examine his or her own lectures and readings for ethically inappropriate material; the former needs to establish guidelines which seek to head off the all-too-normal tendency of students consciously or unconsciously to defend bigoted positions or use biased terminology.

Classroom action is dominated by student interaction in electronic text, some of it carefully considered and revised, but much of it delivered with the immediacy and heat of oral discourse. What is "said" in a classroom debate can be glossed over and forgotten, but what is "written" in a classroom debate has a frightening permanency and an inordinate sense of existential validity. Yet the instructor must not attempt too great a control over the creative efforts of the students, or the personal, problem-solving nature of the collaborative classroom will devolve back into the time-honored emphasis of the traditional classroom: "give the teacher what the teacher wants, no more, no less."

Regarding the content of classroom text when students are the principal authors of such text, it is crucial that nothing should be said which would endanger a collegial working relationship. I ask each writer to imagine that the classroom readership constitutes a support team specifically assigned to help the writer achieve the highest level of writing skill (and grade) possible. Since this support team is composed of a variety of human beings who may view things quite differently from the writer, it is important that the writer anticipate hurtful content. Comments which antagonize readers subvert the collaborative relationship the course tries to engender; being careful of one's biases in such a classroom should encourage the same enlightened self-interest that real-world authors feel as they hope to avoid repelling their readers.

This is all very abstract, of course, and when presented in the abstract usually attracts the same sort of sleepy nods that the reading of any general information attracts. But one of the first tasks I require in the networked classroom is an electronic discussion concerning precisely those kinds of comments which might so antagonize a reader/colleague. Students, communicating in text synchronously over networked computers, muse about what indeed could distort the relationship between writer and reader or student and colleague, and some very specific remarks are held up to examination. But because these remarks are being discussed

objectively and are not being hurled as invectives, no one gets up-
set. In fact, a surprising air of maturity often surrounds such discussions which carries over throughout the semester.

The "ground rules" for avoiding biased expressions are therefore established at the outset. As instructor, I often prompt certain
conclusions from my students, but there is usually in such discussions, as in the course itself, a sense that the students themselves,
in collaboration, have arrived at a generally agreed upon notion of
sensible language behavior. Certainly this is the case with comments regarding race, religion, or economic status. Such a general
agreement regarding gender-biased comments is much more difficult to achieve since many if not most of my students are either
unaware that such bias exists or refuse as a matter of principle to
see such a bias as wrong. Both men and women argue that "differences" between the sexes and how the sexes are treated are
natural and good and that attempts to establish the proverbial
level playing field are subversive in socially harmful ways.

The instructor exists as the enforcer-of-last-resort when biased
comments arise, but I emphasize the "last resort." The students
themselves become good at discovering and censuring such comments. In fact, it is often the instructor's job to keep reactions
against alleged slurs or prejudice within reasonable limits, since
there can be a tendency in a collaborative classroom for other students to attack the offender with more virulence than that expressed in the original offense. If the instructor does intervene, it is
usually in the form of a private e-mail message warning the offender, or perhaps a sly remark in a synchronous electronic discussion which signals to the offender that he or she has stepped over a
line. Usually this is enough. Occasionally, especially when an offender has been backed into a corner and has called upon a cher-
ished (and often crude) "principle" of human behavior as a defense, a face-to-face conference is necessary.

The ethical issue of restricting biases in the classroom is hardly
news to the traditional instructor. But it also obviously presents a
particularly troublesome issue for the instructor in a computer-
based networked classroom since networks are used to allow students to form their own classroom discourse communities. The effectiveness of the networked writing classroom lies in its ability to
empower the students' own rhetorical authority, their own sense
of how text forms and informs a community of ideas. Too much in-

tervention and control, even for the best of motives, seriously undermines this instructional dynamic. So, as we have seen, the issue for the instructor in a networked classroom is not what to control, but how to encourage in students the awareness that some things should be controlled in their own best interests. Again, this can be done, though never perfectly, by opening up the questions of bias and self-defeating language behaviors as a proper investigation for the class as a whole—with the instructor remaining a "moderator" (in all senses of the word) for the group investigation and subsequent enforcement.

The Ethics of Exploitation

The computer-based collaborative classroom generates a considerable amount of electronic text, since most of the classroom interaction—classroom discussions, peer critiques and private messages, and evaluations by the instructor—is written exchange. The fact that so much of what happens in a computer-based classroom is captured in electronic text presents a marvelous opportunity for the researcher to investigate a wide range of collaborative processes which stimulate effective writing.

For example, the instructor can examine the dynamics of how the sexes interact in classroom discussions by reviewing synchronous discussions and noting the markers of interaction, such as terms of response, agreement, disagreement, apology, and rudeness. The instructor can examine the critical reading skills of students by surveying volumes of peer critiques. The instructor can assess the effect of collaborative interactions on revision by closely following the "paper trail" of numbers of drafts leading up to final essays, all of which continue to exist in the classroom database. Some of this can be performed electronically. Analysis mechanisms can be programmed that review vast amounts of electronic text and produce statistics from easily quantifiable data such as sentence lengths, frequency of punctuation use, syllable counts, and so forth. In fact, it seems likely that as familiarity with studying this sort of computer-based collaborative text increases, the ways in which writing behaviors can be analyzed (by examining the whole spectrum of classroom messaging) will extend far beyond what we now, at the very beginning of this kind of study, can anticipate.

But we should consider again, now at more length: is it fair play, in theoretical and/or practical terms, for all this (readily available) student-student and student-teacher collaboration to be appropriated by the instructor for his/her own research purposes? This question hinges on questions (already suggested) about what classroom writing represents, what it is intended for, and whether the instructor, by using the writing for research studies, subverts the instructional purposes and intentions of student writing. These questions—neither trivial nor obvious nor easily answered—warrant further investigation.

If in using classroom writing the researcher somehow passes off student ideas as his own or otherwise neutralizes the value of uniquely personal or commercially viable student work, then such use is wrong. But student writing, in the vast majority of cases, does not fall within these categories. This is true almost by definition. Student writing, as student writing, is inherently unusable in a commercial or even personal sense because of the unpracticed nature of the effort. In all but extraordinary cases, if student writers were producing viably commercial or importantly private text, they wouldn't be students in a basic composition course.

But this line of argument is stymied, in part, by the adamant effort in the computer-based collaborative classroom to dispel the notion that students write merely student text—to assert that even unpracticed students can generate valuable writing which informs and influences readers. So there exists an ethical paradox of sorts. If student writing is essentially worthless as property, then appropriation of it by researchers should be acceptable. But if student writing is indeed worthwhile property, then researchers should not appropriate it for their own uses. The very classrooms in which such valuable writing *can* be appropriated in extremely effective ways, the computer-based writing classrooms, are the same ones which seek to emphasize the substantiality of student writing.

The only way out of this dilemma is, as always, to collaborate with the students. Bring them in as researcher-colleagues. Make the writing course not only a means by which they can expand personal writing ability, but a means by which their efforts can affect writing instruction in many other places. Just as they should hash out questions of bias in text, they should grapple with the ethical questions of what use is to be made of their classroom writing. This approach is not without serious problems. It can happen (and has) that members of the class, for a variety of reasons not necessarily related to those described in this essay, simply refuse to cooperate. If any student refuses to participate in allowing his/her writing to be processed, analyzed, or disseminated for purposes of research, then I consider that classroom to be closed to research. To do otherwise would be to devalue the students or their writing—and in the process, the idea of collaborative effort itself.

Further (the above-described okay having been granted), if a student's identity is to be made public in presentation or publication subsequent to the class (which it almost never is in the broad, text-based research I do), then specific written permission should be obtained. I would not, however, require specific permission for simply identifying students by sex, race, or other generic category, given the agreement negotiated by the class as a whole. While it is unlikely that students can ever be completely informed as to the nature of any research, the sorts of things we do in networked classrooms and the results we look for are easily understood and almost always perceived as a natural and non-threatening extension of an essentially collaborative situation.

The Ethics of the Technology

Technology in the twentieth century has been assumed by many to be the prime agency of control and oppression, manifested in the popular imagination by devices such as Huxley's sleep-teaching machine and Orwell's spying television set. Since computers (including those used in the collaborative classroom) provide a frightening capability for acquiring and managing data, they are juicy targets for a romantic view of the individual exploited by large, faceless management systems. A number of people who feel an instinctive resistance to computers do so for this reason (although I personally feel that an equally large, if not larger, number simply experience a lack of confidence in operating unfamiliar devices and would consciously or unconsciously prefer to disguise it as a matter of conscience). There are those who would claim that simply by putting computers in writing classrooms and emphasizing them so strongly in the pedagogy, writing instructors are forcing students into a cold-blooded, data-ridden existence.

From a somewhat different angle of attack, the question often arises from faculty and the occasional student as to whether by requiring students to use computers for writing classes we are in effect imposing a kind of ideological technophilia. Of course, no student I've ever taught or supervised has actually been required to remain in a computer-based class, but in such a view, simply offering computer-based classes puts us in the position of tempting innocents. And there *is* an undeniable pressure for students to "take advantage of" computer-based instruction. The pressure comes from a society increasingly reliant on computer use and from an accompanying belief that success as a professional will require not only familiarity with but even affection for computers.

In defense of computer-based writing, I would argue that if society is pressuring students to learn how to use computers, it is mostly because computers are indeed effective tools for managing the complex processes and information of contemporary human life. And in the classroom, not only do I not see computers or computer networks as an inherently insidious invasion of "machine-think," but on the contrary, I am impressed by the directly humanizing effect of collaboration facilitated by the computer networking—by which students see themselves as forming a *community* of writers, thinkers, and language users.

"Research" in instruction, by definition, involves trying unfamiliar methods and examining unfamiliar results, putting students into strange environments, or at the least, examining their behaviors in possibly uncomfortable new ways. Many of the particulars of our concern as researchers derive from the social context in which we are operating. The romantics of Frankenstein's day perceived natural man and technology in a naïve opposition. I think that we, on the other hand, can more easily recognize that technology is not a corruption of natural tendencies but rather an extension of them. The point here is that any ethical arguments which hinge on the presumed inherently dehumanizing and destructive character of computers or networks should be held strongly problematic. In researching the use of computers in instruction, we should not assume an inherent antagonism between people and machines, but rather a facilitating relationship which requires experience and knowledge to ensure. Seen in this light, the study of how new technologies affect learning begins on a firmly human and social-ethical base, and it is up to the researcher to keep it that way. In fact, the wooden, shoe-box classroom with the squeaky chalkboard and the droning teacher could be seen, in the not-too-distant future, as a form of deprived, isolationist instruction a modern society should eliminate.

What Do You Think?:
Collaborative Learning and Critical Thinking in the Business Writing Class

Ellen Andrews Knodt

Improving students' abilities to think critically or reason abstractly has received increased attention nationwide in the past ten years. Such programs as ADAPT (Accent on Developing Abstract Processes of Thought) at the University of Nebraska and STAR (Steps to Abstract Reasoning) at Metropolitan State College in Denver show the effort many institutions have begun to give to improving critical thinking skills. Other studies, including those of Lunsford and McKinnon, have found that sizable proportions of college students are unable to synthesize ideas or "cope with abstract propositions" (Sternglass 154). The perception that students lack these skills is so widespread that, as Mike Rose warns, there is a danger of confusing students' problems in reasoning with an inherent inability to think abstractly. In his excellent meta-analysis of studies of cognitive abilities, Rose sees no convincing evidence of an innate inability of students to think and reason. Instead, he suggests that students lack instruction and practice in these skills, especially as they relate to writing (285). As he points out, specific instruction in critical thinking can yield "dramatic results on performance" (284).

While critical thinking skills should be a focus of all writing courses, business writing instructors may be in a unique position to devise instructional techniques and assignments that provide practice in critical thinking. For one thing, students in business writing may be motivated to learn writing techniques perceived as more "practical" than those taught in other composition courses.

Furthermore, the time-honored "case study" method of business schools is well adapted to problem-solving writing situations.

Before discussing specific assignments and outcomes, we need to consider a working definition of the term "critical thinking." Common attributes of critical thinking as defined by sources from the College Board to B.F. Skinner include the following characteristics:

1. recognizing and questioning assumptions, separating fact from opinion;
2. identifying problems and actively searching for alternatives to solve them;[1]
3. drawing reasonable conclusions based on evidence.

Many students have had little exposure to these skills, having learned to memorize and merely parrot information on multiple choice tests without questioning or needing to synthesize information, as they would have to do in essay responses. If students are confronted with a problem-solving situation, they frequently jump to conclusions, seizing on the first possible solution without analyzing the situation fully and examining alternatives—a tendency aptly described as a "stampede to closure."

Two approaches seem especially fruitful in enhancing students' critical thinking abilities and are particularly well adapted to business writing classes:

1. using peer-group collaboration in prewriting or invention activities;
2. developing problem-solving assignments through careful attention to purpose and audience.

The nature of business writing, which is particularly goal-oriented, makes collaboration among classmates more appealing than it is for the kinds of rhetorical situations posed in most other composition classes. That is to say, students may welcome help from peers in solving a business problem while they may resent collaborating with peers on a more sensitive "personal experience" assignment. Furthermore, students are aware that, in business, writing tasks are frequently group projects.

While many studies of collaborative writing focus on the peer group's role as audience in the drafting or revising process (see Carroll, Beavan, et al.), the involvement of peer groups at the prewriting or invention stage may be even more important in fostering critical thought by exposing students to others' opinions and delaying the stampede to closure. In a recent article on the role of collaborative planning in the business writing classroom, Rebecca Burnett agrees: "Collaborative planning encourages students to become more skillful planners; they become problem solvers who consciously explore various rhetorical elements, such as purpose, audience, organizations, and design" (9–10). This is not to dismiss questions about peer group effectiveness and inequity of power relationships among the members of some groups, particularly female and ethnic minority group members (for example, see Danis). However, on balance most researchers agree with Wendy Bishop that, "In general, collaborative peer writing groups do benefit the student" (120). George Hillocks, Jr., mentions two studies of college freshman composition classes (Craig, 1982 and Myers, 1980) which sought to determine whether peer discussion at the invention stage made a difference in the final product. While Craig found no significant difference, Myers' more extensive study found that the group that had discussed the assignment in collaborative pairs prior to writing did significantly better on three types of essays (narrative, expository, and argumentative) than did the control group which had studied grammar, punctuation, and outlining (175). Hillocks himself conducted a study with Kahn and Johannessen (1983). An experimental group learning to write extended definitions of abstract concepts worked in small-group discussions on three scenarios which set up a number of situations illustrating the concept of courage; a control group studied nine model definitions and did not discuss the scenarios. The experimental group had significantly better scores than the control group on post-test papers overall, especially in the areas of the use of criteria and examples (184–85).

This last study is particularly interesting because by using both peer group collaboration and scenarios, the researchers involved students in an inquiry: what constitutes real courage? Such problem-solving assignments seem a promising way to foster critical thinking among students and improve their writing. In his metaanalysis of composition experiments, Hillocks concludes that "Studies which make inquiry an integral part of their experimental treatments all show significant effects for inquiry either in pre-to-post effects, in experimental/control effects, or in both" (186).

Since scenarios or case studies are a common pedagogical tool for business schools, and such cases provide excellent opportunities for rhetorical situations with specific audiences and purposes, many business writing instructors have found them appropriate for writing assignments—and, I decided, a natural for a collaborative approach to problem solving. (For a similar approach, see also Renshaw.) To test the effectiveness of collaborative learning on students' writing and thinking, I decided to see whether there was any difference between a student's solitary analysis and response to a case and her analysis and response after small-group discussion. Each case presents a complex situation which might be dealt with in one of several ways. Students are given a role (for example, "You are the Purchasing Manager"), an audience to whom they will write, and the pertinent facts of the case."[2]

Before they read a case, I discuss a problem-solving strategy with each class, which includes the following steps:

1. Define the dilemma or problem;
2. Get the facts;
3. Consider options for solving the problem;
4. Evaluate options: are they legal, moral, beneficial?;
5. Make decision.

(adapted from *The Wall Street Journal*)

We discuss the importance of working through each step and not moving to the last step without fully implementing the others. It is useful for students to know that many people do not consider a given problem sufficiently to be sure even that what they think is the problem really is the problem. Sometimes it turns out that the real problem is not obvious at all! The following case cited as the Sandia Case illustrates this point.

* * *

The Sandia Case
(adapted from *Technical Writing Teacher*, 1978)

You are a member of the staff of Sandia, Inc., a think tank organization similar to The Rand Corporation. Sandia does planning work for high-level governmental and military projects.

The company employs 135 professional men and women who represent the best or near-best in several fields: the physical and social sciences, education, urban planning, etc. In addition to their professional qualifications, all possess the quality that Sandia finds most valuable: a flair for independent and original thought. They are hard to find and highly paid. However, budgets for both recruiting and salaries have traditionally not been a problem for the company. Sandia could easily afford to hire more and could pay well if the proper people could be induced to come. The average salary for all professional personnel is slightly over $100,000.

Even non-professional help—secretaries, technicians, clerks, etc.—are expensive, largely because each must be cleared for highly classified work. Sandia employs 150 such people and pays them an average salary of $500 per week.

One day you receive the following memo from the Director of Research Projects, who is your boss and ranks just below the President of Sandia.

TO: You
FROM: R.T. Ralston, Director
SUBJECT: Lunch Room Use

I cannot help noticing how little use our lunch room facilities are getting lately. As you know, the company laid particular stress on the quality of food service and the attractiveness of the lunch room appointments when this building was designed. I doubt if there is a better dining facility in industry.

More serious, in going out to nearby restaurants, our people are taking more time for lunch than is justifiable. Although I have made no systematic study, I'm sure we lose several hundred man hours each week because of overlong lunch hours.

Please look into this matter immediately and give me your assessment and recommendations.

Some discreet observation over the next two weeks confirms Ralston's suspicions. The excellent lunch room, designed to accommodate 350 people easily, serves an average of 100 lunches per day, mostly to clerical help. Only about 25–30 of the professional staff eat there regularly. You are hard-pressed to explain why. The food is good (no complaints have ever been registered) and inexpensive—the cost of a typical lunch is $7.00. The nine full-time lunch room employees (average salary $350 per week) are efficient and courteous. Seating is at small tables rather than at long benches.

More observation reveals that those going out to lunch return 15–30 minutes late on the average. When a late-returner one day notices you conspicuously looking at your watch as he walks past, he tells you to "mind your own business."

In a memo to Ralston, analyze the problem and propose a solution.

* * *

The problems appear to be the lack of lunch room use and late returning by employees who have gone out for lunch. Certainly the evidence substantiates that the lunchroom is underused and that employees are returning 15–30 minutes late on the average. But given the nature of the company, the highly trained and independent nature of the employees, and our lack of information about employee productivity, the fundamental problems may not be so clear-cut. If employee productivity is satisfactory, the late return from lunch may not actually be a problem, and the lunchroom facility may need to be scaled down. If the writer of the memo takes this tack, however, he or she must be prepared to justify the findings to Director of Research Ralston. The problem then becomes a matter of satisfying Ralston rather than changing the employees' behavior. On the other hand, if the problem is defined as Ralston presents it, then the solutions will focus on late returns and lack of lunchroom use. Students need to understand that their definition of the problem will determine the feasible approaches to the problem and ultimately their choice of solution. One of the goals of problem-solving is to get students to see this complexity.

After defining the problem and getting the facts, we discuss the necessity for considering all possible options before censoring any—subverting the desire to latch onto the first solution thought of. Keeping an open mind is a struggle for many students because they do not tolerate ambiguity well. Once the possible solutions have been listed, students must evaluate these options to determine, in so far as they can, the possible consequences. So, for example, if one is considering requiring Sandia employees to punch a time card, or sign in and sign out for lunch (a popular "quick fix" solution proposed by many students), one must consider the effect this solution could have on highly trained, hard-to-get employees, who might be hostile already to such monitoring (as suggested in the case description through one employee's reaction).

Following the discussion of this problem-solving strategy, the members of one class were assigned to individually read the case again and respond in writing to each step of the problem-solving strategy. I collected their individual responses and then asked them to write the memo, based on their decision as to how to solve the problem.

The other class was broken into heterogeneous groups of four or five members. The members of each group were asked to discuss the case among themselves and write down a group response to the case, following the steps of the problem-solving strategy above. After completing this task, group members wrote memos individually.

Analysis of the strategy papers revealed similar definitions of the problem. However, the students working in groups found more alternatives for solving the problem and analyzed more fully the implications of those alternative solutions. That is, the groups seemed to recognize more clearly advantages and disadvantages that might result from certain decisions.

Students from both classes turned in their memos anonymously (using social security numbers for identification). Without regard to which belonged to which class, I graded the papers as I would normally grade a business writing assignment, looking for evidence of solving the problem while taking the facts of the case and the intended audience into account (grammar and punctuation also counted). The results of the papers from the two classes were dramatically different. The average grades were as follows:

Class 1 (group discussion before writing)	84.24 aver.
Class 2 (individual work on case)	75.88 aver.

A second trial of the experiment used a case of my own devising—The "Gill" Case. This time I had the second class discuss the problem-solving steps in small groups and write out their analyses. The first class followed the procedure of individually responding to the case. As before, both classes then wrote their responses individually and anonymously, and I pooled the papers and graded them as before.

The Gill Case was described as follows:

* * *

The Gill Case
© Ellen A. Knodt

You are the Purchasing Manager for Gill Products, Inc., a firm that makes ignition systems for cars, trucks, and farm and construction equipment. You sell your parts directly to General Motors, Navistar, and other large manufacturers of the final product. In turn, you require some small switches to be supplied to you by another firm, Safety Switch, Inc. You buy approximately $175,000 yearly in switches from Safety just for the ignition systems that you sell to GM.

Due to foreign competition, all the manufacturers that you supply with ignitions are experiencing declining sales. Navistar will close a plant for two months, laying off 1,500 workers. GM is attempting to stimulate sales by starting a new car rebate program. To fund such a program, GM is asking all its suppliers to reduce their prices 2 percent for a 6–month period. GM has several different suppliers for ignition systems and other parts, so if one supplier doesn't go along with GM's request for the cost reduction, it is possible that a competitor will get GM's business. GM says publicly, however, that it does not plan to punish suppliers who can't go along: "If they turn us down, they turn us down. That's their prerogative," says a GM spokesperson.

Your company, Gill Products, is inclined to go along with the reduction because GM is a very good customer. However, you feel that you can't reduce prices unless Safety Switch reduces its prices as well. As Purchasing Manager, analyze your options and write a letter to the Vice-President of Sales at Safety Switch, John O'Malley.

* * *

The Gill case poses different problems from those in the Sandia case. In Sandia the problem or problems need to be defined before the writer can propose solutions. In Gill, however, the problem is defined within the case: the writer needs to ask a supplier to reduce the price of the product. The difficulty here is primarily rhetorical: how can the writer explain the problem to the supplier in such a way as to gain the company's cooperation? But for the request to be convincing, the implications of each suggested approach have to be well thought out.

The results of the Gill case letters were not significantly different between the classes, but it is interesting to note that the second class improved remarkably over its average in the Sandia case:

Class 1 (individual work on case)	82.33 aver.
Class 2 (group discussion before writing)	83.50 aver.

Although the fact that the Gill case was largely a rhetorical problem may have accounted for the similar class performances, I think that the experience of working on the first case in small groups also helped to give the students in Class 1 a better idea of how to work through a problem even on their own. Their individual planning strategy papers were quite complete, and they had clearly considered many alternative ways to approach Safety Switch as well as the consequences of the alternatives.

The results of these experiments in business writing classes corroborate the conclusions reached by O'Donnell et al. in their studies of collaborative writing among psychology students. They concluded that cooperative work on one writing assignment not only improved performance for that assignment but also enhanced performance when students subsequently worked alone on another writing assignment. Therefore, collaboration appears to have positive effects directly and on transfer tasks.

If these conclusions are correct, then small-group work to foster problem-solving skills need not be done for every problem or every assignment. Perhaps instructors might use this technique when introducing a new or more complicated problem but would not have to structure classes this way routinely. Small-group discussions do take extra time. The class using this method took two class periods to complete preliminary work, whereas the class working individually used just one.

Repeated trials of this experiment have yielded mixed results in the grades of the papers produced, with some classes scoring nearly the same on papers whether discussed in groups or done individually. However, in all cases the planning papers issuing from the first group discussions yielded more alternative suggestions and more consideration of implications than did the planning papers of the students working individually. This evidence suggests, at least, that invention stage peer-group collaboration in conjunction with problem-solving situations enhances critical thinking and is one more reason to include collaboration as a teaching technique in writing classes.

Notes

1. See, for example, such sources as the College Board's *Academic Preparation for College*, Watson and Glaser's *Critical Thinking Appraisal*, Skinner's *The Myth of Teaching for Critical Thinking*, or Whimbley and Lockhead's *Problem Solving and Comprehension* among others.

2. In my experience, students prefer cases based on real-life situations and like to compare their responses with those of real-world problem solvers. Instructors might consider asking business people for problem-solving letters and memos and then building cases based on the pertinent facts.

Works Cited

Beaven, Mary H. "Individualized Goal Setting, Self-Evaluation, and Peer Evaluation." *Evaluating Writing: Describing, Measuring, Judging*. Ed. Charles R. Cooper and Lee Odell. Urbana, IL: NCTE, 1977, 135–56.

Berthof, Ann E. "Is Teaching Still Possible?" *College English* 46.8 (Dec. 1984): 743–55.

Bishop, Wendy. "Helping Peer Writing Groups Succeed." *Teaching English in the Two-Year College* 15.2 (May 1988): 120–25.

Burnett, Rebecca E. "Benefits of Collaborative Planning in the Business Communication Classroom." *The Bulletin of the Association for Business Communication* 53.2 (June 1990): 9–17.

Carroll, J.A. "Process into Product: Teacher Awareness of the Composing Process Affects Students' Written Product." *New Directions in Composi-*

tion Research. Ed. Richard Beach and Lillian S. Bridwell. New York: Guilford Press, 1984, 315–33.

Danis, Francine. "Weaving the Web of Meaning: Interactions Patterns in Peer-Response Groups." Paper presented at CCCC, San Francisco, March 1982. ERIC ED 216 365.

"Ethics on the Job." *The Wall Street Journal*, July 14, 1986: 21.

Hillocks, George, Jr. *Research on Written Composition.* Urbana, IL: NCTE, 1986.

————, E.A. Kahn, and L. Johannessen. "Teaching Defining Strategies as a Mode of Inquiry: Some Effects on Student Writing." *Research in the Teaching of English* 17 (1983): 275–84.

Lunsford, Andrea. Address at Penn State Conference, July 1985.

O'Donnell, Angela, D. Dansereau, T. Rocklin, J. Lambiotte, V. Hythecker, and C. Larson. "Cooperative Writing: Direct Effects and Transfer." *Written Communication* 2.3 (1985): 307–15.

Renshaw, Debbie A. "In Class Collaborative Cases." *The Bulletin of the Association for Business Communication* 53.2 (June 1990): 63–65.

Rose, Mike. "Narrowing the Mind and Page: Remedial Writers and Cognitive Reductionism." *College Composition and Communication* 39.3 (October 1988): 267–302.

Skarzenski, Donald. "A Problem Solving Case for the Technical Writing Course." *Technical Writing Teacher* 5.3 (1978). Original Case Written by Caroline Eckhardt and James Holahan, Penn State University.

Sternglass, Marilyn S. "Integrating Instruction in Reading, Writing, and Reasoning." *The Writer's Mind: Writing as a Mode of Thinking.* Ed. Janice Hays, et al. Urbana, IL: NCTE, 1983.

Section IV

What Makes a Collaboration Successful?

Kicking Dr. Johnson's Rock:
An Inductive View of Collaboration

Robert Murray Davis

Theoretical discussions of collaborative writing often make the process seem unlikely, if not impossible, because it is just too complicated. Discussions of actual collaborations don't make the process seem much simpler, but at least they focus on something being accomplished. In fact, very much the same kinds of collaborative work have continued to be done, at all levels, from the sixteenth century through the present, and ranging in commercial/aesthetic intent from the most popular genres to the rarefied aesthetic realms inhabited by the likes of William Butler Yeats and George Moore.

In pursuit of some of these things and their implications, I have, like Samuel Johnson, who thought that by kicking a rock he refuted Bishop Berkeley's theory that all events take place in the mind, gone out looking for things to fall over—or, to descend to the literal, surveyed more than fifty books and articles, ranging from "how-to" advice in *Writer's Digest* to Yeats' *Autobiographies*, to discover practical, if partial, answers to several closely related questions:

1. Why are writers, a notoriously individualistic breed, driven to collaborate?

2. What do writers—and publishers, agents, and lawyers—*mean* by collaboration?

3. What are the results of collaboration, not only in specific products but in the effect on the collaborators' future writing?

4. What use can writing teachers and others make of information about collaboration?

As is often the case, Dr. Johnson, one of the first writers to earn a living directly from his writing, provides the simplest and most direct answer to the question of why writers collaborate: "No one but a blockhead ever wrote except for money." Putting it a little less crassly, we might say that writers collaborate because they wish to make something which individually they could not make, or, having made, could not successfully push through the rest of the publishing process to market. In other words, a writer collaborates when she or he has been driven to it by inefficiency, insecurity, or inability. Or, less defensively, when he or she uses the process to illustrate—or in the most interesting cases to discover—an original theory or aesthetic rather than simply to produce a single work.

On the most commercial level, descriptions of motive and process for collaboration—largely related to inefficiency or a desire for greater efficiency—suggest the workings of an assembly line. For example, Renni Brown's agency, The Editorial Department, acts as a kind of super copy-editor, working with—as well as for—the publisher, but the organization also acts as a kind of super-agent, or even producer and director, finding writers to collaborate on books already contracted or—like the movie business—to use a bankable name to convince a publisher to invest in an idea (Carter 30–31).

This process might seem to have little to do with real collaboration, since it reduces writers to cottage-industry piece-workers, chained to their word processors. But something very much like this has been happening in drama for centuries. In the Renaissance, Philip Massinger was frequently called upon to write opening and closing scenes, as if, Cyrus Hoy says, he had been "employed for the express purpose of setting a play in motion, and providing it with a finale" (52), rather like a framer as opposed to a joiner or cabinet-maker.

A desire for efficiency is often connected with a sense of one's inabilities and an appreciation of another's talents. John Dryden, for instance, brought in Nathaniel Lee to write violent, passionate scenes for two plays (Brown 12). And sometimes a modest appreciation of one's abilities can verge over into insecurity. George Bernard Shaw, that scourge of conventional, commercial theater, got his start as a dramatist when William Archer brought him in to write the dialogue for a scenario which Archer had proudly constructed but felt unequal to scripting (Shaw x). In another genre, the even more illustrious pair of Joseph Conrad and Ford Madox Ford were brought together because their advisors felt that their talents could supplement each other's shortcomings: the one had substance and the other style (Morey 27). The closest student of the Mark Twain-Charles Dudley Warner collaboration on *The Gilded Age* speculates that Twain "may have had a certain timidity at facing a novel for the first time alone" (French 57).

The second question—"What do writers (and others) mean by collaboration?"—is even more interesting than the first. The answer is at one level contractual. Seen as a division of labor and as the conversion of raw material into a product, the collaborative work has to do with credit, rights, money, and power. Commercial publishing recognizes a clear hierarchy—though the assignment of levels may vary (and a ghost does not exist at all on this scale)—ascending from "a *as-told-to* b" to "a *with* b" to "a *and* b." Like all hierarchies, this involves power: "a" has veto rights over "b's" embodiment in the "as-told-to" work; "a" has the stronger negotiating position in "with"; "a" and "b" presumably have equal power over the fully compound work (Barbato, Levine). However, in the actual process of writing and revision, these hierarchies tend to dissolve.

One of the most common sorts of collaboration is not officially recognized as such: collaboration of writer and editor. It seems that the best kind of editor, one who attains sympathetic understanding or, in the root sense, can "feel with" the initiating author's subject and form, will subordinate his or her own style and vision to the author's, like Maxwell Perkins' to Thomas Wolfe's. Collaborative editing at this level is largely confined to cutting and re-ordering. A more complex kind involves the actual writing of new material in the spirit or language of the original work. For example, Richard Bridgman notes that Dr. Johnson "supplied the final four lines of Goldsmith's *The Deserted Village*" and speculates that Goldsmith called upon Johnson because he could not face the conclusion which his argument made inevitable (269, 271). Less problematic— or more, depending upon your point of view—is the case of Conrad's *Nostromo*, fifteen pages of which Ford seems to have written (Morey 117). In apportioned or assembly-line work, the collaborator becomes less an editor and more a writer, but he or she does not help to plan the work or determine its ultimate shape.

There are various ways of describing the composition process itself, but in dealing with collaboration, I prefer to call the stages preparing, producing, and polishing. The simplest kind of preparing, at least in theory, occurs in "as-told-to" writing, where one partner has the experience and the other gives it shape or form as well as a voice. As I have pointed out, the writing partner is more than a stenographer or an interviewer, or even a therapist directing the conversation; ideally, he/she is a real coauthor seeking, with the experiencing partner, the inner shape of a segment of experience or a whole life. The "as-told-to" kind of collaboration involves separation of responsibility for content and form. As various commentators have noted, the term "as-told-to" cannot adequately describe the actual process. Ford claims to have taken dictation from Conrad for *A Mirror of the Sea* and *Some Personal Reminiscences*, but he went beyond the role of mere amanuensis to prod his friend for details which Conrad thought unimportant or had suppressed (Morey 28). Ford's techniques sound very much like those described decades later in Cecil Murphy's "Getting Them to Tell-To." Albert E. Stone makes a crucial distinction between memories, which belong to the subject, and imagination, which belongs to both collaborators, and indicates some of the ways in which the subject attains a different sense of self as the result of being audited and edited (154).

Next, at least in theoretical complexity, is "a *with* b" writing, speaking here of power rather than billing, in which the senior partner provides the basic outline and assigns fairly specific tasks to the junior. As we can see in the case of Philip Massinger and his colleagues, in the Dryden-Lee collaboration, and in the Auden-Isherwood *The Ascent of F-6* (Mendelson), drama seems particularly suited to this process, or at least makes it particularly easy to trace, because various collaborators can work independently. But this is also possible in fiction—as Bryant Morey French indicates of *The Gilded Age*, in which Twain, apparently the senior partner, provided certain characters and incidents, Warner others. In fact, French has ascribed the relative failure of the novel to the substitution of "mechanical division of labor" for careful planning of the plot as a whole (81).

The original blend of two or more individual talents in full collaboration, "a *and* b," is the most interesting kind of collaboration both practically and theoretically because it is the least predictable and the most problematic, and, for the composition theorist, because it contains in most complex fashion the various elements of the composition process. This is particularly true of the preparing stage. As in single-author writing, this stage is crucial. In fact, in the tri-part collaboration of "Marion Margery Layne" on *The Balloon Affair*, a novel, and the subsequent article "Nine Steps to a Published Novel," six of the nine stages deal with preparation.

Of course, collaborators, like individual writers, often discover the final shape of a work during the course of producing it. This is probably the touchiest area in collaboration because, even with computers, this process is difficult to share completely. Someone has to have control of the instrument at any given moment even if the revising/editing process is as nearly simultaneous as possible. In practice, one of two things happens. One partner can write and another edit, though in full collaboration this tends to result in mutual revision of each other's work. Or each partner can do a draft and the collaborators can either take features from both, as Twain and Warner did, or take some kind of vote—perhaps from an outside source like Twain's and Warner's wives, or an outside editor, who becomes, in the broad sense, another collaborator.

In practice, both preparing and producing go on more or less continuously. Raymond T. Brebach has traced eight stages in the intricate interplay of suggestion, revision, reconsideration, and effects of the Conrad-Ford collaboration on "Part Fifth" of *Romance*. On the other hand, Keith Laumer offers the following description of his collaboration with Rosel Brown on the science-fiction novel *Earthblood*, for which he had the basic plot idea and she immediately modified it:

> We got together and talked over the general outline of the book ... and worked out the ground to be covered in the opening canto. Then we both wrote same, met again, compromised on the inconsistencies.... Then one of us rewrote it, drawing on both versions.
>
> This was a lot of work. Thereafter, we discussed the upcoming chapters in pairs, each picked one, and wrote it. We met about once a week and swapped chapters, resolved any discrepancies, and repeated the process. When we finished, each gave the ms. a

final revision to put back in all the good stuff the other had axed.
(Laumer 216)

As the contrast between the Conrad/Ford and the Laumer/Brown collaborations suggests, commercially-oriented writers seem more likely to write alternate sections in the interests of speed and efficiency. Frederick Pohl and C.M. Kornbluth began their collaborative career by using Pohl's outline as the basis of a Kornbluth first draft which Pohl would then revise and publish—in his own magazine if nowhere else. Later, under pressure of a book deadline, the two wrote a novel in eight days "by writing turn and about, four pages at a time, around the clock. It worked—well enough so that we kept to that method of writing first drafts from then on." On one book, a little benzedrine helped speed things up still further (Pohl 102–9).

Pohl and Kornbluth had resolved a problem which Laumer does not mention: polishing is a necessary and natural continuation of the producing stage, but finally, however much consultation, concession, and consensus there may be, someone has to be able to say that the project is finished. Sometimes this issue is solved by legal or other formal agreement. Sometimes it is resolved on psychological grounds, as is the practice of the husband-and-wife team of romance writers, Judith Barnard and Michael Fain. They devote considerable time to a first draft of each chapter. Then,

> Judith, the more intense and compulsive of the two, writes the first version on her word processor, and Michael makes notes for the next one on his processor. They pass the chapter back and forth until Michael, at least, is pleased with it. (Mills 68)

Michael has final power to release a manuscript because Judith is never satisfied. But sometimes the issue is decided by outside control, like that of Mrs. Clemens and Mrs. Warner. Finally, if the collaboration has been at all successful—and more have miscarried than produced teratological specimens—a work results.

This brings us to my third question, about the direct results and the longer-range effects of collaboration. Of course, the question of why a work did not result can be as interesting as the analysis of a successfully completed work. In the case of so-called serious literature, collaborative works are either not regarded as collaborative (Goldsmith, *Nostromo*) or not rated highly in the canon of either collaborator (Twain/Warner, Ford/Conrad, Moore/ Yeats, Steinbeck/Ricketts). Even the joint authors of a recent scholarly essay on collaboration suggest that greater academic credit be given to singly-authored works. One might ask whether the lesser esteem for collaborative work is the result of accurate evaluation of its quality and, if so, whether the process of collaboration itself necessarily produces second-rank results. Is collaboration regarded by the authors themselves as a kind of elaborate parlor game or training exercise or apprenticing or mentoring, depending on one's place in the literary pecking order? Or could authors, critics, or both have a romantic prejudice in favor of the single, lonely, inspired author?

If these questions are difficult, it is easier to answer questions about the effect of collaboration on the future work of specific pairs. In a sense, of course, writers never stop collaborating, and formalizing the process of collaboration at one stage may make the general process easier. But there are more specific effects: Twain, Shaw, and Ford were able to begin careers in new genres as a result of collaborating. Or the collaboration may affect the style or method of a collaborating author. Ford certainly, and Conrad arguably, went in new fictional directions as a result of the theories of construction and style which they developed during their partnership. Or the effect can be less happy: William Butler Yeats argued that his collaboration with George Moore, in which he dominated in the choice of words, Moore in construction, had a deleterious effect on both men, citing his loss of a sense of coherence in his conception of later dramatic work and Moore's beginning a "pursuit of style that made barren his later years" (Yeats 293).

Answers to my fourth question—how can teachers, especially teachers of writing, use this information?—are in one sense obvious, though the question needs answering in concrete ways. By using examples of collaborative writing, the teacher can show students that the process of peer editing they are being asked to work through is quite normal and can be productive. Also, students themselves can be seen as junior partners in a collaborative writing enterprise, and seeing professional writers in analogous situations may allow them to feel less threatened. Perhaps they will be encouraged by this knowledge to find, or invent, the friend-collaborator-audience-editor-analyst who can serve the function which their peers and teachers assume in writing classes. And, finally, they can learn from the practice of collaborative writers some of the techniques by which they can become senior partners in control of their own texts.

Works Cited

Barbato, Joseph. "Giving up the Ghost." *Publishers Weekly* 229 (January 10, 1986): 34–38.

Brebach, Raymond T. "The Making of *Romance*: Part Fifth." *Conradiana* 6 (1974): 171–81.

Bridgman, Richard. "Weak Tocks: Coming to a Bad End in English Poetry of the Later Eighteenth Century." *Modern Philology* 80 (1982): 169–72.

Brown, Richard E. "The Dryden-Lee Collaboration: *Oedipus* and *The Duke of Guise*." *Restoration* 9 (1985): 12–25.

Carter, Robert A. "When the Author Needs a Helping Hand." *Publishers Weekly* 228 (October 4, 1985): 30–32.

French, Bryant Morey. *Mark Twain and "The Gilded Age": The Book That Named an Era*. Dallas: Southern Methodist UP, 1965.

Hoy, Cyrus. "Massinger as Collaborator: The Plays with Fletcher and Others." *Philip Massinger: A Critical Reassessment*. Ed. Douglas Howard. Cambridge: Cambridge UP, 1985. 51–82.

Laumer, Keith. "How to Collaborate Without Getting Your Head Shaved." *Turning Points: Essay on the Art of Science Fiction*. Ed. Damon Knight. New York: Harper, 1977. 215–17.

Layne, Marion Margery. "Nine Steps to a Published Novel." *Writer* 95 (December 1982): 20–22, 95.

Levine, Mark L. "Double Trouble." *Writer's Digest* 65 (March 1985): 34–35.

Mendelson, Edward. "The Auden-Isherwood Collaboration." *Twentieth Century Literature* 22 (1976): 276–85.

Mills, Barbara Kleban. "Judith Barnard and Her Husband, Michael Fain, Jointly Conquer the Romance World as 'Judith Michael.'" *People Weekly* 22 (October 8, 1984): 67–68.

Morey, J.H. "Joseph Conrad and Madox Ford: A Study in Collaboration." Unpublished dissertation, Cornell U, 1960.

Murphy, Cecil. "Getting Them to Tell-to." *Writer's Digest* 65 (April 1985): 30–31.

Pohl, Frederick. "Reminiscence: C.M. Kornbluth." *Extrapolation* 17 (May 1976): 102–9.

Shaw, George Bernard. "The Author's Preface." *Bernard Shaw's "Widower's Houses": Facsimiles of the Shorthand and Holograph Manuscript and the 1893 Published Text.* Ed. Jerald E. Bringle. New York and London: Garland, 1981.

Stone, Albert E. "Collaboration in Contemporary American Autobiography." *Revue française d'études americaines* 14 (May 1982): 151–65.

Yeats, William Butler. *The Autobiography of William Butler Yeats.* New York: Collier, 1965.

Collaboration in Political Science: The Research-Writing Nexus

Robert P. Steed

Collaborative writing is not new to political science—the work of Karl Marx and Friedrich Engels, for example, stands as an excellent example of collaboration in the production of powerful political theory. Certainly, if we adopt the broader definition of collaboration offered by Jeanette Harris in this volume (in her essay "Toward a Working Definition of Collaborative Writing," pp. 77–84) as including "any substantive modification of the interior or generative or even the completed text that occurs as a result of one writer's conscious and deliberate interaction with another," probably all writing in political science has been collaborative. The involvement of various of the framers of the United States Constitution in the production of *The Federalist Papers* qualifies those classic works as collaborative in this sense even though the final versions were clearly the product of the solitary writer (John Jay, James Madison, or Alexander Hamilton, depending on the particular papers under consideration).

However, if we utilize the narrower, more traditional definition of collaborative writing to mean the shared act of physically producing the final text, collaboration has become relatively widespread in the discipline only over the past half-century. Without rejecting the argument that the broader definition is legitimate and should be incorporated into our understanding of collaboration, I would suggest that the more limited definition is more instructive as an aid to understanding the contemporary development of political science as a discipline and for helping us compare collaboration in political science with what is ostensibly the same enterprise in other disciplines. It is, therefore, this narrower sense of the term that I would like to consider in discussing the collaborative production of text by political scientists and the degree to which such collaboration is fundamental to achieving the goals of modern political science research.

The rationale for collaboration in political science is generally quite similar to the rationale for collaboration in drama, literature, history, or the natural sciences. As Robert Murray Davis argues in his essay in this volume, "a writer collaborates when she or he has been driven to it by inefficiency, insecurity, or inability." There are numerous examples of coauthored books or journal articles for which the division of labor was clearly based on the respective skills and/or specialized training of the writers involved. The texts for introductory survey courses (e.g., Introduction to Political Science or American National Government) are frequently collections of chapters written by a variety of specialists; in this operative mode, for example, the materials on constitutional law and the judiciary are supplied by experts in that field while the materials on the presidency, political parties, interest groups, Congress and the legislative process, public opinion, public policy, and electoral behavior are supplied, in turn, by specialists in those fields (Janda, Berry, and Goldman, 1989; Keefe, Abraham, Flanigan, Jones, Ogul, and Spanier, 1986; and Prewitt, Verba, and Salisbury, 1987). A slight variation of this approach, frequently occurring in the preparation of more technical research papers or journal articles, involves utilizing the services of a specialist (for example, a statistician) to provide technical advice for a manuscript written almost entirely by another. Similarly, the involvement of a graduate research assistant in preparing some part of a report or in doing some of the preliminary legwork in the early stages of the project typically results in yet another sort of coauthorship (Sears, Citrin, and Kosterman, 1987; and Hopkins, Lyons, and Metcalf, 1986). In short, there are many instances of collaborative writing in political science covering a wide range of approaches. Here, the major deviations from other disciplines lie in the subjects being examined and the type of writing being done (e.g., data analysis as opposed to dramatic dialogue).

The rationale for collaborative writing in political science, however, goes well beyond the necessity of collective action in the production of the final physical text. It is not accidental that the expansion of collaborative writing in political science has paralleled rather closely the development of the technology and methodology that make quantitative research possible. The groundbreaking voting behavior studies of the 1940s (Lazersfeld, Berelson, and Gaudet, 1944; and Berelson, Lazersfeld, and McPhee, 1954) were collaborative, as was the seminal work on southern politics at mid-century (Key, 1949); and, in fact, a considerable portion of the behavioral research in the years since has been collaborative. While traditional political science research and writing—focusing mainly on political theory and legal and institutional analysis— were quite amenable to solitary work, the development of quantitative, systematic, empirical techniques opened new doors and created new imperatives for researchers in the discipline.

Indeed, in much of this type of political science writing, the nature of the research design itself necessitates collaboration as a forerunner leading almost inevitably to collaboration in the creation of the final report, whatever form it may ultimately take. While this is not necessarily unique to political science—it logically applies to other social sciences and to the natural sciences, as well—it is certainly critical for an understanding of collaboration in political science. The physical inability of the solitary individual to meet the demands of contemporary research reduces the feasibility of isolated effort. Very significant limitations of time and money dictate some type of joint undertaking to collect and prepare the data. Invariably, in my personal experience, this has been the single most crucial underlying factor in the decision to engage in collaboration. An examination of one such project begins to elaborate the point.

In mid-1983, two colleagues and I began to plan a multi-state survey of delegates to state party conventions in the thirteen states which would select their 1984 national convention delegations through a caucus-convention process. A project of this type would have been inordinately expensive for a single researcher, and, as it developed, was well beyond the financial resources of the three of us. Even if funding had been available, the timing of the state conventions (a total of twenty-five, many on the same days or almost the same days, hundreds of miles apart) would have been an insurmountable obstacle. The conventions represented a one-shot opportunity to collect the data, unlike library or archival materials which continue to be available if one or two visits are insufficient for the collection of information; so we did not have the luxury of spreading the data collection phase of the project over a longer, more manageable period. The answer in this case was to adapt an approach utilized by Alan I. Abramowitz, Ronald Rapoport, and John McGlennon in a similar project organized in 1980.

We organized research teams in each of the states to be surveyed, constructed a common questionnaire, agreed upon a standard set of operating procedures and coding practices, and gave each team responsibility for conducting surveys in their respective states. Ultimately nineteen individuals were involved in the project. Beyond administration of the surveys, the massive task of preparing the data for analysis dictated a division of labor among the research teams as well. Since almost 12,000 delegates responded to the surveys, coding the data and entering it into the computer was a task far surpassing the capabilities of a single researcher. We constructed a common codebook, and each research team assumed responsibility for coding data and preparing a computer tape (or computer scan sheets), which was then sent to us for combination into a single, inclusive dataset. Even with the energetic involvement of all nineteen researchers in the project, this data preparation required almost a year to complete (although, to be sure, each of us was having to work on this project in combination with a full schedule of faculty duties). Once the combined dataset was finished, we supplied copies of the resulting tapes to each of the state research teams.

Given the collective nature of the data-gathering and preparing processes, collaborative writing among the researchers involved was natural as well. The alternative to collaborative writing in such a case is for every participant in the project to do whatever analyses of the data she or he wishes. This is unattractive as a writing strategy because it not only carries a high risk of competitive and duplicative writing, but also is likely to bruise feelings and rupture professional associations as various participants find that the data they were especially interested in reporting have already been mined by others. At the outset of the project, we made it clear that while every research team would have unlimited access to the data from its state, the full dataset would be off-limits for analysis until some agreements were negotiated regarding who would develop which analyses. Through a series of informal discussions and written communications, agreements were reached among the various researchers to coauthor a variety of specifically designated papers and articles. In some cases, these arrangements fell rather naturally into place as two or three of the researchers identified topics of common interest upon which they could collaborate; in other cases, one of the research group would identify a topic of interest and invite another to collaborate on the report. Once these initial agreements were negotiated and the resulting writing was completed, all restrictions on the data were removed, and researchers were free to pursue whatever other analyses they might wish. In some instances these were jointly authored, in other instances singly authored. Of the roughly four dozen professional papers, journal articles, and book chapters ultimately resulting from this project, however, the vast majority were collaborative. Even the one book based on these data (itself a joint effort) consisted of a series of integrated research reports which were largely coauthored rather than singly written (Baker, Hadley, Steed, and Moreland, 1990).

While the particular details and strategies differ from project to project, the underlying logic of the type of extensive collaboration used in the 1984 state convention survey applies to a broad range of quantitative research and writing in political science. For example, similar necessity prompted collaboration in the above-mentioned 1980 survey of state convention delegates co-directed by Abramowitz, McGlennon, and Rapoport. As with the 1984 study, practically all of the writing done from this research was collaborative, involving either various combinations of the state research teams or the principal investigators themselves (e.g., Rapoport, Abramowitz, and McGlennon, 1986; and Abramowitz and Stone, 1984). And a variation on this approach is currently being employed by Lewis Bowman, William Hulbary, and Anne Kelley in organizing a joint data-gathering and writing project focusing on precinct party officials in the eleven southern states.

Within the context of contemporary research complexities, even studies which have enjoyed more financial and institutional support have frequently found joint data collection, and ultimately joint writing, to be attractive, if not absolutely essential. For example, the research and writing undertaken by the Survey Research Center (now the Joint Center for Political Studies) at the University of Michigan has often been collaborative. The mention of one of the outstanding seminal works in voting studies, *The American*

Voter (1960), brings to mind its four authors, Angus Campbell, Philip Converse, Warren E. Miller, and Donald Stokes. Another prime example involves the landmark study of southern politics directed by V.O. Key, Jr., in the late 1940s (Key, 1949). This was a project funded by a generous grant from the Rockefeller Foundation and supported institutionally by the Bureau of Public Administration at the University of Alabama; even so, the scope of the research—covering all eleven states of the former Confederacy and involving the collection of massive numbers of election and demographic statistics along with lengthy personal interviews with 528 political leaders, journalists, and academicians in the region—was sufficiently extensive to require Key to enlist the help of two professional colleagues (Alexander Heard and Donald Strong) plus significant clerical support from the University of Alabama. As it turned out, the project still took three years to complete. Additional examples include, among others, studies of national conventions (e.g., McClosky, Hoffmann, and O'Hara, 1960; and Sullivan, Pressman, Page, and Lyons, 1974) and the multistate study of political party organizations in the United States undertaken by James L. Gibson, Cornelius P. Cotter, John F. Bibby, and Robert J. Huckshorn (Gibson, Cotter, Bibby, and Huckshorn, 1983; and Cotter, Gibson, Bibby, and Huckshorn, 1984). In short, the logistics of collecting and preparing massive sets of quantitative data commonly lead to collaboration regardless of the financial backing available for a project.

In most instances, as in our 1984 survey, once a decision has been made to make the research collaborative, the entire development of the research design for the project becomes collaborative. It is logical, as well as politic, for the principal investigator(s) to discuss the nature of the research design and the plans for future analyses with those colleagues invited to participate in the collection and preparation of the data. Inasmuch as a variety of scholars have participated in planning and executing the research, it then becomes reasonable, and professionally ethical, for all to have an opportunity to participate in the presentation of results through papers and publications. Under these circumstances, it is practically impossible to separate the collaborative writing process, the production of final texts, from the larger collaborative research enterprise.

A final variation on this theme involves the decision by two or more individuals to combine materials from separate but similar research projects. In most cases of this type, the projects have been undertaken independently, and the researchers became aware later of the overlapping elements of the materials and the potential for expanding their separate analyses through collaboration. Indeed, one of the major benefits of participating in professional conferences is the opportunity to identify similar research interests and existent projects which might provide bases for future collaboration of this sort. There are, of course, undeniable difficulties in collaborative writing. Many of these are not unique to political science; however, the particular blend of research and writing collaboration described above creates the potential for some peculiar problems less likely to arise in, for example, the humanities.

There are, in the first place, the usual aggravations of coordinating joint research. Scholars, even those working in generally the same terrain, have their own specific research interests, agendas, and priorities; reaching agreement on the project's focus often requires some delicate negotiation. Ultimately, the project coordinators have to make some operational decisions about such matters as what questions will be included in the questionnaire and then convince colleagues to continue their affiliations with the project even though some of their preferences have been partly or even totally overridden. In our experience with the 1984 delegate survey, there was never any serious threat that one of the state research teams would withdraw, but this was only because great care was taken to include in the construction of the survey design at least some of the suggestions each had made. There were some items which in themselves were so important to one or more of the teams that their exclusion very probably would have led to the teams' withdrawal; a key to the project's success, therefore, lay in our ability to identify those items and include them even at the cost of omitting other items we considered important. Such negotiations are tedious, time-consuming, and often frustrating, but they are absolutely essential to joint research.

Similar problems may arise in conjunction with making decisions on data preparation. For example, should the respondent's age be coded by the actual year (a code giving greater accuracy but requiring more computer space and, in some ways, complicating the ultimate analysis), or should the data on age be collapsed into broad categories and coded accordingly (a code giving less accuracy but facilitating analysis at lower computer cost)? Again, these questions can usually be resolved, but only after some time and energy has been devoted to multiple communications among the researchers. The same type of problem arises in the process of deciding who does the analysis of which part of the dataset. This is more difficult to resolve inasmuch as many of the researchers commonly share interests in various parts of the data and therefore view those topics as the choicest for analysis. Frequently, some workable compromises may be reached among competing parties, perhaps including an agreement to write together. But in those rare cases of failure in the assignment process, a project may collapse altogether.

While complete dissolution of a project in a tangle of ill will and hurt feelings is the worst possible outcome of collaborative effort, fumbled responsibilities and missed deadlines do not rank far behind as a source of headaches for collaborators. In fact, it could be argued that this problem ranks ahead of any potential for a collapsed project simply because it is so much more likely to occur. Research involving many people is more vulnerable, of course, than that involving two or three collaborators because there is much greater opportunity for some sort of delay somewhere along the line. In many cases such difficulties are not primarily the fault of the collaborators involved, but friction among collaborators is likely when the delays inevitably ripple out to disrupt the project schedule for everyone else. In the 1984 delegate survey, for example, computer problems in one state delayed for approximately one month the creation of the final full dataset. In two other states, the research teams could not convince the state party leaders to give them access to the convention floor, so the questionnaires had to be mailed out to a sample of delegates following the conventions. Again, this was beyond the control of the research teams in those states, but the delays in obtaining data changed the project schedule for all. An even more serious problem of this type arose during the delegate survey in Massachusetts, where the convention hall cleaning crew accidentally threw all the questionnaires out with the trash the night before the Democratic convention, thus effectively eliminating Massachusetts from the study; needless to say, this required some serious reconsideration as to how data from the remaining states could be most effectively analyzed, and caused some delay in the execution of the altered research design.

At the writing stage, missed deadlines and failures to supply expected contributions to the paper (or book or report) are also, unfortunately, not uncommon. To some degree, the likelihood of this problem depends on the writing strategy adopted. For example, if each contributor is responsible for writing a specified portion of the paper, the failure of any collaborator to supply a given section on schedule delays completion significantly. If, on the other hand, one collaborator assumes responsibility for writing a first draft which will then be reviewed by the other(s) for suggested revisions, the failure of the reviewer(s) to operate on schedule can be overcome if necessary by energetic action by the initial writer either to downgrade the contribution of the reviewer(s) or to pressure and solicit them for verbal, if not written, suggestions for revisions. Such a resolution of this problem is usually possible in collaborative writing based on collaborative research such as the 1984 delegate survey; it is not likely that one collaborator (the writer of the first draft) will be totally at the mercy of the other contributors inasmuch as all have been involved in the design of the project and in the collection of the data. Ideally, such problems should not develop among professional colleagues at all, but the possibility that they might requires project directors to plan alternative writing assignments or pairings if they should be needed. And even the initial assignments/pairings should be made with the potential for this problem in mind.

Under the best of circumstances, much of the collaborative writing in political science is complicated by the physical distances separating those involved and the attendant necessity to ship materials, data, drafts, and revisions back and forth. While this problem has in some cases been alleviated by the advent of contemporary computer networking systems and fax machines, this new technology of communication is not yet universally available. That is to say, solitary writing in political science remains easier in some ways than collaborative writing. Certainly the administrative headaches, the problems of coordinating multiple schedules and personalities, and the sense of dependence on the sometimes unpredictable performance of others can be largely avoided by working alone. There are, however, identifiable benefits to collaboration. The clearest benefits, described earlier in this paper, revolve around the researcher's ability to engage in projects which simply would not be possible otherwise. There is, however, an additional benefit which should be recognized. In political science (as in all academia), key purposes of scholarship, broadly defined as the research and writing enterprise, are simultaneously to teach others in the discipline and to learn more about the discipline.

We write to share our learning with others and to advance scholarly understanding of the discipline, but at the same time we write because that activity requires us to learn and to refine and articulate what we have learned. In collaborating with others, this joint learning and teaching is frequently enhanced well beyond levels that can be easily attained through solitary research and writing. There is, to borrow from economics, a type of multiplier effect in collaboration which pushes our personal understanding of the topic, and our ability to articulate that understanding, further than we might normally or reasonably do by ourselves. This is not unique to collaboration in political science, but it certainly applies with great force to political science. In my personal experience with joint research and writing, the exchanges of ideas and the necessary sharpening of both research design and resulting writing have ultimately been the core of the experience and the principal payoff of the work. This has invariably easily outweighed the frustrations and problems associated with collaborative activity.

Works Cited

Abramowitz, Alan I., and Walter J. Stone. *Nomination Politics: Party Activists and Presidential Choice*. New York: Praeger, 1984.

Baker, Tod A., Charles D. Hadley, Robert P. Steed, and Laurence W. Moreland, eds. *Political Parties in the Southern States: Party Activists in Partisan Coalitions*. New York: Praeger, 1990.

Berelson, Bernard R., Paul F. Lazarsfeld, and William N. McPhee. *Voting: A Study of Opinion Formation in a Presidential Campaign*. Chicago: U of Chicago P, 1954.

Campbell, Angus, Philip E. Converse, Warren E. Miller, and Donald E. Stokes. *The American Voter*. New York: John Wiley and Sons, 1960.

Cotter, Cornelius P., James L. Gibson, John F. Bibby, and Robert J. Huckshorn. *Party Organizations in American Politics*. New York: Praeger, 1984.

Gibson, James L., Cornelius P. Cotter, John F. Bibby, and Robert J. Huckshorn. "Assessing Party Organizational Strength." *American Journal of Political Science* 27 (March 1983): 193–222.

Hopkins, Anne H., William Lyons, and Steve Metcalf. "Tennessee." *The 1984 Presidential Election in the South: Patterns of Southern Party Politics*. Ed. Robert P. Steed, Laurence W. Moreland, and Tod A. Baker. New York: Praeger, 1986.

Janda, Kenneth, Jeffrey M. Berry, and Jerry Goldman. *The Challenge of Democracy: Government in America*. Boston: Houghton Mifflin, 1989.

Keefe, William J., Henry J. Abraham, William H. Flanigan, Charles O. Jones, Morris S. Ogul, and John W. Spanier. *American Democracy: Institutions, Politics, and Policies*. Chicago: Dorsey P, 1986.

Key, V.O., Jr. *Southern Politics in State and Nation*. New York: Knopf, 1949.

Lazarsfeld, Paul F., Bernard Berelson, and Hazel Gaudet. *The People's Choice: How the Voter Makes Up His Mind in a Presidential Campaign*. New York: Columbia UP, 1944.

McClosky, Herbert, Paul J. Hoffmann, and Rosemary O'Hara. "Issue Conflict and Consensus Among Party Leaders and Followers." *American Political Science Review* 54 (June 1960): 406–29.

Prewitt, Kenneth, Sidney Verba, and Robert H. Salisbury. *An Introduction to American Government*. New York: Harper and Row, 1987.

Rapoport, Ronald B., Alan I. Abramowitz, and John McGlennon, eds. *The Life of the Parties: Activists in Presidential Politics*. Lexington: U of Kentucky P, 1986.

Sears, David O., Jack Citrin, and Rick Kosterman. "Jesse Jackson and the Southern White Electorate in 1984." Laurence W. Moreland, Robert P. Steed, and Tod A. Baker, eds. *Blacks in Southern Politics*. New York: Praeger, 1987.

Sullivan, Dennis G., Jeffrey L. Pressman, Benjamin I. Page, and John J. Lyons. *The Politics of Representation: The Democratic Convention 1972*. New York: St. Martin's, 1974.

Collaboration as Conversation: Literary Cases

Laura Brady

> "There is an assumption I wish to challenge: it is
> that people sit in garrets and write books on their
> own."
>
> Dale Spender (*Man Made Language* x)

The way we teach and study literature implies that writing is a solitary act. Although numerous examples of literary collaborations exist, few cases are acknowledged or included in the anthologies that package literature for mass student consumption. T.S. Eliot's *The Waste Land*, for example, is seldom published with manuscript pages showing Ezra Pound's revisions; Thomas Wolfe's editorial collaborator, Maxwell Perkins, appears only on the acknowledgements or dedication pages of Wolfe's novels. The collaborative works of writers such as Henry James (*The Whole Family*) and Samuel Clemens (*The Gilded Age*) are considered among their more "obscure" of "minor" works, and receive attention only for the individual contributions of each author. Such cases of literary collaboration challenge our usual conception of single/solitary authorship and thus require a new model for the production, circulation, and teaching of literature.

Collaborative models vary depending on the writers, the purposes, and the contexts. In recent research, Lisa Ede and Andrea Lunsford distinguish between two general types of collaboration: hierarchical and dialogic. They describe the hierarchical mode as "structured, driven by highly specific goals, and carried out by people playing clearly defined roles." Within this mode the "realities of multiple voices and shifting *authority* are seen as differences to be overcome or resolved." The dialogic mode, by contrast, is flexibly structured and the roles of each participant remain fluid: each person may occupy several roles as the project progresses (133).

The conversational metaphors often used by Ede and Lunsford suggest that there are certain discursive conditions which aid or impede collaboration. Linguistic methods for the analysis of conversational discourse, informed by studies of the social construction of gender, enhance the usefulness of Ede and Lunsford's schema and provide a powerful model for the analysis of literary collaboration.

Three co-written novels illustrate what I will call monologic, dialogic, and conversational collaborations. I am deliberately varying Ede and Lunsford's terms to represent a wider range of points along a continuum of collaborative practices. "Monologic" collaboration roughly corresponds to Ede and Lunsford's hierarchical mode: only one voice is heard at a time, and the individual speaker often refuses to yield the "floor" to let others take their turns, or interrupts a speaker who has the floor. The word "dialogic" etymologically implies only two speakers participating in an equitable exchange of ideas. This is a more narrow construction than Ede and Lunsford give the term, but I reserve it for cases where collaborators agree to yield the "floor" of the text at predetermined points. In my definition of dialogic collaboration, the speakers/writers do not compete for control, but neither do their voices overlap; they maintain individual authority. "Conversation" is an inclusive term: it denotes social interaction without delimiting the number of voices, and it leaves authority (or ownership) unspecified. I use this term to describe collaboratively produced texts where the participants discuss and reach consensus on every point.

The "Cooperative Principle" and *The Whole Family*

Collaboration, like conversation, depends on common goals and purposes. According to H.P. Grice, the most basic conversational assumption is that when people speak and listen to each other, they intend to communicate effectively and purposefully; Grice termed this the "Cooperative Principle." The cooperative effort inherent in conversation applies to written discourse as well:

participants discuss and clarify their understanding of goals, negotiate differences, establish commitment, and so forth. When participants do not share goals, nor discuss and negotiate differences, nor trust and respect each other's judgment and talents, communication—and collaboration—fails. The collective work of William Dean Howells and others entitled *The Whole Family* (1908) exemplifies failed collaboration: the authors compete for control of the text, disregard the need for any logical sequence or coherence, and frequently contradict each other's contributions. What prevented the participants from fulfilling the Cooperative Principle?

The patchy surface of the finished novel, rife with contradictions and incoherences—sometimes amusing, more often confusing—reflects the oddities of its origins. Many critics, upon reviewing the book, referred to the collaborative project as mere literary game-playing, and directed specific comments to individual authors. The *Nation* provides a typical review:

> This must have been good fun for everybody involved, though how it all came about is a question for the *curious*. Their joint *performance* was, we believe, the subject of a *guessing* contest. But ... did all the participants come willingly into the game, or were certain of them under strange compulsion? The result is sufficiently *amusing*, as occasional in its nature as a *parlor charade*.... It is *pure vaudeville*, but many of the "turns" are characteristic and amusing; none more so than that of Mr. [Henry] James, who holds the stage ... twice as long as most of the others. (552–53; emphasis added)

The participants' inability to "take turns" (exemplified by James, and observed by the reviewer) edges the game metaphor with tones of rivalry.

From the outset of the project, William Dean Howells and Elizabeth Jordan, *Harper's Bazaar* editor, tried to impose a plot and structure on the contributing members of *The Whole Family*. This plan, which illustrates Ede and Lunsford's definition of the hierarchical mode, privileged authority rather than cooperation. Howells, who initiated the collaborative project, not only dictated the general process for producing a collaboratively written novel, but tried to control the specific content and purpose of the text as well: "What I wish to imply is that an engagement is much more a family affair, and much less a personal affair than Americans usually suppose" (*Life in Letters* 223). According to Howells' proposal, each chapter in the novel (beginning with his own contribution) would represent a different family member's response to the engagement of the daughter. Howells professed these ideas to be a "general plan to the other contributors," and told Jordan not to expect anyone to "conform rigidly or at all" to his conceptions of the several characters; in fact, Howells stated, "I will conform my ideas to theirs. They must be left in entire freedom" (*Life in Letters* 223). Howells further stipulated in a letter to Jordan that she submit his "scheme" to ten other writers "without letting them know who is to do the others ... and letting each imagine the family for him or herself" (*Life in Letters* 224).

The fact that Howells established the direction and purpose is not, by itself, a problem. But he created irresolvable tensions: he dictated a plan, but refused to reveal that plan fully to the participants. He expected coherence and clear connections in the development of the novel, yet endorsed "entire freedom" and the anonymity of the other writers. The project never relied on consensus or commonality of goals; there was no opportunity for direct communication among the participants. On the few occasions when the writers expressed themselves, they spoke to an intermediary—editor Elizabeth Jordan. The writers themselves never met, conversed, or corresponded with each other.

Dialogue was prevented in two ways: through Howells' initial condition of anonymity and through Jordan's selection of contributors. Since the commercial purpose of *The Whole Family* was to display *Harper's* talent, Jordan chose contributors based on their individual work for the magazine; she did not try to form a congenial group who knew and respected one another's writing. As a result, Jordan recounts that "[e]ach judged [the book] from the viewpoint of his own part and each had grave doubts about the abilities of his associates" (*Three Rousing Cheers* 279–80).

In no sense did the contributors to *The Whole Family* fulfill the Cooperative Principle. In fact, what began as a lack of communication deteriorated into intentional efforts to confuse the other participants. Some writers closed plot options prematurely and complicated the writing task for those who would follow. Howells' expository chapter, for example, details the personalities of the characters who will comprise the other chapters in the novel. The sister-in-law is "not without the disappointment which endears maiden ladies to the imagination, but the disappointment was of a date so remote that it was only a matter of pathetic hearsay, now" (*The Whole Family* 19); the son "will never be the man his father is" due to his "easy temperament" and artistic inclinations (13); the engaged daughter is "shy," "charming," and "unworldly" (18). Others attacked their fellow participants by adding self-reflective comments and scenes. Consider, for example, the statement that opens Chapter Six. The son-in-law's comments (written by John Kendrick Bangs) bear upon professional problems as well as upon the novel's fictional relationships:

> On the whole I am glad our family is no larger than it is. It is a very excellent family as families go, but the infinite capacity of each individual in it for making trouble, and adding to complications sufficiently complex, surpasses anything that has ever before come into my personal or professional experience. (124)

The Whole Family thus became a story of a family divided by conflicts—most of which resulted from family members who (like their authors) did not talk to one another and often made false assumptions about others' actions.

Ede and Lunsford argue that multiple voices and shifting authority are problematic in the hierarchical mode of collaboration: the participants do not value innovation; changes are seen as deviations or obstacles (133). After Howells' exposition of an "average American family," for instance, many of the other writers accused Mary E. Wilkins Freeman of deliberately causing problems by creating a non-traditional "Old-Maid Aunt" in Chapter Two. Instead of filling in Howells' outlines for a demure spinster who was the object of "pathetic hearsay," Freeman created "Aunt Elizabeth" as a young, independent, and flirtatious woman. Something of a vamp, Aunt Elizabeth, we learn, already knows her niece's fiancé—and he is attracted to her.

Although some of the writers (including editor Jordan) were grateful to Freeman for creating some interesting complications, others, including Howells, felt that she had sabotaged the originally intended plot (again belying Howells' statement that he wanted to allow complete freedom for all of the writers). Instead of negotiating these differences, the individual contributors were each left to deal with the character of Aunt Elizabeth in any way they chose. By Chapter Eleven (written by Alice Brown), the aunt is once again a somewhat pathetic figure.

By the middle of the book the rivalry was so acute that James entreated Elizabeth Jordan to let him take over the rest of the novel, beginning with his section, "The Married Son" (Chapter Seven). In the introduction to the new (1986) edition of *The Whole Family*, Alfred Bendixon quotes James's letter to Jordan (October 2, 1907), in which James voices his frustration:

> I had engaged to play the game & take over the elements as they were & hated to see them so helplessly muddled away when, oh, one could one's self (according to one's fatuous thought!) have made them mean something, given them sense, direction and form. It was, & still is, I confess, for me, the feeling of a competent cook who sees good vittles messed. (qtd. in Bendixen xxx)

Although James refers to the whole process as a "game," he was reluctant to relinquish control of the text once it was his turn to write. In conversational terms, he refused to yield the floor to another speaker.

Factors That Influence Collaboration:
Two Explanatory Models

Two models help explain the resistance to turn-taking systems: one draws again upon linguistic analysis of conversational discourse, the other upon studies of culturally learned behaviors in males and females. In discourse analysis, turn-taking refers to the distribution of talk among participants in a conversation. One of the mechanisms that govern turn-taking is "a sharing device, and 'economy' operating over a scarce resource, namely control of the 'floor'" (Levinson 296–97). "Turns" at talk are divided into units, with the length of each unit largely determined by the speaker. In cooperative conversations, the speaker will make some sort of signal when she is ready to hand over the floor: a gap to be filled, a new topic, a question, a direct invitation, etc. Turn-taking does not, however, guarantee order or equal distribution of turns. Speakers violate the cooperative principle when they refuse to yield the floor and let others take their turn. In these situations speakers compete for control.

Turn-taking and competition also characterize other forms of social interaction, including games. Carol Gilligan's studies of psychological theories and women's development, for example, argue that boys' play depends on rules and competition, while girls' play is more concerned with relationships and turn-taking. Gilligan gives the following example (based on a study by Lever): "Traditional girls' games like jump rope and hopscotch are turn-taking games where ... success does not necessarily signify another's failure" (10). As a result of these patterns of behavior, Gilligan reports that various studies concur with Piaget's observations that "[g]irls ... have a more 'pragmatic' attitude toward rules.... [They] are more tolerant in their attitudes toward rules, more willing to make exceptions, and more easily reconciled to innovations" (10). This flexibility leads Piaget to conclude that the legal sense (crucial to his model of moral development) is "far less developed in little girls than in boys" (qtd. in Gilligan 10). Piaget's conclusions on development endorse male, rule-bound competition while devaluing female flexibility.

These observations would suggest that there are gender-related differences that might influence both conversational cooperation and written collaboration: women employ cooperative strategies (and thus are "natural" collaborators) while men are competitive. But not only would such a conclusion overgeneralize; it would also perpetuate stereotypes about the aggressive nature of men and the more nurturing nature of women. In the specific case of *The Whole Family* it would ignore the fact that Elizabeth Jordan was the project's editor, with authority over all decisions regarding the text, including the authority to veto Howells.

Deborah Cameron, a feminist linguist, offers another example that disputes the essentialist stereotype of competitive men and cooperative women. She analyzes a linguistic sample in which the women speakers were notably less cooperative than a corresponding group of men. Both groups requested equal amounts of information and both made expressions of agreement, but the women interrupted more (violating turn-taking and the cooperative principle) and disagreed more. Cameron finds the reason for this "fairly obvious." She explains:

> It happens that in the data specimen I chose, the men are discussing a subject on which they agree. The women in contrast, do not agree with each other. A number of facts in the situation determine whether the participants will be "cooperative" or "competitive," notably, if banally, whether they agree, whether they

like each other, what they are trying to accomplish in talk and so on. (42)

In the context of *The Whole Family*, Mary E. Wilkins Freeman's portrait of Aunt Elizabeth may be seen as a competitive or "masculine" move: she creates a conflict that determines, and thus controls, much of the succeeding text. Alternatively viewed from the perspective of innovation (a "feminine" trait), Freeman's chapter opens up new possibilities, and favors flexible characterizations over conformity to rigid stereotypes. Cameron argues that the discursive context must always be considered; she cautions against generalizations "on the basis of so gross a variable as speaker sex" (42).

Yet Ede and Lunsford do make gender discriminations in describing hierarchical and dialogic modes of collaboration. Within hierarchical collaboration, a senior member or leader will establish goals, assign roles (and "turns"), and supervise production. Shifting authority is a problem. This mode of collaboration is, according to Ede and Lunsford, "typically conservative" and a predominantly "masculine mode of discourse." The loosely structured dialogic mode, characterized by fluid and shifting roles is, they argue, "predominantly feminine" (133). There is an implicit distinction between male and masculine, female and feminine. A "male" or "female" mode of discourse implies a difference in nature; a "masculine" or "feminine" mode implies that the difference is "conventional"—i.e., socially and culturally constructed.

The process of collaboration is—like games that value turn-taking, innovation, and flexibility over rule-bound competition—usually devalued in favor of traditional conventions of individual authorship. Prevailing attitudes, which privilege solitary writing, would have us accept that all collaborative writing, with its shifting voices and authority, is difficult and inferior to individually authored works. But this prevailing outlook is based on a diminished sense of "collaboration," one which, in the context of the present discussion, could be called the "Whole Family Fallacy." Only in some collaborative processes do multiple voices and shared authority constitute a problem. Collaborations that insist on a linear process and hierarchical authority and that, like *The Whole Family*, have a remote or artificial origin, are destined for obvious difficulties. In this case, the participants did not know each other, talk to each other, or agree with each other or with the idea of collaboration. As a result, the participants devalued the flexibility and dialogue necessary to negotiate differences and challenge conventions. Because it denies any sort of Cooperative Principle, *The Whole Family* does not represent a process of co-labor so much as a composite portrait of competitive family members.

Turn-Taking and *The Gilded Age*

In contrast to the linear, monologic model, the "dialogic mode" of collaboration finds the process of articulating and working together to achieve goals "as important as the goals themselves" (Ede and Lunsford 133). The composition of *The Gilded Age*, although not fully conversational, at least represents a cooperative process in which Clemens and Warner took turns developing the structure, characters, conflicts, and details of the novel. These collaborators resemble relay runners, who depend on each other despite the fact that they are never on the field at the same time except to exchange places.

The success of one partner depended on the success of the other; they worked cooperatively rather than competitively to achieve their goals. Clemens, for instance, created the central plot revolving around the Hawkins family, their Tennessee land, and Colonel Sellers' various business and land ventures; he also initiated much of the plot's political intrigue in Washington. The characters, along with the elements of "intrigue," created openings for Warner's burlesque of the sentimental novel. Warner, in turn, introduced several subplots and additional characters such as Senator Dilworthy, who served as a vehicle for Clemens' political satires.

Clemens and Warner maintained separate turns throughout the composition of the novel. The two writers wrote alternately—first Clemens, then Warner, then Clemens, and so on. For instance, Clemens wrote the book's first eleven chapters (some 399 pages); at the end of this burst of writing, Warner took over the book for the next twelve chapters, and then returned it to Clemens. Clemens and Warner wrote the remainder of the book by exchanging the manuscript every two or three chapters (French, appendix).

The advance advertising of *The Gilded Age* made much of the fact that the two well-known authors were collaborating. Clemens scholar Bryant Morey French cites the following account printed in the *New York Tribune* (April 22, 1873):

> It is called "The Gilded Age"—a name which gives the best promise of the wealth of satire and observations which it is easy to expect from two such authors.... An immense audience is already assured beforehand; and it is fair to conclude that writers who have displayed so much wit, insight and delicacy and fanciful observation in former works, will not be unprovided with the equipment which is necessary to successful fiction. (qtd. in French 13)

Although Clemens and Warner wrote sections separately, and at times settled for tenuous connections between their different subjects, they based their collaboration on a social critique of post-Civil War America. Clemens mainly satirized current political and economic situations, while Warner burlesqued popular culture with his own version of a sentimental novel. Clemens, in the first eleven chapters, created several threads that Warner could choose to pick up, if he wanted to. Clemens recognized Warner's right to determine certain patterns within their jointly woven text. In terms of conversational cooperation, Clemens had both projected topics and invited Warner's participation. In his turn, Warner took up these ideas, especially developing Clemens' character, Laura, as a sentimental heroine who suffered cruel deceptions.

As the novel continues, Laura becomes a lobbyist and social belle in Washington (through plot twists involving other, secondary characters). Warner plays with her position in politics and in society, often involving Laura in various scandals (such as shooting her former lover). Her actions frequently provide both Clemens and Warner a vehicle for social satire. For instance, they both play with an episode in which Laura, as lobbyist, succeeds in securing a majority vote for Senator Dilworthy—a friend of the Hawkins family—who is sponsoring the Knobs Industrial University Bill. Laura obtains a key opposition vote by blackmailing a senator. When the bill passes, the Hawkins family's "Tennessee Land" (Clemens' invention) is suddenly worth a fortune as the future site of a university. Because of connections between the Senator who sponsored the bill and the Hawkins family (Washington Hawkins, the Squire's son, is the Senator's personal secretary; Laura Hawkins acts as a lobbyist for Dilworthy), scandal envelops the Hawkinses.

At this point the sentimental and political satires intertwine; the characters and plot inventions have been mutually developed by Clemens and Warner, thus reflecting the cooperative efforts and mutual rhetorical goals of the two writers.

The partners were scrupulous about acknowledging each other's contributions to *The Gilded Age*. Clemens and Warner could provide manuscript evidence (if necessary) of their shared writing practice; their turn-taking process of composition demonstrated their mutual agreement about the division of writing. Instead of admiring the "joint work" that had been anticipated with some interest, several critics, upon reading the novel, felt that Warner and Clemens had taken advantage of their reputations and of their readers' expectations. Clemens' *Autobiography* reflects some of his anger toward those who accused him and Warner of exploiting their readership:

> I believe [the reviewer for the *Atlantic Monthly*] did not deal mainly with the merit of the book or the lack of it but with my moral attitude toward the public. It was charged that I had used my reputation to play a swindle on the public—that Mr. Warner had written as much as half of the book and that I had used my name to float it and give it currency—a currency which it could not have had without my name—and that this conduct of mine was a grave fraud upon the people. (298–99)

The reviewer for the *Chicago Tribune* also condemned the collaboration, and implied that the two pure-bred writers had co-labored to produce a "mongrel" (qtd. in French 17).

It is true that Clemens and Warner relied on the established value of their names to guarantee large advance sales by subscription (and because of this the book sales were little affected by the negative response of the critics). But the critics' accusations that Clemens and Warner deliberately exploited the public by claiming joint authorship are unfounded: "swindle," "fraud," and "deceit" are all charges made against the process of collaboration—not against the content of the book.

Despite critical condemnations of their collaborative work, the two partners were far more successful than the co-authors of *The Whole Family* in producing a jointly written novel. In terms of conversational analysis, Clemens and Warner successfully fulfill the Cooperative Principle's conditions of quantity, quality, relation, and manner. Grice defines "quantity" as providing sufficient information for the purposes of the exchange (45). In the case of *The Gilded Age*, each collaborator is careful to introduce a new element with enough expository information that the other can pick up that piece of the story if he chooses: each explains, for instance, who a new character is and how that character is connected to the other characters and action of the novel; at the same time, each provides enough options to allow his co-author to develop the character further. "Quality" relates to the truthfulness of the exchange: "Do not say what you believe to be false. Do not say that for which you lack adequate evidence" (Grice 46). Unlike the co-authors of *The Whole Family*, Clemens and Warner do not try to confuse or contradict one another; each works with the intention of collaboratively producing a single, coherent text. "Relation" and "manner" are cooperative conditions that directly affect the process of a conversational exchange: the focus and relevance of an exchange affects shifts and changes (turn-taking); clarity, length, and order also make possible the transition from one speaker or writer to another (Grice 46). Warner and Clemens employ cooperative turn-taking strategies: each projects topics through the plots and characters, and each invites the other's contributions.

The cooperation evident in the drafting of the novel was not, however, mobilized in the revisions of the text: critics, with some justice, attacked *The Gilded Age* for not achieving sufficient structural coherence. Some aspects of the plot are dropped completely, and others are resumed so much later in the novel that the events are disjointed. It is not that Clemens and Warner did not cooperate at the final stages of producing *The Gilded Age*, but that they simply did not revise at all. The writers did not coordinate their efforts to give the final text greater continuity than the drafts. Instead, they organized the book by "numbering the chapters and working them in together in their appropriate places" (Clemens, *Letters*, April 26, 1873)—which amounted to their submitting the text in the same order that they wrote it in, with little attention to editing or organization. Consequently, their process was a truncated conversation. The final manuscript is more like a series of letters—a correspondence between two writers—than an integrated and overlapping dialogue.

Collaboration as Conversation in *Love Medicine*

The Gilded Age provides an instance of two peers maintaining individual control over separate sections of a jointly produced novel—accommodating one another's choices, but not compromising any of their individual preferences and not extending their collaborative dialogue to editorial revisions made with the entire finished product in mind. *Love Medicine* (1984) and the other four novels written by Louise Erdrich and Michael Dorris (*The Beet Queen*, 1986; *A Yellow Raft in Blue Water*, 1987; *Tracks*, 1988; *Crown of Columbus*, 1991) exemplify fully conversational collaboration, in which the writers themselves claim not to remember who was responsible for any particular section, but instead remember conversations that shaped the text.

Ironically, these collaborators have—until their latest novel—listed only one of their names as author of their jointly written texts. Louise Erdrich is listed as author of *Love Medicine*, *The Beet Queen*, and *Tracks*; Michael Dorris' name appears on the jacket of *A Yellow Raft in Blue Water*. In numerous interviews the writers explain that the name on the title page is the person who instigated the project and who had "final say" on decisions about the text. Nonetheless, all of the books acknowledge the other partner as collaborator. For example, *Love Medicine* is dedicated to Michael Dorris: "I could not have written [this book] this way without Michael Dorris, who gave his own ideas, experiences, and devoted attention to the writing. This book is dedicated to him because he is so much a part of it." *A Yellow Raft in Blue Water* reads: "For Louise / Companion through every page / Through every day / Compeer." Each of these dedications is more than a passing acknowledgment of support; each refers to the essential, integral role the other plays in the writing of the text. Erdrich and Dorris' 1991 novel *The Crown of Columbus* lists for the first time both their names as author.

Despite the division of names on the book jacket (presumably an attempt to avoid the marketing problems often associated with collaborative works) Erdrich and Dorris, when interviewed, explain that they are not able to specify who wrote which sections of their five collaborative novels, that it is impossible to separate their contributions. They argue that, even if they could identify ideas or portions of the text as clearly "Louise's" or clearly "Michael's," specifying individual work contradicts the collaborative process. In a 1986 *Publishers Weekly* interview with Miriam Berkley, Erdrich describes the way that she and Dorris write all of their fiction. Erdrich emphasizes the degree to which she and Dorris talk about the characters and scenarios, read aloud and discuss drafts, and continue a pattern of talking and writing until they "achieve consensus on literally every word" (Berkley 59). Erdrich describes the process as "a true kind of collaboration: we both really influence the course of the book. You can't look back and say which one made it go this way or that way, because you can't remember. You just remember that you had that exciting *conversation*" (Berkley 59; emphasis added).

The recurrent references to conversation and discussion in Erdrich's description of the collaborative process resonate with Ede and Lunsford's emphasis on dialogue. Dorris continues:

> Nothing goes out of the house without the other person concurring that this is the best way to say it and the best way of presenting it. One of the beauties of the collaboration is that you bring two sets of experience to an issue or an idea, and it results in something that is entirely new. (59)

Erdrich takes up the thread of the conversation once again:

> Some people don't believe it's possible to collaborate that closely, although we both have solitude and private anguish as well. You develop this very personal relationship with your work, and it seems fragile; you're afraid to destroy it. But I trust Michael enough so that we can talk about it. (59)

The text, through conversation, becomes a joint work as Erdrich and Dorris strive to "achieve consensus."

The content and structure of *Love Medicine* echo Erdrich and Dorris' thorough conversational process of collaboration. Interviewer Charles Trueheart points out that the connections, associations, and family ties across generations in this book (as in their other books) are not always easy for the reader to pick up. Erdrich responds: "Our idea was that it would be like stepping into a community for anyone. It didn't make it easy for the reader, it's true. But stepping into another culture or community is never easy. And in a way it doesn't matter how people are related so much as how people treat each other" (Trueheart B8). *Love Medicine* invites the reader to join the conversation of its characters, and appreciate its tensions.

The novel concerns several generations of a Native American community as it explores tensions between white and Chippewa cultures, between Catholicism and Chippewa beliefs, between traditions and innovations or adaptations. Both alienation and integration are central themes. The language and setting of the novel also integrate diverse cultures: the characters speak a mixture of English, Chippewa, and French; the Turtle Mountain Chippewa reservation is located near both the International Peace Gardens and the line of intercontinental ballistic missile silos that stretches across North Dakota (Jahner 100).

In traditional Chippewa culture (as in many cultures), the telling of myths and stories is an important part of the culture's process of passing along its values and concepts. The oral tradition is reflected in the narrative structure of *Love Medicine*. We hear "stories" from several different narrators who represent different generations, different cultural perspectives, different attitudes. The multiple narrative perspectives, themselves creating a type of conversational collaboration, represent the "multi-voiced and multivalent" dimensions that Ede and Lunsford find inherent in any collaborative venture (133). Erdrich and Dorris use the novel's narrative structure not only to represent different points of view, but also to emphasize the importance of family and community: all but three chapters (and well-marked sections of two others) are told in the first person. Whenever the third-person voice is used, it refers to a character who is no longer part of the community, a character who is alienated from family and tribal connections, someone excluded from the immediacy of conversation.

Thus the book begins with a third-person narration of the death of June Morrisey, a woman distanced physically and emotionally from her family and community. In the opening scene, June is "killing time before the noon bus arrived that would take her home" (1). She delays her trip to spend time with a stranger whom she meets in a bar. "He could be different she thought. The bus ticket would stay good, maybe forever. They weren't expecting her home on the reservation. She didn't even have a man there, except the one she divorced" (3). June has no definite ties. She never physically returns home: she dies in a snowstorm, attempting to walk the long journey back to the reservation. It's unclear whether the death is a suicide or the ironic result of "natural causes" (the cause stated by her insurance company).

Bev Lamartine, another dislocated character whose story is narrated in the third person, lives in the Twin Cities and sells after-school homework books to parents with dreams for their children's success. The narrative voice tells us that "part of Bev's pitch ... was to show the wife or the husband a wallet-sized school photo of his son.... The back of the photo was inscribed 'To Uncle Bev,' but the customer never saw that" (78). The photo is Bev's only tie to his family, but even this is undermined by falsification. The third-person account of Bev's life emphasizes his remoteness. This is further signified by his setting: Bev lives away from the land, away from the reservation, selling a commercial product in a city.

At the center of these complex narratives is the character of Lipsha Morrisey. Lipsha is the son of June Morrisey, and he has family ties to the three families who narrate the events. Lipsha is the point of intersection for many of the narrative and thematic lines: as a central receiver (listener) for the stories, he integrates different perspectives and sources of knowledge and belief, while also representing links to the older generations and traditions. Finally, Lipsha and June Morrisey—representing mother and son, male and female, death and life, alienation and community—merge in the last lines of the novel. The book ends with a return to community—a literal and figurative homecoming on a clear morning in spring, when the character of Lipsha crosses a river back toward the reservation, bringing home the spirit of his mother, June Morrisey: "So there was nothing to do but cross the water, and bring her home" (272).

Love Medicine emphasizes context; it reflects the traditions of an oral culture with its multiple yet integrated narratives; it parallels the importance of conversation and integration in Erdrich and Dorris' collaborative writing process.

All of their novels incorporate the elements of community and storytelling found in *Love Medicine*. *The Beet Queen* and *Tracks*, for example, center on characters and events that connect to the stories and characters in *Love Medicine*. *A Yellow Raft in Blue Water*, like the other three novels, tells its story from multiple perspectives, representing different generations, different responses, different types of knowledge. In *The Crown of Columbus* the narrative is carried by the voices of the two central characters—Vivian Twostar and Roger

Williams. The two characters represent different ethnic backgrounds, different attitudes on family, and different approaches to Columbus as a subject of study (Roger is a poet and Vivian is an anthropologist). The two negotiate personal and professional tensions throughout the course of the novel. In this latest novel, as in their other fiction, the reader must listen to all the voices to learn the whole story. As in a conversation, no one voice dominates.

Collaboration in Context

Like those in *Love Medicine*, the narrative structures of *The Whole Family* and *The Gilded Age* reflect the particulars of the collaborative processes that produced them. The plot of *The Whole Family* contains numerous contradictions and incoherences; familial conflicts ironically provide the only unifying theme. The serialized publication of the novel encouraged competition over collaboration: *Harper's Bazaar* invited its readers to compete in attempts to unmask the individual author of each chapter. The magazine listed the names of all twelve contributors at the beginning of each installment, with the note, "the intelligent reader will experience no difficulty in determining which author wrote each chapter—perhaps." This device kept the reader intrigued throughout the yearlong serial, and prompted the writers themselves to display recognizable individual styles. The magazine revealed the name of the writer of each chapter in the final installment, and again when the serial novel was published as a book.

Conversational collaboration increases in proportion to the amount of flexibility and cooperation among those involved in the process. The conditions that aid or impede collaboration are conventionally described as "masculine" or "feminine" patterns of discourse: "masculine" monologic (or hierarchical) systems do not value multiple voices or innovations; "feminine" cooperation and turn-taking characterize a less orderly but more inclusive system that recognizes multiple voices and values flexibility. But the participants in *The Whole Family*, *The Gilded Age*, and *Love Medicine* go far toward demonstrating that gender does not by itself determine the nature of collaborative practices. Collaborative writing, like conversation, depends on a variety of specific, contextual conditions.

In the paradoxically monologic collaboration that produced *The Whole Family*, multiple voices and differing perspectives were seen as problems, not advantages. The participants did not negotiate their differences, and as a result the project quickly became a battle of wills in which some of the writers wanted simply to take over the text—to the exclusion of other contributions. Neither the editor nor the writers attended to the interconnected processes of discussion, negotiation, and writing. Too much emphasis was given to the final (anti-collaborative) goal for the text: a showcase of individual talent.

Clemens and Warner did not engage in counter-productive competition; instead, they composed *The Gilded Age* in relays. Each took turns inventing and developing the structure, characters, conflicts, and details of the novel. Despite their cooperative practice, however, the final novel is disjointed: their version of the relay system did not provide for the conversation necessary to reorganize and revise the text. *The Gilded Age* thus illustrates partial collaboration. Clemens and Warner shared control of the text by taking responsibility for specific sections; each accommodated the other's ideas within the separate sections, but there was little integration. As a result, the events in the novel connect tenuously, and the table of contents reveals more by way of digressions than of coherency. While certain inconsistencies can be attributed to the writers' burlesque of the sentimental novel, the rough collective style shows the difficulties of collaboration without thoroughgoing discussion and joint decision-making at every turn.

Erdrich and Dorris' conversational collaboration on *Love Medicine* shaped the global and specific features of the text through constant discussion and consensus. Unlike either monologic or dialogic collaboration, there is no division of labor or authority; all aspects of the composition are shared. As Erdrich and Dorris emphasize, "Nothing goes out of the house without the other person concurring that this is the best way to say it and the best way of presenting it.... [W]e ... achieve consensus on, literally, every word" (Berkley 59).

The cases of *The Whole Family*, *The Gilded Age*, and *Love Medicine* confirm that different types of collaboration correspond to differing degrees of authority, agreement, dialogue, and negotiation. No matter where these cases fall along the continuum of monologic, dialogic, and conversational collaboration, all three contradict the assumption that writing is a solitary (or silent) practice. These cases of collaboration begin to demonstrate that while we cannot ignore the significance of authors and texts as fundamental units of the literary canon, our constructions of literary knowledge must also reexamine the ways in which texts are (should be?) created—not only to accommodate specifically co-written work but to re-evaluate our general understanding of authorship and textuality.

Works Cited

Berkley, Miriam. "PW Interviews Louise Erdrich." *Publishers Weekly* 230 (Aug. 15, 1986): 58–59.

Cameron, Deborah. *Feminism and Linguistic Theory.* New York: St. Martin's, 1985.

Clemens, Samuel. *The Autobiography of Mark Twain.* Ed. Charles Neider. New York: Harper and Row, 1917, 1959, 1975.

———. *Mark Twain's Letters.* Ed. Albert Bigelow Paine. 2 vols. New York: Harper, 1917.

Clemens, Samuel, and Charles Dudley Warner. *The Gilded Age: A Story of To-Day.* Hartford, CT: American Publishing Company, 1873, 1890.

Dorris, Michael. *A Yellow Raft in Blue Water.* New York: Holt, 1987.

Dorris, Michael, and Louise Erdrich. *The Crown of Columbus.* New York: Harper, 1991.

Ede, Lisa, and Andrea Lunsford. *Singular Texts/Plural Authors.* Carbondale: Southern Illinois UP, 1990.

Erdrich, Louise. *Love Medicine.* New York: Bantam, 1984.

———. *The Beet Queen.* New York: Holt, 1986.

———. *Tracks.* New York: Holt, 1988.

French, Bryant Morey. *Mark Twain and* The Gilded Age: *The Book That Named an Era.* Dallas: Southern Methodist UP, 1965.

Gilligan, Carol. *In a Different Voice: Psychological Theory and Women's Development.* Cambridge, MA: Harvard UP, 1982.

Grice, H.P. "Logic and Conversation." *Syntax and Semantics 3: Speech Acts.* Ed. Peter Cole and Jerry L. Morgan. New York: Academic Press, 1975, 41–58.

Howells, William Dean. Vol. 2 of *Life in Letters*. 2 vols. Ed. Mildred Howells. Garden City, NY: Doubleday, 1928.

————, et al. *The Whole Family*. 1908. Introduced by Alfred Bendixen. New
York: Ungar, 1986.

Jahner, Elaine. Review of *Love Medicine*, by Louise Erdrich. *Parabola* 10
(1985): 96, 98, 100.

Jordan, Elizabeth. *Three Rousing Cheers*. New York: Appleton-Century,
1938.

Levinson, Stephen C. *Pragmatics*. Cambridge: Cambridge UP, 1983.

Piaget, Jean. *The Construction of Reality in the Child*. New York: Basic Books,
1954.

Review of *The Whole Family*. *The Nation* (Dec. 3, 1908): 552–53.

Spender, Dale. *Man Made Language*. London: Routledge & Kegan Paul,
1989.

Trueheart, Charles. "Marriage for Better or for Words: The Erdrich-Dorris
Team." *The Washington Post* (Oct. 19, 1988): B1.

Mark Twain and Dan Beard's Collaborative *Connecticut Yankee*

M. Thomas Inge

The story of how Daniel Carter Beard came to illustrate Mark Twain's *A Connecticut Yankee in King Arthur's Court* has been told several times.[1] I will, therefore, summarize it briefly here, with a few new details, as background to my main intent—which is a more thorough analysis of the illustrations than they have been accorded in order to establish the actual relationship they bear to the text of the novel. I hope to demonstrate that they are not mere illustrations or decorations but essential to an understanding or appreciation of the novel as Twain intended, as it was read in 1889, and as we should read it today.

Having already learned the value of the illustrations in selling a book by the subscription method, and having been not entirely happy with those in his earlier books, Twain was determined that *A Connecticut Yankee*, which he spoke of as his final major work, would have the best illustrations possible. As he wrote notes to himself during the course of composition sometime after November 1886, Twain was already considering the illustrations, but with no particular artist in mind. One note was a reminder to include "Fine heliotype portraits of Arthur & Lancelot in armor. 'Getting their first photographs taken.'" Another suggested a "Picture: The first locomotive tearing along, & priests, people & steel-clad knights breaking in every direction for the woods."[2] Neither of these scenes would appear in the book, but they suggest a design to have Hank introduce the art of photography and the invention of the steam engine to the Middle Ages, though only the latter idea was developed. The anachronistic incongruity in both images, however, contains an element of humor that retains its appeal even today. The reader can easily visualize them for his own amusement, suggesting that Twain himself had a talent for creating visual humor with words, something he may have learned from the humorists of the Old Southwest.

As the manuscript neared completion, Twain suggested that the publisher consider for the job Frank T. Merrill, who had illustrated *The Prince and the Pauper* in 1881; and by the time he finished, he suggested Reginald B. Birch, who had done the drawings for Frances Hodgson Burnett's *Little Lord Fauntleroy* in 1886. In both he admired the attention to accuracy of detail and fine draftsmanship. Then he picked up the March 1889 issue of *Cosmopolitan* magazine and found his man. Here was the second part of an eight-part serialized novel, "Wu Chih Tien, The Celestial Empress. A Chinese Historical Novel. Translated from the Original by Wong Ching Foo."[3] The five drawings Twain saw here were striking examples of Daniel Carter Beard's best action and adventure style. They were full of details obviously based on careful research into Chinese dress and culture, demonstrated a skillful use of the kind of cross-hatching and light-and-dark contrast possible in pen and ink renderings, and brought his figures alive on the printed page with exaggerated and lively poses. At the time, Dan and his older brothers Frank and Harry were among the most popular cartoonists and illustrators in New York.

Dan and Harry shared a studio and were featured with photographic portraits of themselves and their studio in the May issue of *Cosmopolitan* in an article by Elizabeth Bisland, "The Studios of New York." She reported that "Dan and Harry work in partnership at 191 Broadway, where dried monkeys, stuffed birds, and queer relics and fragments are thickly clustered, with a much-exercised manikin whose frantic efforts to furnish dramatic poses have made him prematurely decrepit."[4] After an initial inquiry, the following letter was posted June 14, 1889, by Charles L. Webster & Co. to both Dan and Harry Beard:

Gentlemen;—

Your favor received. Mr. Clemens would like to have you take the first thirty or forty pages of his new book[,] read it over and make a drawing choosing just such portion of the text for illustrating as you think best, —of course we leave [the] character of the illustration to you. On receipt of drawing we will submit it to

"I SAW HE MEANT BUSINESS."

Figure 1

Mr. Clemens and on hearing from him we will be able to talk
with you definitely one way or the other regarding the illustrating of his book. Of course if the drawing should not prove satisfactory to him we will expect to pay you for your trouble just the
same.[5]

The sample drawing (Figure 1) was submitted by Dan of a
knight charging Hank Morgan, who has shinnied up a tree, with a
comic decorative design in the lower left-hand corner. The illustration, which would become the book's frontispiece, greatly pleased
Twain, who agreed to Beard's terms of $3,000 for producing be-
tween 250 and 260 drawings. On July 19, Twain dictated a note to
his agent:

> I prefer to contract this time for the very best an artist can do.
> This time I want pictures, not black-board outlines & charcoal
> sketches. If Kemble illustrations for my last book [*Adventures of
> Huckleberry Finn*] were handed to me today, I would understand
> how tiresome to me that sameness would get to be, when
> distributed through a whole book, & I would put them promptly
> in the fire.[6]

Apparently Harry Beard was not a contracting party, although it
was presumably understood that he would help out in meeting the
deadlines. None of the drawings bear his signature, and in all of
the later discussions of the event, Harry is mentioned by Dan
Beard only once as having drawn the face for the royal figure being
carried by peasants in Chapter 8. Harry's drawing style was similar to Dan's, so the possibility of further collaboration on his part,
particularly as the pressures of deadlines developed, is not to be
entirely discounted.

For a number of reasons, Dan Beard must have relished the
idea of illustrating Mark Twain's book. In his autobiography,
Hardly a Man Is Now Alive, Beard proudly proclaimed on the first
page, "I am a Connecticut Yankee."[7] Although he was born in
Ohio and raised in Kentucky, his forebears of British yeoman stock
had arrived in Boston in 1637 before moving into the wilderness to
settle an estate carved out of the Connecticut forest. Beard strongly
identified with the pioneer and frontier spirit of America as depicted in legend and lore. He told stories about prominent folk
heroes who lived before his time as if he had known them personally and recounted events from his infancy he could only have
heard later in his life. He loved the boisterous life in a frontier

town and the games a boy could play on a country farm. His own experience was much like that of Mark Twain, and he described a kind of backwoods society in which Huckleberry Finn and Tom Sawyer would have been right at home.

The actual sources of much of the America that Beard described as personal experience are not hard to find. In his autobiography, we learn that he had read many popular books in his youth, including James Hall's *Western Tales*, *The Life of Abraham Lincoln* by Josiah G. Holland, Beadle's dime novels, and a special favorite, *The Young American's Picture Gallery*, with photographs of famous leaders and heroes; these fired his imagination with regard to folk mythology.[8] More importantly, he heard his brother James tell "firsthand stories of river pirates, highwaymen on the Natchez trace or the wilderness trail, Indians and wild animals." Beard exclaimed, "Why Daniel Boone, Simon Kenton and Mike Fink, with the red feather in his hat, were as real to me as my father."[9] He once noted in a letter to Cyril Clemens,

> In twenty-odd years intimate association with Mark Twain, coupled with the fact that we both spoke the same language, gives me, I think, an understanding of his real character which is not superficial. I also grew up in the river bottom among the Huck Finns and Tom Sawyers of the Ohio valley, among steamboats, rafts, and flatboats, in fact, I believe in the same atmosphere as that breathed by our great philosopher himself.[10]

Thus Beard had participated in the mythic American experience and its propagation as fully as had Mark Twain, who would come to be regarded as the quintessential American—though perhaps Beard would have a more profound influence in some ways than Twain through his synthesis of the frontier and wilderness experience in the guide books and rituals of the Boy Scouts of America, which he would found in 1910. Beard would take great pride, during the height of his career as an illustrator, in being known as "the Mark Twain of art."[11]

Before he began work, Beard was summoned to Twain's office for personal instructions. He recalled the interview over twenty years later:

> "Mr. Beard, I do not want to inflict any mental agony upon you nor subject you to any undue suffering, but I wish you'd read the book before you make the pictures."

I assured him that I had already read through the manuscripts three times, and he replied by opening a prominent magazine at his elbow, to a very beautiful picture of an old gentleman with a smooth face, which the text described as having a long, flowing white beard, remarking as he did so:

"From a casual reference to the current magazines I did not suppose that was the usual custom with illustrators."

"Now," he said, "Mr. Beard, you know my character of the Yankee. He is a common, uneducated man. He's a good telegraph operator; he can make a colt's revolver or a Remington gun—but he's a perfect ignoramus. He's a good foreman for a manufacturer, can survey land and run a locomotive. In other words, he has neither the refinement nor the weakness of a college education.

"In conclusion, I want to say that I have endeavored to put in all the coarseness and vulgarity into the Yankee in King Arthur's court that is necessary, and rely upon you for all the refinement and delicacy of humor your facile pen can depict. Glad to have met you, Mr. Beard. Goodbye."[12]

In his autobiography, written almost fifty years after the interview, Beard recalled an additional piece of advice from Twain:

"In regard to the illustrations you are to make," he said, "I only want to say this. If a man comes to me and wants me to write a story, I will write one for him; but if he comes to me and wants me to write a story and then tells me what to write, I say, 'Damn you, go hire a typewriter,'" meaning a stenographer.[13]

Whatever the veracity of this additional statement, remembered half a decade later, Twain did indeed grant Beard free rein to follow his own inspiration, as witnessed by a memo from Twain to the publisher dated July 24, at Elmira, New York:

Upon reflection—this: tell Beard to obey his *own* inspiration, and when he sees a picture in his mind put *that* picture on paper, be it humorous or be it serious. I want his genius to be wholly unhampered. I shan't have fears as to the result. They will be bullier pictures than if I mixed in and tried to give him points on his own trade.

Send him this note, and he'll understand.[14]

Beard was pleased to receive this vote of confidence and the artistic license to pursue what he later identified as "an experiment on my part," an attempt "to illustrate the ideas expressed there as well as the narrative itself."[15] Since there seems to be no model for what Beard was attempting, and he cited no example or source, we can only speculate about its origin. Perhaps it was the falling together of kindred spirits and the amicable meshing of ideas and ideology that inspired Beard; Beard's strong identification with Twain and Twain's admiration for Beard surely provided a potent impetus for their collaboration. *A Connecticut Yankee* was the kind of socially conscious book Beard would have liked to write (and he would indeed try his hand at his own version later), and Beard had the kind of acerbic satiric sensibility Twain would have shown had he been able to draw. But at the same time, the division of labor for *A Connecticut Yankee* was clear: Twain had written the text, and Beard would draw the illustrations—each without interference from the other. Although the result would be a mutual dependence, the process was carried on without substantial give-and-take.

As each batch of drawings was sent in, Beard received encouraging notes of appreciation from Twain. There was a psychological element in this, since Twain was determined to see the book published in time for Christmas sales, and all participants—author, illustrator, typesetters, proof-readers, and publisher—were working under incredible pressure. After a month's work was completed, Twain wrote Beard enthusiastically on August 28, again from Elmira:

> I have examined the pictures a good many times, and my pleasure in them is as strong and fresh as ever. I do not know of any quality they lack. Grace, dignity, poetry, spirit, imagination, these enrich them and make them charming and beautiful; and wherever humor appears it is high and fine, easy, unforced, kept under mastery, and it is delicious. You have expressed the King as I wanted him expressed; both face and figure are noble and gracious, and set forth the man's character with a satisfying eloquence. And he is clothed as he should be clothed—it was a proper subject for the dainty workmanship of the pencil. You have made a darling of Guenevere, and the architecture setting adds effect to her soft young grace and beauty. I like the Yankee every time; you have got him down fine where he is naked in the dungeon, supporting the initial letter. I enjoy the humor of the Sky-towering Monster (the fineness of the work, too) and of the interview between the Yankee and the page in the dungeon, and the Yankee's opening adventure with Sir Kay [the frontispiece]— enjoy it exceedingly; there is something about the smile of that

SANDY RODE BY ON A MULE.

Figure 2

helmet in the left foreground of the latter which is a perpetual delight to me. I could go into much further detail without saying all my say and expressing all my pleasure—but what I mainly wanted to put on paper was the fact that I appreciate the pictures and hold myself your obliged servant.[16]

Using as a gauge the drawings from Chapter 5 mentioned by Twain, Beard had finished at least twenty-two in the first month, only ten percent of the total, so a boost like this had to have a good effect.

Since he had other commitments to fulfill, the strain on Beard must have been severe. He was still finishing the illustrations for "Wu Chih Tien, The Celestial Empress," scheduled to run in *Cosmopolitan* through the September issue—which perhaps explains why some of the drawings for the last chapters of the Chinese novel were less detailed and carefully rendered than the earlier ones. It may also explain why Beard borrowed from several of his *Cosmopolitan* drawings for work that appears in *A Connecticut Yankee*, specifically renderings of an explosion in the midst of combat, a woman being burnt at the stake, and a heraldic device with symbols of despotism—the crown, the whip, and the manacles of slavery.[17] Given the speed at which he was working, it is remarkable that numerous mistakes did not enter the drawings, but Beard was a careful reader and collaborator. There is, however, at least one possible error. In Chapter 21, Twain had noted that the side saddle "was to remain unknown in England for nine hundred years yet," but Sandy seems to be using one in a drawing (Figure 2) for Chapter 36 as she rides a mule searching for Hank.[18] If Beard made no major mistakes, he acted as a collaborator by saving Twain from one. Twain had listed a turkey as being an item on a list of goods purchased for the dinner with Marco and his friends in Chapter 32, until Beard observed that the fowl would not be known until the discovery of America; so the turkey was changed to a goose.[19]

According to Beard, the drawings were finished in seventy working days, at which point he collapsed, physically exhausted,[20] but Twain cheered him up on November 11 with a frequently quoted note:

Hold me under everlasting obligations. What luck it was to find you. There are a hundred artists who could have illustrated any other book of mine, but there was only one who could illustrate this one. Yes, it was a fortunate hour that I went netting for lightning bugs and caught a meteor. Live forever.[21]

A Connecticut Yankee was published on December 10, 1889. Most of the American reviewers were also impressed by Beard's work. For example, Sylvester Baxter of the Boston Sunday *Herald* said, "These drawings are graceful, picturesque and thoroughly characteristic of the spirit of the book,"[22] and William Dean Howells noted in *Harper's*, "Throughout, the text in all its circumstance and meaning is supplemented by the illustrations of an artist who has entered into the wrath and the pathos as well as the fun of the thing, and made them his own."[23] In the most negative American review the book was to receive, in the Boston *Literary World*, Beard also received his share of the condemnation. The anonymous commentator concluded, "If anything could be less of a credit to our literature than the matter of this book, it certainly is the illustrations which disfigure it."[24] Since many British reviewers were offended by the novel, it was to be expected that they too would dislike the drawings—and they did. The most extended critique was provided by the anonymous reviewer for the London *Speaker*:

> They are very badly arranged; they seldom occur at the right place; and they break into text, making the task of reading very difficult. The task was hard enough, too, without that. We hope—we may even believe—that we have seen the artist at his worst; we certainly have not seen the author at his best.[25]

It is interesting that no American or British reviewer liked the text but not the drawings, or vice-versa. In general, they seemed to accept the drawings as an integral part of the book and noted their close correspondence to the text.

But there was another kind of negative response that Beard did not expect. As he reported it,

> Sad to say, the illustrations which so pleased Mark Twain and delighted people all over the world grievously offended some advertisers. The offending illustrations were removed from further editions. Not only did the book feel the force of the displeasure of this group, but it is significant that after its publication Mark Twain was ruined financially and my work was boycotted for many years by all the prominent magazines, with the exception of *Life* and *Cosmopolitan*. I, too, went practically broke, but Mark Twain died a wealthy man and I lived to find my work in great demand.[26]

When Beard was queried for more information about the reasons for this boycott in 1936, he responded,

> In regard to the illustrations, I am afraid that they showed Mark Twain's thought too much to please them. You must realize that when Mark Twain tread [sic] upon any social, political, or ecclesiastical corns, the owners of those corns assumed that his remarks were only meant to be funny; but could not assume that when Mark Twain's thoughts were put into the form of cartoons and illustrations. You know, Mark Twain once said that I not only illustrated the stories, but I illustrated the thoughts of the author when he was writing the story, and that may be where the shoe pinched.[27]

Such comments, to the extent that they are reliable, bespeak a very close relationship and sense of identification between author and artist, between the text and the art work—an intimacy the initial reviewers, both pro and con, seemed inclined to accept.

Subsequent criticism, on the other hand, tended more toward a view of the illustrations as external to the text. Henry Nash Smith has said that Beard should be considered "the first reviewer of the book" and the drawings his own "interpretation" of Twain's novel. Smith was not happy with the ideas and thoughts in the drawings, and like other critics, was inclined to see them as separate, if not entirely unrelated to Twain's actual beliefs.[28] I wish to argue the contrary, that whatever divergences may exist between the meaning of the text and the pictures, or between Twain and Beard, we have no choice but to consider *A Connecticut Yankee* as a work of willful and intentional collaboration, and that to consider the narrative without the illustrations is to consider an incomplete work. To make that argument requires addressing some complex questions.

Exactly to what degree has Dan Beard simply illustrated *A Connecticut Yankee*, to what degree expanded upon or provided a gloss on Mark Twain's text, and to what degree gone beyond the text to make additional commentary on the subjects with which the novel is concerned? These are questions which have not been directly addressed by previous scholarship but which I wish to consider through an analysis of the illustrations and their relationship to the text.

I have been able to divide the drawings into four distinct groups or categories:

1. Illustrations of specific scenes, characters, and events described by Twain in the text.

2. Decorations using designs, figures, and settings appropriate to the time and place of the narrative (a good many of the chapter initial letters fit into this group, although many of them serve as illustrations as well).

3. Interpretations of the text—that is, symbolic scenes and figures not mentioned in the text but reasonable extrapolations of the meaning and substance of what seems to have been Twain's intent.

4. Independent commentaries by Beard expressing pictorially his point-of-view on the political and social topics under discussion by Twain but without specific support by the text.

Twain contracted with Beard for between 250 and 260 drawings, 300 were advertised in the prospectus, and Beard recalled producing about 400; yet only 220 appear in the book. At least 222 were completed, if we include the single drawing rejected·by Twain (two knights preparing to charge each other) and the one that appeared in the publisher's prospectus but not in the book.[29] This was probably due to the tight publication schedule rather than any dereliction on Beard's part. Of the 220 drawings published in the book, according to my analysis, 152 (69%) are purely illustrative, another 15 (7%) are decorative, 44 (20%) are interpretive, and 9 (4%) are independent statements. The usual functions of the illustrator are to portray scenes, characters, and events from the novel and to provide decorations appropriate to the work; slightly over 75 percent of the art work fulfills those conventional functions. It is, however, the remaining quarter that makes the difference—defining for Beard a unique place in the importance of the novel by virtue of the dialogue his non-traditional "illustrations" carry on with Twain's text.

Even in the straightforward illustrations, Beard took some unusual liberties by inserting contemporary faces and well-known personages in them. Some of these insertions are fairly innocent, such as the appearance of Sarah Bernhardt as Clarence (Figure 3) and Annie Russell as Sandy (Figure 4), as well as many relatively unknown people, such as George Morrison, a real-life Yankee from Connecticut who happened to be working on some inventions in the office next to Beard's studio, as Hank Morgan (Figure 5); R.J. Lowden, the captain of Beard's rowing club, as a sentinel (Figure 6); the baby daughter of a banker, named Will James, as a foundling (Figure 7); and assorted bench-warmers from Central Park, a destitute French waiter, and Beard himself in several instances.[30] I say innocent, although Richard Bridgman has placed some unusual constructions on the Bernhardt drawing in an article which he says attempts to answer the question, "Why did the illustrator, Dan Beard, give Hank Morgan's page the face and figure of Sarah Bernhardt and go on to found the Boy Scouts of America?" What Bridgman suggests, but does not actually say, and probably with tongue in cheek, is that both Beard and Twain were latent homosexuals and pedophiles, among other things.[31] I will not address his evidence here, except to say that in the case of the Bernhardt drawing, I would suggest it was the costume that she wore in a photograph, in which she portrayed a boy troubadour, rather than the feminine figure that attracted Beard's attention in seeking out a model (she was frequently cast in masculine roles on stage). As Beard himself explained, "In making the illustrations ... I referred to a collection of photographs of people of note. When I wanted a face or a figure to fit a character in the story I looked over this collection of photographs and made free use of them, not as caricatures or portraits of the people themselves but for the dress, pose, or their whole figure and features as best fitted the character I was to depict."[32]

Other famous people who appear do seem intended as editorial comments and expand upon Mark Twain's meaning, such as the appearance of Alfred Lord Tennyson as Merlin (Figure 8), a brilliant touch by Beard, using the contemporary figure most closely associated with the idealization of Arthurian chivalry as a way of satirizing the feudal values which still held an appeal for the nineteenth century. Less subtle, but also relevant to the royalty-bashing in which Twain liked to engage are the appearances of Queen Victoria as a bewitched old sow and, as themselves but identified as "chuckleheads" (Figure 9), the Prince of Wales (later Edward VII), his eldest son Albert Victor, Duke of Clarence and Avondale, and the Emperor of Germany, Kaiser Wilhelm II (the last twice, once in caricature and the second time in full figure dressed in battle armor [Figure 10]).[33]

(continued on page 190)

"GO 'LONG," I SAID, "YOU AIN'T MORE THAN A PARAGRAPH."

Figure 3

"SHE CONTINUED TO FETCH AND POUR UNTIL I WAS WELL SOAKED."

Figure 4

Figure 5

Figure 6

Figure 7

Figure 8

Figure 9

"ARMOR IS HEAVY, YET IS IT A PROUD BURDEN,
AND A MAN STANDETH STRAIGHT IN IT."

Figure 10

(continued from page 181)

The most notorious of the drawings featuring contemporary figures is the slave driver with the face of Jay Gould, financier and Robber Baron (Figure 11). As Beard later explained, "I wanted a face which showed a high order of intelligence, but was absolutely heartless, cold brutally and cruel. I found such a face among my photographs of prominent people and used it."[34] Beard never publicly identified the face as that of Gould, but when a New York *Times* correspondent so identified the figure to Mark Twain, he did not deny it.[35] Since Twain was already on record with his opinion of Gould as a swindler and stock manipulator, there was little surprise there. Recent research has also indicated that other Robber Barons appear in the drawings, such as "Diamond Jim" Fisk, William Marcie "Boss" Tweed, and John T. Hoffman, as well as some figures greatly admired by Beard, such as Edward Bellamy and Henry George.[36]

What might have been Beard's intent in including these contemporary faces, other than to add an amusing guessing game for the reader? Aside from the actresses and the individuals known only to Beard, the others do underline the parallels Mark Twain wanted his readers to draw between the sixth and the nineteenth centuries, especially the degree to which his British contemporaries were still suffering under the delusions of chivalric ideals and belief in benign monarchy. The unscrupulous American business interests become a counterpart to the ruthless nobility of Britain's past, and romantic necromancers of the word like Tennyson become modern representatives of the forces of ignorance and superstition represented by Merlin. These implied parallels do not, however, entirely support one of Twain's stated intentions: "I think I was purposing to contrast ... the English life of the whole of the Middle Ages, with the life of modern Christendom and modern civilization—to the advantage of the latter, of course."[37] But the text is also equivocal on this point, and the criticism of modern business, science, and technology becomes as severe as that of the Middle Ages, particularly considering Hank's bleak failures; and Hank comes to long more for the old world than for the new. Thus, Beard's illustrations seem to capture Twain's intention (as expressed in the novel) better than Twain's own statements on the subject. Twain is famous for his works getting out of hand and galloping off in their own directions. Beard agreeably goes along for

Figure 11

Figure 12

the ride in this case and encourages his mount to follow wherever they are led.

As noted earlier, Mark Twain was reported as having said, "Dan Beard is the only man who can correctly illustrate my writings, for he not only illustrates the text but he illustrates my thoughts."[38] If, as I have suggested, this is true to some extent even of drawings in the "purely illustrative" category, it applies still more fully to the more than forty drawings I would categorize as interpretive drawings which have their source of inspiration in an idea or sentence expressed by Twain but which constitute an explication of the meaning. The very first of these (Figure 12) is prefatory to Chapter 1, a symbolic depiction of Hank Morgan tickling the nose of a huge lion with a straw, thus a description of Twain's intent to rib British society through satiric ridicule. Tickling, of course, is not a very pleasant way to elicit laughter.

It isn't until Chapter 8, entitled "The Boss," however, that Beard begins seriously to expand on Twain's thoughts and introduce a variety of pictorial satiric strategies of his own. In fact, three of his major techniques are displayed here—those of comic exaggeration or hyperbole, the animal fable, and the editorial cartoon. The prefatory drawing (Figure 13) begins the anti-church theme by portraying a monk greedily guzzling down a mug of liquor with a devil's head (instead of a halo) encouraging him from behind, a serpent wearing a bishop's mitre before him, one foot on the King's crown, and the other on Hank's Yankee Doodle hat, with the legend "That was the Church." This drawing and two others in the chapter represent a type of visual exaggeration and symbolic hyperbole used by Beard throughout the book—one (Figure 14) portraying Hank as a figure towering over a Lilliputian king, and the other (Figure 15) a fat monarch (who looks like "Diamond Jim" Fisk) resting on a bed of roses, while beneath three peasants wearily support the heavy load with briars cutting their feet and wolves hungrily nipping at their heels. Another illustration in this chapter adopts the method of the animal fable, to which Beard frequently resorts later in the book. A lion is depicted as a king being fed a rabbit by a priestly fox, with other rabbits—the common people—awaiting their turn.

The final two drawings in Chapter 8 adopt the visual strategies of the editorial cartoon, which was in its heyday in the last part of the nineteenth century with such cartoonists as Thomas Nast, *(continued on page 197)*

Figure 13

Figure 14

"INHERITED IDEAS ARE A CURIOUS THING."

Figure 15

(continued from page 193)
Bernard Gillam, and Homer Davenport at their most influential. In the cartoon of social and political protest as developed by such artists, symbolic figures are used to represent ideas or classes of people, but they are clearly labeled to make their meaning explicit. Thus in one cartoon by Beard (Figure 16), the sun, labeled "Divine Right of Kings VI Century," is about to be eclipsed by a moon labeled "The Earth Belongs to the People XIX Century," with a silhouetted throng below praising the event. In the second (Figure 17), a scroll emblazoned with the words "All men are free and equal" is exploding with such a bright light that a king is losing his crown and robe, a bishop his mitre and vestment, and a slave his chains, while Satan scurries away.

It is in the first of these two political cartoons, labeled in the list of illustrations as "The Earth Belongs to the People," that Beard begins to follow his own ideology and more forcefully to alter the ideological complexion of Twain's text. This is the first instance of what Henry Nash Smith noted as a tendency on Beard's part to ascribe to Twain "a number of slogans and battle cries of current left-wing groups such as the Single-Taxers and the Anti-Monopolists with whom he had no previous associations"; and of this drawing specifically Smith said that it almost certainly misrepresents the views of Twain, "who was never disposed to question private rights in property.... The passage near which the drawing is placed does contain a denunciation of the divine right of kings by the Yankee, but there is nothing in the text to support Beard's single-tax doctrine about ownership of natural resources."[39] In other words, Smith feels that it is the spirit of Henry George (proponent of the single tax) that resides behind the drawing rather than that of Twain; but George was a man admired by both Beard and Twain at the time, and Twain entered no objection to this political cartoon or any other. He accepted it as part of his novel, and thus assumed a collaborative responsibility for it.

Perhaps Beard's most elaborate political cartoon is the last drawing (Figure 18) for Chapter 30, where he takes as his text the phrase "A tree is known by its fruits." A tree labeled "The Golden Rule," with its roots of several freedoms planted in the "Soil of Common Sense," has produced an abundance of fruit in the arts and sciences (poetry, education, music, chemistry, mechanics, etc.),
(continued on page 201)

Figure 16

Figure 17

"A TREE IS KNOWN BY ITS FRUITS."

Figure 18

(continued from page 197)

topped by an angel of peace. Actually this is more elaborate than an effective editorial cartoon should be, simplicity and directness being major criteria. Except for the inclusion of free trade and free land among the roots, it is a non-partisan statement in accord with the spirit of the text. The bleakest editorial cartoon is the one (Figure 19) prefatory to Chapter 30 and a counterpart to the one just discussed. Here is the tree rooted in vested rights, religious intolerance, and the soil of selfishness, and from its blasted limb hangs the body of a peasant, with Satan sitting above. The entire sketch is strongly reminiscent of the engravings of Francisco de Goya, *Los Desastres de le Guerra* (1809), which had caused a sensation 80 years earlier and with which Beard was undoubtedly familiar. Several of the drawings employ a blasted tree, an emblem frequently used by Goya, as a part of the background. In general, the tree becomes a standard motif for Beard, as do the scales of justice.

The scales figure in five of the illustrations in a variety of ways, usually under the control of or tipped in favor of royal privilege, self-interest, or the church. In one (Figure 20), entitled "Two of a Kind," the scales are evenly balanced between a fat monarch and a worthless hobo of the nineteenth century, while in another (Figure 21), the Boss—representing science, independence, and freedom—outweighs a monarch, a bishop and a magician. A striking one (Figure 22), more purely in the editorial cartoon style, shows two figures of justice conspiratorially winking at each other from beneath their blinds across the centuries, with the scales rigged to their big toes so as to tip them in favor of title over labor in the sixth century and money over labor in the nineteenth. The title is "Sister Your Blind Is Disarranged." Beard, then, not only draws parallels between the inequities of both centuries, but he suggests as well that the principle of Justice herself is open to collusion and corruption, a fairly radical statement for either artist or author. It is one thing to find the authorities of the law degenerate (as in the cartoon prefacing Chapter 25) but another to find justice corrupt and open to barter.[40]

In a drawing for Chapter 28 (Figure 23), Beard anticipated Twain by introducing a parallel that would later be discussed in the text. Picking up on the statement, "Brother!—to dirt like that?," made by King Arthur, who is shocked at the idea of calling an or-
(continued on page 207)

Figure 19

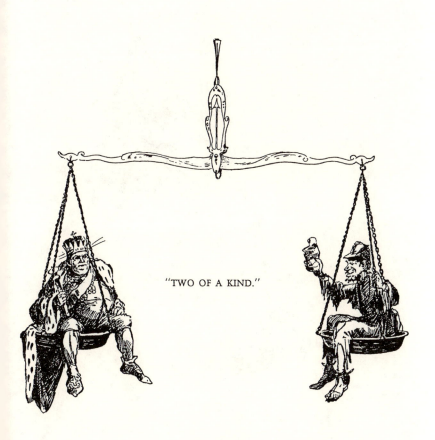

"TWO OF A KIND."

Figure 20

Figure 21

Figure 22

Figure 23

(continued from page 201)
dinary man a friend or brother, Beard provides a triptych of pictures with a king looking down his nose at a slave, a Southern
plantation owner doing the same at an African slave, and an American industrialist scorning a laborer. The face of authority remains
the same, but the source of power changes in each picture from a
sword of oppression, to a law book, to money bags. This is another
effective effort to make clear the parallels between two centuries,
but the introduction of Southern slavery in the second picture as
another parallel is new.[41]

It was inevitable that the similarities between medieval and
Southern slavery would be mentioned by Twain. While writing the
novel, he was using as a major source of information on the effects
of slavery an American slave narrative, Charles Ball's *Fifty Years in
Chains* (1837). The South is not mentioned in the novel, however,
until Chapter 30, where Southern "poor whites" are discussed fa-
vorably, and again in Chapter 31, where wages between the North
and South during the Civil War are compared. Then, in Chapter
34, Twain draws a direct parallel between the lot of the Southern
slave and that of the sixth-century slave when it dawns on Hank
Morgan that he has been enslaved himself, and he comments, "a
thing which had been merely improper before, became suddenly
hellish. Well, that's the way we are made." In this instance, then,
Beard's drawing colors the text by anticipating and planting in the
reader's mind a theme later to be developed by Twain.[42]

It is interesting to note that by placing the Southern slave
against the industrial wage-earner, quite unintentionally I am sure,
Beard was harking back to one of the most provocative defenses of
slavery to come out of the South, William Grayson's lengthy didactic poem *The Hireling and the Slave* (1854). Intended to counteract
the influence of *Uncle Tom's Cabin* (1852), by Harriet Beecher
Stowe, Grayson's argument in heroic couplets asserted that the life
of the wage slave in the Northern factories was far more precarious
and difficult than the life of a bond slave in his rural and paternal-
istic security. That certainly is not the argument of Beard or Twain;
but by bringing the two economic systems into conjunction this
way, the effect of Twain's text and, to an even greater degree,
Beard's illustration is to find both objectionable as humane ways of
life. An unreconstructed Southern reader, of course, might have
taken some small comfort in even this conclusion.

Beard's pen as an editorial cartoonist took a very traditional turn by the end of the book. From the start, after having been stripped of his cheap business suit, Hank Morgan was presented as wearing a top hat with three Yankee Doodle feathers in it. The hat, in fact, becomes a symbol of the Boss. By Chapter 41, as the end approaches, we find the hitherto clean-shaven Hank (Figure 24) sporting a goatee and wearing striped pants, as he holds up his child in a tableau in which Sandy in her starry dress takes on the outlines of a Mother Columbia (I suspect some contemporary political cartoon as the source of the figures in this drawing). Hank's transformation is complete by the next-to-last drawing (Figure 25) in the book. He has completely become Uncle Sam in dress and features, as he sits astride a copy of Thomas Paine's *Common Sense*, with macaroni in his hat, poking at a symbol of aristocracy with the mighty pen of truth dripping with ink. Given Hank's character as the consummate American, addicted to common sense, freedom, and pragmatism, despite the book's critique of nineteenthth-century America, this transformation seems a natural result of Beard's artistic tendencies and Twain's vision.

I have categorized nine of the drawings as representing an independent point of view on the part of Beard, pieces which have no clear anchor in the text. I would include in this category the final drawing of Hank as Uncle Sam, since this seems to have been Beard's inspiration, as well as the unexpected introduction of Henry VIII (Figure 26), after a painting by Holbein, prefatory to Chapter 21. Intended to satirize the tendency of Henry to have his wives beheaded, and engage in some weak word play with "head," it is anachronistic to the sixth century and unrelated to the nineteenth. Only in its suggestion of the evils of unrestricted royal authority is it related to the text.[43] I would also include here the odd portrait of the infant prefacing Chapter 22. The list of illustrations tells us that this is "A Foundling," but none of this age is mentioned in the text. I suspect Beard simply wanted to work in a sketch of the baby daughter of a friend, Will James, President of the Long Island Savings Bank,[44] or perhaps he was running out of ideas that day.

The most interesting of the independent illustrations is a five-piece series beginning with the drawing prefatory to Chapter 33 and running throughout the chapter, a kind of editorial cartoon es-
(continued on page 212)

"HELLO-CENTRAL!"

Figure 24

"HANDS OFF! MY PERSON IS SACRED."

Figure 25

"THE POWER OF TRAINING! OF INFLUENCE! OF EDUCATION!
IT CAN BRING A BODY UP TO BELIEVE ANYTHING."

Figure 26

(continued from page 208)

say on the virtues of free trade over protective tariffs. The text of the chapter is devoted to a discussion between Hank and some medieval tradesmen, with Hank defending free trade and the latter protectionism. The real argument, however, devolves into an effort on Hank's part to help them understand that the value of wages is determined by the purchasing power rather than the amount received, an argument he finally loses.

Beard's pictures go off on their own tangent. In the first (Figure 27), which gets its title from a shout of Dowley, a blacksmith, "Rah for protection!," a stork representing "Capital" can reach with its beak into a decanter with a long neck labeled "Protection," while a dog with a "labor" cap on its head can only lap up what water drips from the stork's beak. In the second drawing (Figure 28), the stork asks a dog, "Starving, eh? why don't you grow a nose like mine?" The implication is that protectionism is a natural God-given right to business interests and labor should accept its inferior position as a part of the scheme of things. The third drawing (Figure 29) suggests that this has been a matter of evolution rather, with a beggar devolving into a dog and a businessman (who looks like "Boss" Tweed) evolving into a stork, processes which can be reversed we see in the fourth picture (Figure 30), where dogs and storks profitably cooperate and play together as the sun of "Free Trade" rises and the decanter has lost its high neck, making "Natural opportunity free to all." But the final picture in the series (Figure 31) is chilling. It shows a dead stork hung up by its feet with a pen stuck through its heart.[45]

Are we to assume, then, that the final result of the competition between free trade and protectionism is the total destruction of capital? Twain in 1880 had been a supporter of protective tariffs as outlined by the Republican Party; but during the presidential campaign of 1888, he switched to the Democratic theory that high import tariffs would only raise prices rather than workers' wages.[46] While Twain when he wrote *A Connecticut Yankee* was in agreement about the preference for free trade, it is unlikely that he agreed with Beard's radical conclusion. It should be noted, though, that Twain selected the second drawing in this series as his favorite in the entire book, after the frontispiece, so clearly he voiced no disagreement with the ideas Beard expressed.[47]

(continued on page 217)

Figure 27

Figure 28

EVOLUTION.

Figure 29

DISCREPANCY IN NOSES MAKES NO DIFFERENCE.

Figure 30

Figure 31

(continued from page 212)

Radical in another way is Beard's final drawing for the book (Figure 32), the last in the independent category. In it, Beard decided to give the novel another ending. As he commented in a hand-annotated edition of *A Connecticut Yankee*, "It was only a few centuries which separated the Yankee from his wife, Sandy, and his little baby. I had not the heart to kill him as did the author; so I put death at the throat of time, thus killing all that separated the man from his wife and uniting them again." Beard then added a cryptic note: "The pen, which I had used to make all the illustrations in the book, broke as I signed my name to this illustration."[48] If the pen was broken, his intent was clear—to make *A Connecticut Yankee* as much his book as Twain's, even to the point of offering his own alternative ending.

The point I want to make is, I trust, clear by now: *A Connecticut Yankee* should be read as it was received by the readers of 1889—basically a collaboration between artist and author. Twain thoroughly approved of all the drawings in the book, even those which departed freely from the text. Henry Nash Smith found Beard's departures "indefensible," yet Twain stated, "to my mind the illustrations are better than the book—which is a good deal for me to say, I reckon."[49] Smith could only offer this as an explanation: "In the general humanitarian and Populist enthusiasm, fine shades of doctrine were of little interest to the writer or his readers."[50]

It is an interesting sequel to this story of collaboration that after completing work on *A Connecticut Yankee*, Beard decided to again try his experiment of producing a book in which both words and pictures tell the story and reveal the meaning, except this time he would be both author and illustrator. We know the manuscript was finished sometime within a year after the *Yankee*, since he received a letter from Twain's publishing firm dated December 12, 1890, saying that they had read his manuscript and were interested in discussing its publication.[51] The book appeared in 1892 from Webster & Company as *Moonblight and Six Feet of Romance*, actually two works in one volume, both fully illustrated by Beard.

The inspiration for the two works, according to Beard in the foreword, "came from a land beyond his ken, and would, like birds of passage, have flown on, and left nothing to tell of their existence had not their strange notes attracted his attention and interest."[52] The second of the two is but a brief sketch first published

Figure 32

in *Cosmopolitan* magazine in 1889, a fantasy about an artist who falls asleep to dream a reverie about his shoes and boots which walk around on their own.[53] It is only the first story, *Moonblight*, which is relevant to *A Connecticut Yankee*—a short novel intended, Beard says, to undermine the "wall called Vested Rights" which "*must* fall"; then only "will the poor tramp, the beggar, and the white slave begin to show the true color of their manhood."[54] It is a novel of political and social intent that addresses the causes of economic inequality.

The narrator of *Moonblight* finds himself stranded in a dirty, dismal town in Pennsylvania, with his steam yacht out of commission for the winter. In his grim hotel room, he finds some books belonging to the absent usual boarder and begins to read one called *Dreams and Moonblight*, lettered and illuminated by hand. In the bar below, he fails to rouse friendship among the drinking laborers there because, as Sam the bartender tells him later in his room, he is a mine owner and therefore suspect in their eyes. They discuss the extent to which genuine opportunity is still open in America, given the prevalence of vested interest. What begins here is a dramatic enactment of the principles behind Henry George's single tax theory.[55]

After studying a volume of ancient magic among the small collection of books, the narrator suddenly finds himself invested with the ability to "see things as they really are."[56] Looking out of the window, he now sees a group of trudging miners for what they are, "a band of miserable white slaves," and himself, as a capitalist, their part owner.[57] He sees his fellow mine owners as the animals and blood-sucking insects they have become, and he fears visiting his betrothed to see her as she actually is. Through lengthy conversations with his friend, Professor Follium, the bartender Sam, and his mine superintendent, Clint Butts, all honest and clear-sighted men, the abuses of capitalism as practiced in the Pennsylvania coal mines are laid bare. Partly to blame for this economic slavery are "the roots of the old monarchical cancer left in the nation's system," including the cooperation of the church in maintaining it.[58]

The narrator attempts to abolish and replace the old system with an enlightened one in which labor is allowed a greater share of the profits, and constructs a model town, called "Moonblight," as a utopian experiment. He is ostracized by his fellow mine owners and declared a lunatic. In a riot between striking miners, federal troops, and Pinkerton agents, the narrator is shot. Following a delirium, he wakes under the care of the woman he earlier feared to see and who will nurse him back to health.

Advertised as a book which "will take rank with 'Looking Backward'" by Edward Bellamy,[59] *Moonblight* is basically Beard's own version of and comment on *A Connecticut Yankee*. There are numerous parallels with Twain's novel in structure and content. Both narrators begin by coming across manuscripts which open to them a world of magic and mystery, except that in Twain's book we shift to the narrator within the manuscript for most of the narrative. While Beard's hero acquires through necromancy the ability to see things as they really are, Hank has this ability naturally as his birthright as a common-sense Yankee. Both are thought to be magicians, crazy, or possessed by demons as they put into action their rational ideas and idealistic logic, and by pointing out the contradictions and injustices they encounter, they create chaos and only make matters worse by dealing with the world in totally honest ways. Both come up against and are finally defeated by the economic and religious institutions which enslave men, and both are badly wounded at the end, although Beard's hero recovers and Hank (in Twain's text, though not in Beard's illustration) dies. Each has a faithful woman to turn to at the last for comfort, though Hank loses his across the centuries as he returns to his own time. *Moonblight*, it seems, turns the tables by making Twain the unseen collaborator for Beard's text.

The political import of the two works of fiction for contemporary readers was similar: modern man is enslaved by a social and economic system that is built on vested interest and will not easily be altered or improved without violent and radical remedies. And as in *A Connecticut Yankee*, the political message is nowhere more clearly communicated than in Beard's illustrations for *Moonblight*. As was true in the *Yankee*, some of the drawings are political cartoons rather than illustrations of the text, and many of them function quite independently of the text as commentary. Here Beard-the-illustrator collaborates with Beard-the-novelist in much the same way as he collaborated with Twain. Some of the drawings are overt in their symbolism, but others engage in the kind of anthropomorphism employed in the drawings for Twain. Businessmen become snakes and vultures or predatory animals. In one progressive series, a mine owner changes before our eyes into a vicious wolf ready to spring and devour its victim. Several of the drawings would have been as well placed in *A Connecticut Yankee* as here, and they reflect the same kind of combined political and artistic impulse that inspired Beard while he was completing the illustrations for Twain's volume.

Beard was so inspired by Twain's example that he had to write his own version, illustrated in the same fashion and with the same intent of providing a gloss and expansion of the text through pictures that are integral to it. He even imitated Twain's device of inserting in the narrative other fictional texts, written in a distinctively different style, such as the excerpts from Malory and examples of medieval journalism on Twain's part. Certainly without *A Connecticut Yankee* as a model, Beard was not likely to have produced a novel illustrated in this fashion. What worked for Twain, however, did not for Beard. *Moonblight* has been all but lost to literary history, and Beard never tried another novel. He went on to achieve greater success as "Uncle Dan," the founder of the Boy Scouts of America. Here his reform impulse had a greater impact on the world he wanted to change for the better.

Daniel Carter Beard and Mark Twain were to remain fast friends throughout the rest of their lives, and Beard would illustrate other novels and stories by Twain. The nature and closeness of the relationship is perhaps best demonstrated in an anecdote Beard reported about one day when he ran into Twain on the streets of New York:

> "By the way," he said, "I have just written something that you'll like. It is called 'To the Person Sitting in Darkness.' I read it to Howells and Howells said I ought to have that published."
>
> "Of course you're going to, aren't you, Mr. Clemens?" I interjected.
>
> "You didn't let me finish," he retor[t]ed. "Howells also said that I must go hang myself first, and when I asked him what I should do that for he said to save the public the trouble, because when that story appeared in print they would surely hang me."
>
> "But he didn't frighten you off in that way, did he?" I laughed in reply. "You are not so easily scared as that, Mr. Clemens."
>
> "Don't you be so fresh. Howells also said that the story ought to be illustrated, and that there was only one man who could do it, and that man is Dan Beard, so you see you and I have got to hang together."[60]

I believe they should not only hang together but take equal credit for the success and significance of *A Connecticut Yankee*, a work in which picture and text not only complement each other but are to be viewed as an integral whole—an interesting example, perhaps unique in American letters, of how the literary and artistic sensibilities can work together for maximum effect.

We could say, on the basis of his evidently divided intention in *A Connecticut Yankee*, that Mark Twain was an author of two minds who at every turn had to compromise his conflicting intentions by willfully de-emphasizing one side of the conflict. Beard, as collaborative illustrator, seems most often to have championed the side that Twain in his remarks about the novel most frequently denied (or simply avoided): *A Connecticut Yankee* as critique of nineteenth-century American society. Twain's apparently genuine enthusiasm for Beard's illustrations may be an unspoken endorsement of that critique and a recognition of its crucial involvement in *A Connecticut Yankee*. That Beard's illustrations were eliminated after the first edition and that subsequent criticism has insisted on the separateness of Twain's intention from Beard's underscores a prevalent resistance to any tampering with Mark Twain as author figure. And this may be related to a concern over the broader implications of the collaboration.

The case of Twain-Beard as author-illustrator collaboration provides an interesting variation on usual considerations of collaborative process and effect in that the contribution of one partner is most essentially wordless (although the drawings contain a surprising amount of text, some of it Beard-generated) and yet seeks to both read and reinterpret the intention behind the text-as-language-structure. The proposition that Beard's illustrations entered into Twain's text in a way that affected the meaning of the text challenges usual concepts of textuality; that Twain welcomed their entry challenges conventional notions of authorship. The collaboration raises complicated questions about "linguistic" versus "non-linguistic" meaning, about ownership of texts, and about the degree to which written (or spoken) text is a function of authorial intention (either conscious or unconscious). To suppress Beard's illustrations to *A Connecticut Yankee* by denying their relevance to the text is not only to make it a different book from the one Twain published but also to deny the complex nature of authorship and production of text.[61]

Table of Illustrations for *A Connecticut Yankee*

Numbers refer to pages where the illustrations are found in Bernard L. Stein, ed., *A Connecticut Yankee in King Arthur's Court* (Berkeley: U of California P, 1979).

Illustrative (152 drawings): frontispiece, 51, 56, 58, 62, 64, 67, 71, 73, 75, 76, 78, 79, 81, 82, 85, 87, 89, 90, 93, 95, 97, 99, 101, 104, 117, 118, 119, 120, 123, 126, 128, 129, 131, 133, 134, 135, 137, 141, 143, 144, 146, 147, 148, 154, 157, 163, 164, 165, 166, 167, 168, 171, 172, 174, 175, 180, 183, 184, 187, 189, 193, 195, 196, 200, 213, 216, 219, 220, 222, 226, 231, 232, 236, 238, 241, 245, 250, 253, 254, 257, 262, 266, 268, 269, 272, 274, 281, 284, 287, 297, 299, 301, 306, 307, 309, 313, 317, 324, 328, 331, 333, 339, 340, 347, 350, 352, 354, 357, 360, 363, 381, 385, 387, 391, 393, 395, 396, 398, 400, 402, 406, 407, 408, 409, 412, 413, 415, 417, 421, 422, 424, 425, 427, 428, 432, 434, 436, 438, 441, 447, 449, 455, 457, 460, 461, 463, 471, 472, 474, 477, 482.

Decorative (15 drawings): 47, 53, 59, 60, 68, 98, 178, 194, 298, 310, 320, 348, 358, 458, 488.

Interpretive (44 drawings): 55, 107, 198, 110, 112, 114, 115, 125, 151, 152, 155, 159, 185, 205, 206, 209, 225, 261, 271, 277, 283, 290, 293, 319, 322, 323, 335, 336, 344, 368, 382, 405, 411, 442, 443, 451, 452, 454, 464, 479, 485, 487, 490, 491.

Independent (9 drawings): 235, 249, 367, 370, 372, 376, 379, 492, 493.

Notes

1. See, for example, Beverly R. David, "The Unexpurgated *A Connecticut Yankee*: Mark Twain and His Illustrator, Daniel Carter Beard," *Prospects* 1 (1975): 98–117; William V. Kahler, "Mark Twain: Adult Hero of Daniel Carter Beard," *Mark Twain Journal* 18 (Winter 1976–77): 1–4; Henry Nash Smith, "Introduction," *A Connecticut Yankee in King Arthur's Court*, ed. Bernard L. Stein (Berkeley: U of California P, 1979) 1–30, especially 14–17; and Karen Nolle-Fischer, "Selling Mark Twain's *Connecticut Yankee* in America: Marketing and Illustrations," *Revue français d'études americaines*, No. 17 (May 1983): 265–81. This essay was finished before I was able to obtain a copy of Teona Tone Gneiting's unpublished doctoral dissertation,

"Picture and Text: A Theory of Illustrated Fiction in the Nineteenth Century," University of California, Los Angeles, 1977. Her well-researched and impressive chapter on *A Connecticut Yankee* makes the same argument I do but through different means and within a larger theoretical context. Her appendix, which corrects errors in the David article above, is especially important.

2. Bernard L. Stein, ed., *A Connecticut Yankee in King Arthur's Court* (Berkeley: U of California P, 1979) 512.

3. Smith 14. Beginning presumably with Twain in a notebook entry, all commentators and editors since then have mistakenly repeated that "Wu Chih Tien, The Celestial Empress" was a story. The novel began in *Cosmopolitan* 6 (February 1889): 327–34, and continued as follows: 6 (March 1889): 477–85; 6 (April 1889): 564–72; 7 (May 1889): 65–72; 7 (June 1889): 128–32; 7 (July 1889): 289–99; 7 (August 1889): 361–68; and 7 (September 1889): 449–59. In all, Beard did 34 drawings for this series, as well as other illustrations for some of the same issues of *Cosmopolitan*.

4. Elizabeth Bisland, "The Studios of New York," *Cosmopolitan* 7 (May 1889): 22.

5. Charles L. Webster & Co. to H. & D.C. Beard, June 14, 1889, Library of Congress.

6. Cited in Smith 14.

7. Dan Beard, *Hardly a Man Is Now Alive: The Autobiography of Dan Beard* (New York: Doubleday, Doran, 1939) 1.

8. Beard 104–5.

9. Beard 18.

10. Beard to Cyril Clemens, November 21, 1935, Library of Congress.

11. Beard, *Autobiography* 284.

12. Dan Beard, "Mark Twain, the Man as Dan Beard Knew," San Francisco *Examiner* (April 25, 1910): 16.

13. Beard, *Autobiography* 336–37.

14. Samuel Langhorne Clemens to Fred J. Hall, July 24, 1889, Library of Congress.

15. Beard, "Mark Twain, the Man" 16.

16. Clemens to Beard, August 25, 1889, Library of Congress.

17. Compare Stein 317, with *Cosmopolitan* 7 (May 1889) 67; Stein 400, with *Cosmopolitan* 7 (September 1889) 458; and Stein, 155, with *Cosmopolitan* 7 (October 1889) 650 (but note that the heraldic device had first appeared in the March, 1889, issue).

18. Stein 241 and 408.

19. Stein 653. According to James D. Williams, "The Use of History in Mark Twain's *A Connecticut Yankee*," *PMLA* 80 (1965): 102–10, the turkey got in because Twain copied a list of consumer goods used to illustrate prices from one of a series of articles on civilization and economics by Edward Jarvis published in the *Atlantic Monthly* in the fall of 1869.

20. Beard to Cyril Clemens, April 11, 1936, Library of Congress.

21. Cited in Kahler 2. For variant versions of the text, see Albert Bigelow Paine, *Mark Twain: A Biography* (New York: Harper & Brothers, 1912), III, 888; and Beard, *Autobiography* 337–38. Kahler reports that the letter hung framed on Beard's living room wall while he lived and eventually was deposited in the Dan Beard Memorial Room at the Bear Mountain Trailside Museum in Bear Mountain, New York.

22. Sylvester Baxter, review, Boston Sunday *Herald* (December 15, 1887): 17.

23. William Dean Howells, "Editor's Study," *Harper's Magazine* 80 (January 1890): 321.

24. "A Connecticut Yankee in King Arthur's Court," *The Literary World* 21 (February 15, 1890): 52–53.

25. "Didactic Humourists," *The Speaker* 1 (January 11, 1890): 50.

26. Beard, *Autobiography* 338. See also Beard to Cyril Clemens, April 11, 1936, Library of Congress. Beard's son, Bartlett, speculated that the Catholic Church was behind the boycott (Kahler 2). Beard's friend, Hamlin Garland, wrote in 1940, "It surprised me to learn that these illustrations not only brought Beard into disfavor with editors but put him 'on his uppers,' or near it—but nothing in his expression during those lean years gave one any hint of his adversity—and I had no idea that drawings for the *Yankee* were considered heretical" (Hamlin Garland, "Twain's Social Conscience," *Mark Twain Journal* [Summer 1940]: 9). Twain's financial fortunes suffered because of poor investments and not a boycott, so there may be some question as to whether Beard imagined a conspiracy or a boycott actually occurred.

27. Beard to Cyril Clemens, April 28, 1936, Library of Congress.

28. Smith 16.

29. Stein 14, 541, 585, and 624; Beard, *Autobiography* 337.

30. Stein 552, 556, 553, 554, and 568. Beard once reported of George Morrison, "the Yankee himself was very proud of his appearance in the book" (Beard to Cyril Clemens, July 27, 1938, Library of Congress).

31. Richard Bridgman, "Mark Twain and Dan Beard's Clarence: An Anatomy," *Centennial Review* 31 (1987): 212–27.

32. Beard, *Autobiography* 337; Stein 552. See also a letter from Beard to Cyril Clemens, July 27, 1938, Library of Congress.

33. Stein 552, 560, 563, and 654.

34. Cited in Stein 567.

35. Cited in Smith 17.

36. Greg Metcalf, "A Pen Re-Warmed Through Caricature: The Politics of Mark Twain's *A Connecticut Yankee in King Arthur's Court*," a paper delivered at the meeting of the Popular Culture Association, St. Louis, Missouri, April 6, 1989. That other figures remain to be identified is suggested by Beard's statement in a 1941 letter, "My mother recognized more people in the YANKEE cartoons than anyone else, and chided me for making some of them, but I told her not to worry, that she was the only one who would recognize them" (Beard to Cyril Clemens, March 25, 1941, Library of Congress).

37. Cited in Stein 8, note 22.

38. Cited in Beard, *Autobiography* 345. See also Beard to Cyril Clemens, April 28, 1938, Library of Congress.

39. Henry Nash Smith, *Mark Twain's Fable of Progress: Political and Economic Ideas in "A Connecticut Yankee"* (New Brunswick, NJ: Rutgers UP, 1964) 79–80. Louis Budd agrees that Twain was a supporter of property rights in *Mark Twain: Social Philosopher* (Bloomington: Indiana UP, 1962) 210: "As the temper of his social mind is studied from his Hannibal days onward, it becomes clear that he would have sided with the claims of property even if his own bank account had not been sizable after 1870. Seldom in his long life did he doubt that almost everybody makes as much money in the end as he deserves, that property rights are the foundation of the happiest society, that the amount of property a man has largely determines the extent of his right to help guide society, and that political rights are secondary to the need to safeguard the health of private property."

40. See drawings in Stein 151, 159, 277, 285, and 411.

41. Stein 323.

42. Stein 561, 343, 349, and 392.

43. Stein 560.

44. Dan Beard, notes accompanying a letter dated November 20, 1940, from Beard's secretary, in the Mark Twain Museum, Hannibal, Missouri.

45. Stein 367, 370, 372, 376, and 379.

46. Stein 565.

47. Cited in Kahler 2.

48. Cited in Stein 568.

49. S.L. Clemens to L.E. Parkhurst, December 20, 1889, Library of Congress.

50. Smith, *Fable of Progress* 81.

51. Charles L. Webster & Co. to Beard, December 12, 1890, Library of Congress .

52. Dan Beard, *Moonblight and Six Feet of Romance* (New York: Charles L. Webster & Co., 1892) xii.

53. Dan Beard, "Six Feet of Romance, " *Cosmopolitan*, 7 (July 1889): 226–33.

54. Beard, *Moonblight* xiii-xiv.

55. Beard, *Moonblight* 91–94.

56. Beard, *Moonblight* 38.

57. Beard, *Moonblight* 53.

58. Beard, *Moonblight* 122.

59. Beard, *Moonblight* [126], advertisement.

60. Beard, "Mark Twain, the Man" 16.

61. Research for this essay was partially funded by a grant from the Walter Williams Craigie Teaching Endowment of Randolph-Macon College, which help is gratefully acknowledged.

Collaborative Writing:
A Browser's Bibliography

James S. Leonard, Laura Brady,
and Robert Murray Davis

Barbato, Joseph. "Giving up the Ghost." *Publishers Weekly* 229.3 (January 10, 1986): 34–38.

Discusses the escalating scale of "as-told-to," "with," and "and."

Barthes, Roland. "The Brain of Einstein." *Mythologies*. Trans. Annette Lavers. New York: Hill and Wang, 1972, 68–70.

Discusses the mythical dimension of our reverence for individual genius—as epitomized by popular attitudes toward the brain of Einstein.

Bendixen, Alfred. "It Was a Mess: How Henry James and Others Actually Wrote a Novel." *New York Times Book Review* (April 27, 1986): 3, 28–29.

About the ten-author collaborative production of *The Whole Family*.

Bonetti, Kay. "An Interview with Louise Erdrich and Michael Dorris." *Missouri Review* 11.2 (1988): 79–99.

Explores the collaborative process of a successful contemporary novel-writing team.

Brand, Joshua. "A Case of Bigamy." *New York Times Magazine* (May 17, 1987): 100.

About the collaboration of Brand and J. Falsey. Discusses work on the scripts of "St. Elsewhere" and "A Year in the Life." Chats about how this is like a marriage, but nothing very specific.

Brebach, Raymond. "Conrad, Ford, and the *Romance* Poem." *Modern Philology* 81 (November 1983): 169–72.

> Gives versions of the dedicatory poem in the novel, reconstructing the process of how the poem was written, including Conrad's emendations, both suggested and adopted. Effect of the two versions: Conrad emphasized adventure, Ford memory.

————. "The Making of *Romance*: Part Fifth." *Conradiana* 6 (1974): 171–81.

> Traces the eight stages of this part, six in earlier stages. Intricate interplay of suggestion, revision, reconsideration, and effects of all of these stages. Includes discussion of independent revisions.

Bridgman, Richard. "Weak Tocks: Coming to a Bad End in English Poetry of the Later Eighteenth Century." *Modern Philology* 80 (Fall 1983): 264–79.

> Discusses (269–74) Johnson's endings for Goldsmith's poems, moving out into philosophical and literary contexts of the period.

Bringle, Jerald E. "Introduction." *Bernard Shaw, Widowers' Houses: Facsimiles of the Shorthand and Holograph Manuscripts and the 1893 Published Text*. New York and London: Garland, 1981.

> Part of the series, Bernard Shaw, Early Texts: Play Manuscripts in Facsimile. Discusses disagreements about the quality of the play and Shaw's preface. Describes early collaboration on the play: idea by William Archer, which Shaw took over and adapted away from the conventional plot which Archer had stolen from a French drama. Also in this volume is Shaw's preface, which deals in part with the collaboration, quoting Archer's article about it. Shows how an innovative artist took over from a conventional one and changed the spirit while to some extent retaining the plot. And note Shaw's distinction between his term, "story," and Archer's term, "plot."

Brown, Richard E. "The Dryden-Lee Collaboration: *Oedipus* and *The Duke of Guise*." *Restoration* 9 (Spring 1985): 12–25.

> Notes allocation of work/division of labor. Dryden's part is ironic, exhibiting Tory politics; Lee's is violent, passionate. Motives for writing an Oedipus play: testing older drama by rewriting it. Effect of collaboration: parallel and contrast of two moods—irony and pathos vs. wildness of passion, the private vs. the public. Conclusions: Dryden contributed form and theme; "... two authors need not sound

alike—or even have quite the same thematic goals—for a dramatic collaboration to succeed."

Bruffee, Kenneth A. "Collaborative Learning and the 'Conversation of Mankind.'" *College English* 46 (1984): 635–52.

Provides a theoretical and conceptual introduction to the ideas that inform collaborative learning. Specifically, Bruffee presents a rationale for linking thinking, speaking, and writing activities with social relations.

———. "Writing and Reading as Collaborative or Social Acts." *The Writer's Mind*. Ed. J.N. Hays, J.R. Ramsey, and R.D. Foulke. Urbana, Ill.: NCTE, 1983, 159–70.

Moves from rationale to practice as Bruffee explains why and how he uses collaborative learning to teach writing.

Bulletin of the Association for Business Communication. Volume 53, June 1990.

The entire June 1990 issue of this journal is devoted to collaborative writing in business communication. The articles cover a range of subjects, including: the frequency of co-authoring; the use of collaborative case studies; classroom applications; group dynamics of collaboration, such as strategies for increasing coherence and decreasing conflict; the use of computers for collaboration; an annotated bibliography.

Carter, Robert A. "When the Author Needs a Helping Hand." *Publishers Weekly* 228.14 (October 4, 1985): 30–32.

Describes Renni Brown's service, The Editorial Department, which spends half its efforts working with/for publishers—editing in the technical sense—and the other half supplying writers to collaborate on books. Some of these authors get fifty percent of earnings but no credit. Mostly nonfiction. One author faced deadline, another pinch-hit for him, and Brown office helped research, organize, rewrite, type. Tries to match personalities. Believes best books deserve most thoughtful editing, and says most publishers aren't set up to provide tight editing.

Chiseri-Strater, Elizabeth. *Academic Literacies: The Public and Private Discourse of University Students*. Portsmouth, NH: Boynton/Cook, 1991.

While addressing the larger issues and definitions pertaining to academic literacy, this book also explores the responses of students to collaborative work (and to writing in general). Chiseri-Strater illustrates how, for example, collaborative writing can be paired effectively with individual writing. The ethnographic research which provides the basis for this book also illustrates a multi-faceted collaboration between the author and her colleague, Donna Qualley.

Clark, Barrett H. "George Moore." *Intimate Portraits*. New York: Dramatists Play Service, 1951.

Material on collaboration with Moore on pp. 63, 90–104, 119–20, 123–24, 133–34, 146, 148–49. Gives the scattered quality of Moore's conversation, and his short attention span. Failure of dramatic collaboration. Conflict over plot. Each wrote a version, separately, of Act III. Moore's lack of attention to details of planning—until he got the finished product. Dialogue of actual conversation.

Clifford, John. "Composing in Stages: The Effects of a Collaborative Pedagogy." *Research in the Teaching of English* 15 (1981): 37–53.

Clifford designed a study that would "empirically test" theories that claim that collaboration (in the form of peer conference groups) improved students' writing. Using a sample of 92 students, Clifford compared the performance of students in control groups (traditional classroom settings) and students who participated in small groups. He concluded that the collaborative learning group had "significantly higher gains" on a holistically scored writing sample, and that there was no difference in mechanical knowledge or performance, even though the control group was directly taught these skills in every class meeting.

Closson, Kay, and Anita Sheen. "Poetry Collaboration." *MS.* 6 (March 1978): 60–61.

Poems, "Garden Party" and "Night Hunter," and selections to answers to twenty questions on their writing. Have done other collaborations.

Collaborative Writing in Industry: Investigations in Theory and Practice. Ed. Hary M. Lay and William M. Karis. Amityville, NY: Baywood, 1991.

This collection of essays is divided into four sections. The first addresses theoretical concerns; the second provides case-study applications; the third explores the connections between collaborative writing practices and telecommunications and computer-assisted learning; the final section is titled "Current Industrial Concerns: Gathering, Verifying, and Editing Information."

Cross, Geoffrey A. "A Bakhtinian Exploration of Factors Affecting the *Collaborative Writing* of an Executive Letter of an Annual Report." *Research into the Teaching of Writing* 24.2 (May 1990): 173–203.

Curley, Thomas M. "Johnson's Secret Collaboration." In *The Unknown Samuel Johnson*. Ed. John J. Burke, Jr., and Donald Kay. Madison: U of Wisconsin P, 1983, 91–112.

> Johnson's collaborator was Sir Robert Chambers, a lawyer. "Between 1766 and 1770 they fitfully collaborated on a valuable survey of the British constitution and secretly produced *A Course of Lectures on the English Law*." Why they collaborated: Chambers was not very vigorous and was caught up in Oxford social life. Johnson flogged him into producing the lectures.
>
> Previous scholars' assumptions about who did what in the collaboration and who influenced whom. Also covers Johnson's providing material for Boswell's briefs. This raises the broader issue of what collaboration is—where it begins and ends—and not just what it produces, as in a text, but what effect it has on the future thought and work of those involved in the collaboration.
>
> The collaboration is of less interest for the process—which is not recoverable—than for the issue of its effect on the collaborators, in this case Johnson: "his mature thoughts about English government fully crystallized during the collaboration and so prepared him for his political writing in the next decade." Discusses theories in Chambers which are reflected in Johnson's later writings, and not just political writings.

Dahlin, Robert. "Meyer and Kaplan: Two into One Will Go." *Publishers Weekly* 212.21 (November 21, 1977): 46.

> Collaboration of Nicholas Meyer, who also "collaborated" with Arthur Conan Doyle on new Sherlock Holmes stories, "The 7 Percent Solution" and "The West End Horror," and Barry Jay Kaplan, who published Gothics and romances such as *Bettina Kingsley* and who had been a college friend. Alternated drafts of book, seven in all, to get one voice. Some information on how the screenplay had to be enlarged upon.

Daiute, Collette. "Do 1 and 1 Make 2?" *Written Communication* (1986): 382–408.

> Daiute's study of fourth- and fifth-grade writers asked students (using word processors) to write individually, then with a partner, and once more by themselves. Daiute concludes that there are positive patterns of influence resulting from collaborative writing. She also emphasizes the ways in which computers facilitate coauthorship. Daiute's general process provides a practical application of collaborative student writing that is easily adapted to various types and levels of writing.

Davis, W. Eugene. "'The Celebrated Case of *Esther Waters*': Unpublished Letters of George Moore and Barrett H. Clark." *Papers on Language and Literature* 12 (Winter 1977): 71–79.

> Supplements Clark's account (see above), especially on how the collaboration ended.

———. "George Moore as Collaborator and Artist: The Making of a Later *Esther Waters: A Play*." *English Literature in Transition* 24.4 (1981): 185–95.

> Account of Barrett Clark's abortive collaboration on an unpublished version, aborted when Moore refused to consider Clark's version or suggestions. Useful references to Clark's essays on Moore, unpublished and in *Intimate Portraits*. Describes process of Moore's shift, and expands the description of the whole process from Clark and Davis's 1977 article. Gives Clark's tally sheet of Moore's use of Clark's ideas.

De Camp, L. Sprague. "Afterword: Fletcher and I." *The Compleat Enchanter*. By L. Sprague de Camp and Fletcher Pratt. New York: Ballantine, 1975.

> Describes the collaboration of De Camp and Pratt.

Delbanco, Nicholas. *Group Portrait*. New York: Morrow, 1982.

> Especially on the collaboration (classified according to types) of Joseph Conrad and Ford Madox Ford. See especially pp. 95, 98–99, 106–7, 117, 118, 126–27. Notes give direct sources for Conrad's and Ford's comments on the collaborative process; cited as especially important is J.H. Morey, "Joseph Conrad and Ford Madox Ford: A Study in Collaboration," unpublished dissertation, Cornell University, 1960.

Duin, Ann Hill. "Computer-Supported Collaborative Writing." *Journal of Business and Technical Communication* 5.2 (April 1991): 123–50.

————. "Developing Texts for Computers and Composition: A Collaborative Process." *Computers and Composition* 9.2 (April 1992): 17–39.

Duncan, Lois. "Writing the 'As-Told-To' Article." *Writer's Digest* 65.4 (April 1985): 29–32.

> Gives two versions of opening of a story, one in third-person, one as-told-to, and gives other parallel examples. Discusses needs to order, structure, and edit as well as write. The person with the experience gets veto rights over the article only if as-told-to.

Dunning, Jennifer. "Behind the Best Sellers." *New York Times Book Review* 84 (April 15, 1979): 28.

> On Samm Sinclair Baker, who collaborated on the Scarsdale diet, Dr. Stillman, and other self-help projects. Discusses the need for empathy in collaborative work.

Dyson, Anne Haas, ed. *Collaboration through Writing and Reading: Exploring Possibilities*. Urbana, IL: NCTE, 1989.

> Rather than looking at particular collaborative practices, this collection of seven essays (each with a separate preface) explores "collaboration" as a general concept that refers to the social and interactive nature of reading, speaking, and writing. The essays emphasize a contextual approach, and share the view that "the integration of the language arts [is] influenced by the interactions among teachers and students," by students' home cultures, by the specific purposes that guide efforts to use language, "by complex interplay of broad historical and cultural forces" (8, 15–16). The seven chapters present (1) an introduction, (2) a historical perspective, (3) an analysis of the social context beyond the classroom, (4) cognitive influences on reading and writing, (5) the developmental benefits of reading-writing collaborations in elementary and secondary schools, (6) a discussion of the classroom as a collaborative learning community, (7) a final commentary on establishing a framework for reading-writing connections. Although most of the chapters include examples based upon the writers' own teaching experience, the book as a whole offers a conceptual rationale for integrating reading, speaking, and writing. In other

words, the collection provides a framework for creating interactive, collaborative activities rather than describing specific classroom techniques.

Ede, Lisa, and Andrea Lunsford. "Rhetoric in a New Key: Women and Collaboration." *Rhetoric Review* 8 (1990): 234–41.

Part of what may be considered a series of articles on collaboration by Ede and Lunsford, and part of the conclusion of their then-forthcoming book on collaboration (*Single Texts/Plural Authors: Perspectives on Collaborative Writing*). This essay identifies two modes of collaborative writing: the hierarchic and the dialogic. The writers explore the possibilities of the dialogic mode "for subverting traditional phallogocentric, subject-centered discourse," and for re-defining conventional concepts of authorship (238, 240).

———. *Singular Texts/Plural Authors*. Carbondale: Southern Illinois UP, 1990.

Ede and Lunsford's article from *Rhetoric Review* forms part of the final chapter in this book-length study on collaborative writing. Earlier chapters question our traditional assumptions about authorship, examine cases of collaboration in different professions, and draw connections between the practice of writing and the teaching of writing. Much of the work is based on surveys of writing within seven professions. The survey questions, follow-up interview questions, and collaborative writing assignments are all included in ninety pages of appendices.

———. "Why Write ... Together?" *Rhetoric Review* 1 (1983): 150–57.

This essay explores the types and advantages of coauthorship, while giving specific examples to the writers' own experiences as collaborators. Ede and Lunsford examine variables such as the nature and purpose of the project, the relation between writers and audience, and the desire of the writers to work together. The essay concludes with a series of questions that the authors would like to address and see others explore; their list includes questions about features of the collaborative process (as well as the collaborative product), and questions pertaining to the epistemological, technological, pedagogical, and ethical implications of coauthorship.

———. "Why Write ... Together: A Research Update." *Rhetoric Review* 5 (1986): 71–77.

An extension of Ede and Lunsford's 1983 article.

Enos, Theresa. "Gender and Publishing." *Pre/Text* 11 (Fall-Winter 1990): 311–16.

> As part of her survey of male and female publishing ratios, Enos surveys the percentage of collaboratively written articles published by major composition journals in the last ten years. She includes an analysis of the percentage of male-male, male-female, and female-female collaborations.

Felder, Leonard. "Successful Collaboration: When Two Pens Are Better Than One." *Writer* 96 (December 1983): 20–22.

> Distinguishes between a ghostwriter, who "essentially does 100 percent of the writing for a non-writer's book" and a collaborator, who "is a partner who works in tandem with a celebrity author, and each contributes equally to the ideas, outlines, drafts and revisions of their joint effort." Differences in pay and credit: ghost—flat fee, no credit; collaborator—percentage, credit. How to become a collaborator, and how to get pay and credit. Discusses the help Irving Howe received from Kenneth Libo on *The World of Our Fathers*.

Forman, Janis. "Collaborative Business Writing: A Burkean Perspective for Future Research." *Journal of Business Communication* 28.3 (Summer 1991): 233–57.

Foucault, Michel. "What Is an Author?" *Language, Counter-memory, Practice: Selected Essays and Interviews by Michel Foucault*. Ed. Donald F. Bouchard. Trans. Donald F. Bouchard and Sherry Simon. Ithaca: Cornell UP, 1977.

> Analyzes the function of the "author" designation as an index of permissible meaning of a text. Raises questions about differences between actual production of a text and attribution to an author.

French, Bryant Morey. *Mark Twain and "The Gilded Age": The Book That Named an Era*. Dallas: Southern Methodist UP, 1965.

> See especially Ch. 3, "The Collaboration," which shows division of labor, discusses the process of revision and of voting on versions by the authors' wives, and reasons for the relative failure of the book.

Gearhart, Kyle Anne. "A *Collaborative Writing* Project in a Technical Communication Course." *Technical Communication* 39.3 (Aug. 1992): 360–66.

Gebhardt, Richard. "Teamwork and Feedback: Broadening the Base of Collaborative Writing." *College English* 42 (1980): 69–74.

> Gebhardt advocates the use of peer conference groups for invention (in addition to revision and editing). Groups can locate topics, generate details, and provide an initial sense of audience. Gebhardt also acknowledges the emotional support provided by collaboration: it counteracts isolation and loneliness.

Gerber, Helmut E. *George Moore in Transition.* Detroit: Wayne State UP, 1969.

> Discusses Moore as collaborator with Barret Clark, William Butler Yeats, and others.

Gere, Anne Ruggles, *Writing Groups: History, Theory, and Implications.* Carbondale: Southern Illinois UP, 1987.

> Spanning over a hundred years (from 1880 to the present), Gere's study demonstrates that writing groups are neither new nor novel and that they exist both within and beyond the academy. The first two chapters provide a historical perspective on the way writing groups highlight the social dimension of writing. Chapter 1 locates the origins of writing groups in undergraduate literary societies, and continues to show how these groups were integrated into the curriculum, how they fit with educational reforms in the late nineteenth century, and—in Chapter 2—how they evolved into present-day use. Chapters 3 and 4 take a theoretical perspective to examine and critique traditional notions of authorship and Cartesian epistemological approaches to learning. Chapters 5 and 6 assume that writing groups are always connected to issues of literacy and learning. Chapter 5 looks at the factors that help make groups effective and at the central issue of authority; Chapter 6 advances a social constructionist view of literacy that maintains writing groups as a key component to writing and learning. Gere divides her extensive bibliography into two parts: the first half provides a chronological list of books and articles about writing groups, with each entry briefly annotated by a subject heading and a short summary; the second half consists of an extensive list of works consulted.

Goldner, Kathryn Allen, and Carol Garbuny Vogel. "Pros and Cons of a Writing Partnership." *Writer* 100 (September 1987): 24–25.

Golub, Jeff, ed. *Focus on Collaborative Learning.* Urbana, Ill.: NCTE, 1988.

> A collection of brief essays (6–8 pages each) that provide practical teaching ideas for elementary through college-level teachers who are interested in collaborative learning techniques. The book organizes its twenty-three essays into four sections: (I) "Collaborative Learning Skills" provides guides for introducing students to group processes; (II) "Collaborative Learning and Literature Study" and (III) "Collaboration in Writing, Revising, and Editing" include essays which suggest practical peer-group activities for the literature and composition classroom; (IV) the final section, "Additional Collaborative Learning Activities," explores other contexts for collaborative learning skills such as music, scripts, and television projects.

Greenberg, Dan. "How I Overhauled My Mechanic's Novel." *Writer* 98 (Nov. 1985): 5–6; *Reader's Digest* 126 (April 1985): 57–59; *New York Times Book Review* 89 (October 7, 1984): 3.

> Inversion: mechanic doesn't know the jargon or have the tools or skill to fix his novel. Needs a new protagonist, but Greenberg can get him one from another novelist's scrapped trilogy—if the mechanic hasn't worked on the other writer's car.

Griffin, Dustin. "Augustan Collaboration." *Essays in Criticism* 37 (January 1987): 1–10.

> An analysis of collaboration by English writers during the eighteenth century.

Haefner, Joel. "Democracy, Pedagogy, and the Personal Essay." *College English* 54 (Feb. 1992): 127–37.

> Haefner calls for a "recontextualization" of the personal essay that, in part, challenges assumptions of the isolated text and the isolated writer. He suggests that students write collaborative personal essays, or create a mix of "I" speakers to stretch the limits of the first personal pronoun.

Hoy, Cyrus. "Massinger as Collaborator: The Plays with Fletcher and Others." *Philip Massinger: A Critical Reassessment.* Ed. Douglas Howard. Cambridge: Cambridge UP, 1985, 51–82.

> Lists collaborations, including revisions of plays. "The purpose of this essay is to describe the kinds of play to which Massinger contributed: to give some general sense of the sort of plot materials with which the

dramatists are dealing, and of the particular elements of plot which Massinger contributed to the various plays on which he worked." ·

Massinger frequently wrote both opening and closing scenes, as if he had been "employed for the express purpose of setting a play in motion, and providing it with a finale." To frame, in other words. Some examples of his practice and how it tied in with the work of his collaborators.

His work shows us "about the way Jacobean plays were put together, and about the implications of the process for the creative imagination." Massinger's association with Fletcher was bad for him because it went on too long: "Fletcher's style was too powerful and too well established in the favour of theatrical audiences to permit a collaborator any role beyond that of a subordinate assistant." Exceptions to this. Why he isn't first-rate as collaborator or as dramatist.

Journal of Technical Communication. Volume 38 (November 1991).

The entire November 1991 issue of this journal is devoted to collaborative writing. The articles cover a range of subjects, including: collaborative planning of workplace documents; collaboration between business and academia; collaboration between government agencies and academia; effects of collaborative writing research on industry practices.

Karis, Bill. "Conflict in Collaboration: A Burkean Perspective." *Rhetoric Review* 8 (Fall 1989): 113–26.

Karis argues in favor of the value of conflict or "cooperative competition" in collaboration. He cautions against the current emphasis on compromise in collaboration because it limits creativity and dialogue.

Ketterer, David. "The Last Inspirational Gasp of James Blish: *The Breath of Brahma.*" *Science Fiction Studies* 11 (March 1984): 45–49.

Documents preparation for a collaboration with Josephine Sexton which never got very far.

———. "Pantropy, Polyploidy and Tectogenesis in the Fiction of James Blish and Norman L. Knight." *Science Fiction Studies* 10 (July 1983): 199–210.

Mostly about theme, with some material on collaboration.

Kime, Wayne R. *Pierre M. Irving and Washington Irving: A Collaboration in Life and Letters.* Waterloo, Ontario: Wilfrid Laurier UP, 1977.

This is a very thorough account, more descriptive than analytical. The collaborative works seem to be Irving's weakest, or to come from his weakest period.

Kissinger, Henry, and Cyrus Vance. "An Agenda for 1989." *Newsweek* 111 (June 6, 1988): 31–34.

A collaborative essay by two former Secretaries of State, a Republican and a Democrat, advocating international cooperation rather than confrontation. The essay itself is a surprising example of cooperative effort; otherwise, the relevance to collaborative writing is mainly a matter of analogy.

Knox-Quinn, Carolyn. "Collaboration in the Writing Classroom: An Interview with Ken Kesey." *College Composition and Communication* 41.3 (Oct. 1990): 309–17.

Krupat, Arnold. "The Indian Autobiography: Origins, Type, and Function." *American Literature* 53 (March 1981): 22–42.

More description of the genre than of the process of collaboration, but does note that the as-told-to process has to be reciprocal.

Laumer, Keith. "How to Collaborate Without Getting Your Head Shaved." *Turning Points: Essays on the Art of Science Fiction*. Ed. Damon Knight. New York: Harper, 1977, 215–17.

Layne, Marion Margery. "Nine Steps to a Published Novel." *Writer* 95 (December 1982): 20–22, 45.

Pseudonym of Marion Woolf, Margery Papic, and Layne Turkelson, who wrote *The Balloon Affair*. Pre-planning stressed—first six steps. One finally acted as editor to get a single voice.

LeFevre, Karen Burke. *Invention as a Social Act*. Carbondale: Southern Illinois UP, 1987.

While LeFevre's whole book emphasizes social perspectives on invention, Chapter 4 pertains specifically to invention as a *collaborative* act and provides a theoretical foundation as well as examples of collaborative views; it concludes with a discussion of the relation between "collaboration" and the "social collective." In scope, LeFevre's study includes classical rhetoric as well as modern applications. In function, the book demonstrates the integrated and social nature of language use through the presentation of varied examples. The bibliography is not annotated, but is extensive.

Levine, Mark L. "Double Trouble." *Writer's Digest* 65.3 (March 1985): 34–35.

> Advice from a lawyer about legal pitfalls of collaboration, and, a sample "Memorandum of Understanding." Notes distinction of types of credit: (1) "a and b," (2) "a as told to b," (3) "a with b."

Lunsford, Andrea. "Collaboration, Control, and the Idea of a Writing Center." *Writing Center Journal* 12.1 (Fall 1991): 3–10.

Mannocchi, Phyllis F. "Vernon Lee and Kit Anstruther Thompson." *Women's Studies* 12.2 (1986): 129–48.

> More about the emotional relationship between the two women and about their place in the aesthetic theory of the period than about the process of collaboration.

Mather, Nancy, and Betsy L. Lachowicz. "Shared Writing: An Instructional Approach for Reluctant Writers." *Teaching Exceptional Children* 25.1 (Fall 1992): 26–30.

McNenny, Geraldine, and Duane H. Roen. "The Case for Collaborative Scholarship in Rhetoric and Composition." *Rhetoric Review* 10 (Spring 1992): 291–310.

> The authors begin by outlining areas of resistance to collaborative scholarship (e.g., promotion and tenure committees), and then suggest solutions to these problems. Specifically, they cite several advantages to collaboration, such as: a way to foster team spirit; a means of generating collective knowledge; a means of providing recognition for graduate student contributions to research. The article concludes with practical advice for successful collaborations.

Mendelson, Edward. "The Auden-Isherwood Collaboration." *Twentieth-Century Literature* 22 (1976): 276–85.

> Collaboration as anti-romantic. What happened and when; division of labor in *Dog* and *Ascent*.

Miller, J. William, Jr. *Modern Playwrights at Work*, Vol. 1. New York: Samuel French, 1968.

Very useful general material on collaborators of the past and how they worked.

Mills, Barbara Kleban. "Judith Barnard and Her Husband, Michael Fain, Jointly Conquer the Romance World as 'Judith Michael.'" *People Weekly* 22 (October 8, 1984): 67–68.

Description of a husband-wife collaboration.

Mooney, M.E. "Framing as a Collaborative Technique: Two Middleton-Rowley Plays." *Drama in the Renaissance*. Ed. C. Davidson, C.J. Gianakaris, and J.H. Stroupe. New York: AMS Press, 1986.

Moore, George. *Hail and Farewell: Ave, Salve, Vale*. Ed. Richard Cave. Gerrards Cross, Bucks.: Colin Smyth, 1976.

Good on the process of collaboration, especially in questions of choosing dialect and vocabulary.

Morey, J.H. "Joseph Conrad and Ford Madox Ford: A Study in Collaboration." Unpublished dissertation, Cornell University, 1960.

Useful patchwork from Ford's *Joseph Conrad: A Personal Record, Thus to Revisit, Return to Yesterday*, "Conrad and the Sea," and various Conrad and Ford letters.

Conrad died August 3, 1924; Ford finished *Joseph Conrad: A Personal Record* on October 5, 1924. Morey uses the manuscript of this book and in Appendix A includes the portions of it not published in the book version. Discusses Ford's claim to have gone over the manuscript and proofs of *Heart of Darkness* "minutely and with attention"—this from the unpublished portion; also from the unpublished portion, Ford's claim to have worked over every Conrad manuscript between *Heart of Darkness* and *Nostromo*. Ford took dictation from Conrad for Conrad's *A Mirror of the Sea* and *Some Personal Reminiscences*.

Reports the split of Conrad and Ford over *Some Personal Reminiscences*; Conrad thought them finished, but Ford did not. Arguments about form. Discusses Ford's claims about *Nostromo*: his familiarity with the structure of the novel, his ability to imitate Conrad's style, and the fact that Conrad accepted his interpolations "almost without qualification." Notes that nothing much happens in the part of *Nostromo* he wrote. Cites Ford, "On Conrad's Vocabulary" (*Bookman* [June 1928]: 405): "what we worked at was not so much specific books as the formation of a literary theory."

Morgan, Mac, Nancy Allen, Teresa Moore, Dianne Atkinson, and Craig Snow. "Collaborative Writing in the Classroom." *Bulletin of the Association for Business Communication* 50 (September 1987): 20–21.

Muller, Marcia, and Bill Prozini. "Should You Collaborate?" *Writer* 98.3 (1985): 7–10, 45.

> A brief discussion of the advantages of co-writing either fiction or non-fiction, and the elements that these two collaborators consider essential to any successful partnership: trust, willingness to compromise, shared goals which have been clearly outlined, division of work according to abilities. Discusses types of collaboration, including ghost-writing and celebrity collaboration; also touches on typical problems that collaborators may encounter, including the problem of creation of a third voice. Uses mystery stories as example.

Murphy, Cecil. "Getting Them to Tell-To." *Writer's Digest* 65.4 (April 1985): 30–31.

> Tips to get the person to open up. This is closely parallel to the techniques described by Ford in the passages cited in Delbanco.

New Versions of Collaborative Writing. Ed. Janis Forman. Portsmouth, NH: Boynton/Cook, 1992.

> This collection consists of eight essays, a review essay, and reprinted correspondence among the contributors. It examines the importance of context for any consideration and practice of collaboration, and it questions and critiques popular ideas of adapting "real life" collaborative models for the composition classroom. The collection places its emphasis on exploring further the practices and potential of collaborative writing in various contexts.

O'Donnell, Angela M., et al. "Cooperative Writing: Direct Effects and Transfer." *Written Communication* 2 (July 1985): 307–15.

> An empirical study that examines the direct effects of a "cooperative writing experience," and the degree to which students are able to transfer what they learn back to an individual writing situation. The study concludes that the students in the cooperative learning environment "significantly outperformed the individual group on a measure of the communicative quality of the writing on both the initial task and the transfer task" (307).

Petry, Glenn H., and Halbert S. Kerr. "Pressure to Publish Increases Incidence of Co-Authorship." *Phi Delta Kappan* 63 (March 1982): 495.

> Petry and Kerr surveyed "18 leading academic journals in business and economics over a 15–year period." Their findings show 1.29 authors per article in 1963–67, increasing to 1.6 authors per article by 1978. A random sample of single vs. multiple authorship shows no greater frequency of citation, as "an index of quality." The authors suggest greater rewards for those who publish alone.

Pohl, Frederick. "Reminiscence: C.M. Kornbluth." *Extrapolation* 17 (May 1976): 102–9.

> Mostly about what they collaborated on, and a little about shared responsibilities or ideas traded off.

Reiber, Lloyd J. "The Role of Cooperative Writing in the Business Communication Classroom: A Research Direction for the 1990s." *Bulletin of the Association for Business Communication* 55.2 (June 1992): 32–34.

Reither, James, and Douglas Vipond. "Writing as Collaboration." *College English* 51 (Dec. 1989): 855–67.

> The authors define various aspects of collaboration: co-authoring, workshopping, and knowledge-making. They explore the implications of each aspect for the teaching of writing.

Robbins, Peggy. "History's Slighter Side: Pearl Curran and Patience Worth: Strange Literary Partners." *American History Illustrated* 17 (January 1983): 9.

> Patience Worth dictated through a Ouija board; her novels were successful.

Schrage, Michael. *Shared Minds: The New Technologies of Collaboration.* New York: Random House, 1990.

> Surveys new developments in collaborative text production and collaborative decision-making processes in business environments. Focuses on the use of computers and other technological innovations for the creation of "shared space" within which individuals can function together for planning, making decisions, and writing.

Shaw, George Bernard. "The Author's Preface." *Bernard Shaw's "Widower's Houses": Facsimiles of the Shorthand and Holograph Manuscript and the 1893 Published Text.* Ed. Jerald E. Bringle. New York and London: Garland, 1981.

> About the Shaw-Archer collaboration: Archer as constructor, Shaw as writer of dialogue. Plot v. story; ingenuity v. imagination. Why a collaboration failed, or at least failed as a collaboration. But it took this conventional beginning to get Shaw started.

Shloss, Carol. "Foirades/fizzles: Variations on a Past Image." *Journal of Modern Literature* 12 (May 1985): 153–68.

> On the collaboration between Samuel Beckett and Jasper Johns: involves "two artists, two languages, and two media." Influence of the physical conditions of the limited edition as contradicting and canceling the effect of text and pictures.

Smit, David W. "Some Differences with Collaborative Learning." *Journal of Advanced Composition* 9 (1989): 45–58.

> This essay calls for a critical attitude in assessing the research, arguments, implications, and uses of collaborative strategies. Smit surveys much of the major work on collaboration within the field of Composition Studies.

Spear, Karen. *Sharing Writing: Peer Response Groups in English Classes.* Portsmouth, N.H.: Boynton/Cook, 1988.

> The book is divided into two parts: "Challenges of Peer Response Groups," and "Developing Peer Response Groups." The first half provides an analysis of groups and their dynamics (including the problems that may arise in groups) based on theory and research; the second half builds on the theory and research to provide practical applications for peer reading and writing groups in the classroom. Spear includes questions, assignments, and recommendations that can be adapted to individual teacher and student needs.

Starret, Vincent. "Speaking of Ghosts" and "Partners in Print." *Books Alive.* New York: Random House, 1940, 280–91 and 292–308 (respectively).

> Popular summary of various collaborators; very useful background.

Stewart, Donald C. "Collaborative Learning and Composition: Boon or Bane?" *Rhetoric Review* 7 (Fall 1988): 58–83.

This essay provides a brief overview of collaborative learning, its history, and its positive aspects, then presents a critique. Stewart voices two central objections to collaborative learning: he finds the movement to be "historically naive," and he worries about the lack of distinction between *collaboration* and *influence*. Specifically, he finds collaborative learning potentially dangerous, fearing that the movement could lead to "totalitarian societies in which the individual is completely subjected to and subjugated by the will of the group" (74).

Stillinger, Jack. *Multiple Authorship and the Myth of Solitary Genius.* New York: Oxford UP, 1991.

Proposes that acknowledgement of multiple authorship tends to result in devaluation of a literary work. Details unacknowledged or only partly acknowledged collaborative aspects of the works of Keats, Wordsworth, Coleridge, Mill, and T.S. Eliot. Discusses the editorial "collaborations" of Maxwell Perkins and the massive editorial reshapings of such blockbuster bestsellers as *Peyton Place* and *Valley of the Dolls.*

Stone, Albert E. "Collaboration in Contemporary American Autobiography." *Revue française d'études americaines* 14 (May 1982): 151–65.

Suggests that "we must approach the collaboration abandoning belief in literature as a collection of autonomous aesthetic icons and sacred texts and seeing all books—and especially autobiographical narratives—as, in Frederick Crew's [sic] words, 'contingent imperfect expressions of social and mental forces.' If we do so, dual-authorship may cease being a literary *problem* to become rather a cultural solution."

Interested in "the cultural situation which has produced [*Black Elk Speaks, The Autobiography of Malcolm X, The Life of Nate Shaw*] and literally hundreds of other, far more ephemeral life-stories." Distinguishes between memories, which belong to the subject, and imagination, which belongs to both the subject and his/her collaborator. Also the sense of strategy of self of autobiography being audited/edited by someone else. Dialogue translated into monologue in written work. Use/value of foregrounding the role/relationship of subject and writer.

Important distinction between *words* and *voice* of the subject. Emphasis on oral performance, speaker/listener relationship. Some treatment, by implication at least, of the question of *why* as well as *how* the subject agreed to collaborate. Similarities between the three autobiographies mentioned above and single-person autobiographers

248   *James S. Leonard, Laura Brady, and Robert Murray Davis*

who, "often split themselves off from the writing self in order to emphasize their lives' historical or transcendental meaning to others." Analogy of teams of anthropologists vs. single explorers.

———. "Two Recreate One: The Act of Collaboration in Recent Black Autobiography." *REAL: The Yearbook of Research in English and American Literature* 1 (1982): 227–66.

Essentially the same methodology and critical vocabulary as the shorter article, though there is a good deal more description of the individual works than in the shorter piece. Does point out how Haley served as a second, probing consciousness to force Malcolm X to come to terms with his past. Argues that several of the collaborators "play essential roles in helping to recover the historical identities of their several subjects. The cultural critics should, therefore, examine collaborations not simply with a skeptical awareness of their difference and inferiority, but looking for all cues to the cultural context within which the work has been created, the actual interplay of personality and outlook between the two collaborators, the nature of the audiences openly or covertly addressed, and the achieved balance between autobiographical and biographical elements. One should be alert also to indications of recoveries and discoveries of the subject's past as facilitated but not invented by another."

Tomlinson, Barbara. "Characters Are Coauthors." *Written Communication* 3 (1986): 421–48.

Tomlinson provides evidence that fictional characters collaborate metaphorically with authors. This article is part of a larger study, based on over 2,000 published interviews with professional writers, in which Tomlinson examines the metaphors that professionals use to describe their writing processes. She found that many writers cast their characters as collaborators, ascribing independent words and actions to them.

Trimbur, John. "Collaborative Learning and the Teaching of Writing." *Perspectives on Research and Scholarship in Composition.* Ed. Ben W. McClelland and Timothy R. Donovan. New York: MLA, 1985, 87–109.

Trimbur defines collaborative learning as an attempt to "decentralize the authority traditionally held by the teacher and to shift the locus of knowledge from the sovereign domain of the teacher to the social interaction of the learners" (89).

————. "Consensus and Difference in Collaborative Learning."
College English 51 (Oct. 1989): 602–16.

The essay provides a critical perspective on the politics of collaborative learning. Specifically, Trimbur identifies and responds to two
lines of criticism which question the consensual nature of collaborative learning: one line argues that consensus is a potentially totalitarian, conformist practice; the other line argues that the social construc-
tionist rationale for collaborative learning fails to question the hierarchical relations of power that organize knowledge. Trimbur extends
the second of these critiques.

Walters, Ray. "Paperback Talk." *New York Times Book Review* 84
(March 18, 1979): 37–38.

Fiction factory of Lyke Kenyon Engle—John Jakes works for him—
who invents story lines, sells them to publishers, and has authors
write the rest, editing them with his staff in New York State. Mostly
fiction series. And Jim and Carolyn Robertson, who do the same thing
in California, including camera-ready copy, though mostly ecology
and other inspirational books.

Watson-Roulin, Virginia, and Jean M. Peck. "Double Time."
Writer's Digest 65.3 (March 1985): 32–34, 36.

Lists various psychological advantages—range of experience, complementary strengths and weaknesses—in collaboration. How to collaborate, divide work, write. Two types: (a) outline: each do separate
parts; (b) one writes, one edits.

Weber, Bruce. "The I's Have It." *Esquire* 104 (October 1985): 123.

Business angle; Bantam heavily involved in collaborative kind of autobiography. Leo Janos' writing of Chuck Yeager's *Yeager: The Autobiography*. Not very detailed.

Wiener, Harvey S. "Collaborative Learning in the Classroom: A
Guide to Evaluation." *College English* 48 (January 1986): 52–61.

Wiener lists criteria that he has generated as the result of observing
several teachers employing collaborative learning techniques in their
classrooms. The criteria can also function as a good checklist for
teachers who want to *generate* collaborative learning activities since
they provide reminders about preparation, objectives, follow-up activities and so forth.

Yeats, William Butler. *The Autobiography of William Butler Yeats.* New York: Collier, 1965.

> Discusses the W.B. Yeats-George Moore collaboration: two kinds of minds, arguing about words; Yeats triumphed in choice of words; Moore on construction. Yeats believes the collaboration had a bad effect on Moore's style.

Index

DATE DUE

DEC 02 1999	

DEMCO, INC. 38-2931